D1393779

Praise for *Living Supply Chains*

"All executives understand the importance of getting their supply chain right, but few know exactly what that means. In *Living Supply Chains*, John Gattorna offers help. The book begins with customers, and specifically argues for segmenting customers by their dominant buying behaviour, identifies four types of supply chains that respond to the needs of distinct customer segments and argues that successful firms can manage multiple supply chains simultaneously. It is the consistent emphasis on the soft side of making supply chains work that distinguishes this book from many others. This is an excellent contribution to our understanding of how supply chains serve customers and what it takes to get them right."

Donald Sull, Associate Professor of Management Practice in Strategic and International Management, London Business School, and author of *Made in China*.

"The key messages from this book are absolutely fundamental to success in business. I have now worked in five international businesses over more than 25 years; I am very clear that leadership and culture are of crucial importance. John Gattorna is right to emphasize the importance of organizational design, as many companies are plagued with functional silos. He is also right to highlight the need for both the leader and his team to be in touch with both their customers and their market; staying aware of the competition, but making the customer the priority. *Living Supply Chains* will help to connect businesses with their customers, and help business leaders in measuring and managing the engagement of the staff."

Philip Green, CEO, United Utilities

"John Gattorna is well respected as one of the leaders in the field of supply chain management. His new book, *Living Supply Chains*, is a 'must read' for anyone who is keen to learn about the intricacies and underlying mechanisms of corporate logistics networks, and how the human factor, such as leadership style, can affect and influence the effectiveness of these supply chains."

Scott Price, CEO Asia Pacific, DHL Express

"This is an important and valuable book. Yes, it adds much 'science' to the supply chain debate and offers a view of how a leader might navigate his or her way through a supply chain change process, but importantly, for me at least, it reminds the reader of a few basic home truths. John reminds us that a supply chain can and should be a source of competitive advantage, it can be shaped by a leader who is prepared to lead and prepared to influence organizational culture and it should be a means of delighting customers and, through customers, our shared consumers."

Rob Murray, CEO, Lion Nathan

"This book is very timely, presenting new and pragmatic solutions to old problems. Indeed, the search for meaningful supply chain metrics and types is finally solved. John has challenged the various business disciplines with strategic supply chain models, and translated otherwise complicated customer demands into easy to understand observations about supply chain practice in some of the world's leading firms. I particularly like the words John started and finished with: 'Supply Chains *are* the business', which is why only Living Supply Chains will be viable in the future."

Helen Zhao, Director, Lorewin Supply Chain Research Centre, PRC

"The first book to really explore the livelihoods of supply chains, *Living Supply Chains* shows how to mobilize the entire enterprise around delivering what the customers want. Having put the entire subject of supply chain change management into a unique and distinctive perspective, John Gattorna leads us through the challenges – supply chain change-management, managing the customer conversation, implementing multiple strategies, leading from the front, continuous replenishment where relationships matter: lean, agile, flexible supply chains, business alignment models – that deliver the truly living supply chain."
Jalal Ashayeri, Professor of Supply Chain Management, Tilburg University

"Building on his vast experience at the cutting edge of supply chain research and practice with some of the world's leading companies, John Gattorna has melded it with his unique and compelling *dynamic alignment* model to produce a book which will change the way supply chains are understood and managed, now and into the future. I am particularly excited because his book gives the service sector a whole new framework to overcome what he calls its 'supply chain blindness'. It provides ways to extract the huge potential value that exists across many service industries, globally."
Paul McDonald, Executive Director, Committee for Economic Development of Australia (CEDA)

"When I started reading *Living Supply Chains*, I saw very clearly its value to me as Chairman of Berghaus, but did not think I'd find any links with my role as an expedition leader. However, I quickly discovered many parallels in running a successful expedition, which has its own supply chain in the flow of supplies up the mountain and the effective utilization of porters and team members. Equally, effective leadership on a mountain or in any organization is essential for success. John Gattorna has identified all the traits which I recognize as essential to any expedition leader or, for that matter, of any supply chain."
Sir Chris Bonington, Mountaineer and Mt Everest expedition leader

"*Living Supply Chains* not only provides the busy executive with a comprehensive but concise guide to delivering value from their enterprise supply chains, it is also an invaluable tool for the seasoned supply chain practitioner who has to navigate the spaghetti bowl of interdependencies and competing methodologies in order to deliver results."
Nigel Jones, General Manager – Logistics, Sales and Operations Planning, Fonterra Co-operative Group Ltd

"Our research in Value Chain Engineering in the public sector targets the construction of dynamically aligned information systems for a strategically aligned corporation. *Living Supply Chains* provides the key for us to understand *dynamic alignment* and its impact on culture and business process."
James Gibson, Software Engineering Methodologist, Visiting Fellow, University of Wollongong

"A thought-provoking book that will become an authoritative tool for private and public sector executives facing challenges with customers and suppliers in their supply chains."
Susan Mohr, Director, Logistic Support Agency-Navy, Defence Materiel Organisation

Living Supply Chains

FT Prentice Hall
FINANCIAL TIMES

In an increasingly competitive world, we believe it's quality of thinking that gives you the edge – an idea that opens new doors, a technique that solves a problem, or an insight that simply make sense of it all. The more you know, the smarter and faster you can go.

That's why we work with the best minds in business and finance to bring cutting-edge thinking and best learning practice to a global market.

Under a range of leading imprints, including *Financial Times Prentice Hall,* we create world-class print publications and electronic products bringing our readers knowledge, skills and understanding, which can be applied whether studying or at work.

To find out more about Pearson Education publications, or tell us about the books you'd like to find, you can visit us at **www.pearsoned.co.uk**

PEARSON
Education

FT Prentice Hall
FINANCIAL TIMES

An imprint of Pearson Education

Harlow, England · London · New York · Boston · San Francisco · Toronto
Sydney · Tokyo · Singapore · Hong Kong · Seoul · Taipei · New Delhi
Cape Town · Madrid · Mexico City · Amsterdam · Munich · Paris · Milan

PEARSON EDUCATION LIMITED

Edinburgh Gate
Harlow CM20 2JE
Tel: +44 (0)1279 623623
Fax: +44 (0)1279 431059

First published in Great Britain in 2006

ISBN-13: 978-0-273-70614-4   13169327

British Library Cataloguing-in-Publication Data
A catalogue record for this book is available from the British Library

Library of Congress Cataloging-in-Publication Data
A catalog record for this book is available from the Library of Congress

10 9 8 7 6 5 4 3 2
10 09 08 07

Typeset in Plantin 10pt/14pt by 30
Printed and bound in Great Britain by Henry Ling Limited, at the Dorset Press, Dorchester, DT1 1HD.

The publisher's policy is to use paper manufactured from sustainable forests.

To Ella Mae, Charlotte Lucia and Jake Lino

Contents

Publisher's acknowledgements

We are grateful to the following for permission to reproduce copyright material:

Carpenter Ellis (consultants) for Figure 6.4: 'Resultant Metropolitan Distribution Network (MDN)'; Accenture for Figure 9.3: 'Value creation road map'; Gattorna Strategy Consultants Pty Ltd for diagnostic used in Appendix 1A and Geert Hofstede for research data featured in Appendix 3B; Ryder Self Group for Appendix 3A materials and diagram featured in Appendix 3C; Mark Barratt for use of appendices 5A and 5B materials.

In some instances we may have been unable to trace the owners of copyright material, and we would appreciate any information that would enable us to do so.

Acknowledgements

This book has been on my mind, consciously and unconsciously, for more than a decade. Many people have helped to develop my thinking as I struggled to find and fit together all the pieces of the slowly emerging jigsaw puzzle of supply chains. Perhaps the most significant contribution came from those chief executives who believed in me at a very early stage and provided a laboratory (their companies) where we could debate, test and develop ideas. Michael Andrews at Fletcher Challenge (now Tenon), Philip Green and Roger Bowie at DHL, Bob Scott at General Accident (now CGU), John Shasky at Fonterra and, more recently, Scott Price and Stuart Whiting at DHL Asia Pacific and Susan Mohr and Bill Coombes at the Logistic Support Agency-Navy – all have helped me more than they will ever know. Thank you for your respective votes of confidence.

I am also fortunate to have a very supportive colleague and soul mate in the mainstream of supply chain management education, Professor Martin Christopher of Cranfield School of Management. Martin provided me with many opportunities to address post-graduate and post-experience classes at Cranfield, and these interactions helped to further develop and articulate my ideas immeasurably.

My years at Accenture were also very rewarding because of the access I had to very smart people and the resources available to continue developing many of the ideas outlined in this book. Since my retirement from Accenture I have continued to receive great support from Michael Donnellan and Will Lock in London, John Karren and Ming Tang in Sydney and Jeffrey Russell in Singapore.

Apart from my on-going work at Cranfield, I have been most fortunate to be invited to teach MBA classes at the Macquarie Graduate School of Management in Sydney and Asia, the Normandy Business School at Le Havre in France, the Asian Intensive School for Advance Management in Penang, and the Master of Science (Logistics) programme at the University of Wollongong in Australia. These have all been rewarding experiences for me. Indeed, I never cease to be amazed how much I learn from my students; thank you all.

During the past two years, while I have been actively engaged in researching and writing the book, I have received great support from my Research Assistant, Kate Hughes, and my Executive Assistant, Graciela Parker-Day. And the good news: we are all still good friends! Special thanks to both of you. Long-time colleagues Deborah Ellis and Ivana Crestani have always been on hand to provide specialist advice as required. Thanks also to other academic colleagues who have influenced my thinking along the way: Dr Mark Barratt of Arizona State University, Dr Chris Morgan and Professor Richard Wilding at Cranfield, Dr Tim Coltman and James Gibson at the University of Wollongong and Professor Willem Selen at Macquarie Graduate School of Management.

I am also deeply indebted to all those friends and colleagues, too numerous to mention here, who agreed to review drafts of the manuscript at various stages of completion and provided invaluable feedback.

Richard Stagg, Editorial Director at Pearson Education in London, helped to formulate the structure of the book and drove me mercilessly to produce something that executives would find compelling reading. Carmel McCauley of Future Perfect Communications has helped me to achieve this objective, and you the reader will be the final judge as to whether together we have succeeded or not. Professor Donald Sull at London Business School set the benchmark for me with his latest book, *Made in China*, and has been generous with his time and advice. Barry Mellor at the NHS Authority in the United Kingdom has been similarly supportive. And I can always count on Jonathan Norman, Publishing Director at Gower Publishing, for his independent and insightful advice on matters relating to publishing.

Benjamin Roberts, Desk Editor at Pearson Education, took on the task of guiding *Living Supply Chains* through the production process, and Jenny Oates did a superb job copy-editing the original manuscript, eliminating every error along the way. Thank you both for a job well done. Finally, as anyone who has ever engaged in a significant writing project, it is those closest to you that tend to be overlooked. For that reason I owe loving thanks to my wife Lea, for her forbearance while I was both physically and mentally absent for long periods during the preparation of this book.

John Gattorna
Sydney, Australia
26 January 2006, Australia Day

Preface

s there a reason for the supply chains of so many businesses not working well?

Some companies seem to get their products to their customers with glorious ease. Too many others, meanwhile, get caught up in squeezing the costs out of their supply chains, so that customers end up walking out the door. Or, just as bad, they woo customers by providing premium service, only to find that the cost is unsustainable.

For decades we have been trying to find the balance between delivering products to customers and doing so in a smart, cost-effective way. With customers becoming more restless, and the operating environment uncertain, the solution seems as elusive as ever.

The problem starts with the old perception that the supply chain is just that. A chain. A single set of links, admittedly often complex, but a concrete, mechanical structure that, if we only try hard enough – and use enough technology – can be engineered to perform any task we please.

But the reality is that it is people who drive the supply chain, both inside and outside your business, not hard assets or technology. Living supply chains are powered by the energy and expertise of your employees and suppliers; and they are propelled by the changing desires of your customers.

Realizing that living supply chains are organic, not mechanical, will quite fundamentally change your approach to managing your supply chain.

I set out to write this book in order to help chief executives to understand this people component of today's supply chain environment. *Living Supply Chains* describes a new model for understanding your customers, giving you practical ways to allocate your resources to the customers across your many supply chains.

It is all about understanding more about your customers' expectations, so that you'll have a better chance of understanding how they wish to buy your products or services. Ultimately, you'll be in a better position to provide the exact response they desire.

I call this principle of matching changing customer needs and desires with different supply chain strategies *dynamic alignment*. It is dynamic because it more accurately tracks the ebb and flow of people's energy. It is as alive as the people who buy your goods and services; and *dynamic alignment* is exactly what is called for today as businesses get out of their cost-reduction zone and put growth back on the agenda. To grow, you cannot afford to have pain points in the supply chain, blocking the delivery of goods and services or increasing the cost-to-serve.

To secure your space in a new market, you have to get your products out there faster. And the same applies to growing or just keeping existing markets – you need to be the first with new products and the first to match them with particular customer groups.

Through the *dynamic alignment* model, this book provides a structured way of linking customer expectations to the operational side of your enterprise, and systematically modifying fulfillment processes as customers change their buying preferences – as they surely will.

To succeed, you'll need three or four different supply chain configurations in place to 'align' with the equivalent number of dominant buying behaviours of your customers. The best enterprises globally are achieving this multiple supply chain alignment. It is more than possible – it is happening.

These are living supply chains, and designing your strategies around the people who make up today's supply chains will help you to capture new customers, sustain current ones and secure new value for your business.

CHAPTER 1

Supply chains **are** the business

Why not abandon conventional wisdom and discover the customer?

S upply chains and golf have many similarities; for best results, everything must be in *dynamic alignment*. Ask Tiger Woods.

Of course you know who Tiger Woods is. Just like you know Dell, IKEA, Nokia, Zara, Li & Fung. But do you really *know* them? Do you know what lies beneath their dynamic supply chains? Business leaders around the world admire their superior performance; they can deliver products and services to their customers with breakneck speed and in a way that makes it look easy. But not many of us can understand why.

Let us consider the classic business goal of alignment. Many of you will have heard of alignment; companies have been seeking to align their strategies and goals to the needs of the customer for some time. Alignment in the supply chain is similar – but different. It means aligning your supply chain strategies to customer segments. *Dynamic alignment* is something different again.

Dynamic alignment is an idea I have developed after more than 20 years' experience in acting as a consultant to companies worldwide on improving their supply chains. Just as the term suggests, it captures the concept of dynamism, or life, in the supply chain. Seeking *dynamic alignment* means treating your supply chain as a living being, not a mechanical beast: the difference between a golf club sitting in its bag and the swing of a golf club in the hands of Tiger Woods. It is all about energy, execution and the dynamism of people and movement. If you capture that you'll be in 'the zone', with a bottom line to match.

Again, let's look at the performance of some of the world's top brand names. Why is it that Nokia successfully transformed itself from a timber company in the early 1980s to become a world-leading electronics high-technology company? How can we explain the fact that a national icon such as Marks & Spencer can lose its way – and its customers – while others, such as Nestlé, go on to solidify and strengthen their position? We see it is possible for a company such as Dell to change a whole industry through its supply chain innovation, while its competitors are still worrying about removing costs. And Daewoo's Korean shipyards can produce a supertanker every 36 hours, while Dell in Australia can take more than two months to replace the battery in my D800 laptop. Clearly, some can reach 'the zone' while others languish behind them!

Before we explore the detail of *dynamic alignment*, let's start by shedding the old definition of the supply chain. It is no longer all about technology, warehouses and distribution centres, or trucks and planes. Agreed, they are elements – they are the hard assets. But a modern supply chain comprises a lot more than that. We have to embrace a far more liberal view of the supply chain. In effect, the supply chain is any combination of processes, functions, activities, relationships and pathways along which products, services, information and financial transactions move in and between enterprises. It also involves any and all movement of these from original producer to ultimate end-user or consumer; and *everyone* in the enterprise is involved in making this happen.

Solving the problem of complex supply chains

If we accept this new definition of the supply chain, then every enterprise on earth has supply chains of some type or configuration running through them. They could be a manufacturer, a service company, a public sector agency or a private sector firm. Supply chains are omnipresent. They are out there! Most enterprises contain literally hundreds of supply chains that together look more like a bowl of electrified spaghetti than finely tuned conveyor belts.

This has led to two key problems. The first is that many people are largely blind to the presence of these supply chains. They can only see the trackable movement of products and/or the position of hard assets.

Complexity makes the true supply chain invisible. The second problem is that even if people recognize these complex supply chains, they start attacking the complexity issue in inappropriate ways. Failure to see the full extent of supply chains in your company can be damaging. Seeing it but then confronting it with the wrong solutions can be fatal.

If you are a service organization, companies in your sector are the most likely to suffer from supply chain blindness. They think that because their products are intangible, logistics and supply chain principles don't apply; wrong. If you are in the manufacturing or retail industries, companies in your field are likely to see the complexity but attack it with an operational sledgehammer. They are convinced the solution lies in reducing the internal operational complexity that they have to manage. As a consequence, they are busily standardizing and re-engineering processes and installing new technologies, all designed to reduce complexity in the way they deal with customers.

However, these enterprises rarely become easier to deal with from the customer's perspective, quite the contrary. It would be much more productive if they were to accept and confront this inherent complexity, and then set out to master it. The tools and techniques are available, but only the conscious desire – or the understanding – to do so is in question.

Understanding will come from first accepting that the time is here to fundamentally rethink how we design and operate the supply chains that link our own enterprise with suppliers and customers, whether they are 'just around the corner' or around the world. For too long there has been an unhealthy preoccupation with infrastructure and asset utilization, driven mainly by the obsessive desire to cut costs, mostly brought on by the growing requirement for quarterly reporting. Unfortunately, even today many executives think of logistics and supply chains purely as areas for cost-cutting. While acknowledging that ever-lower levels of operating cost are important, achieving and maintaining future competitiveness demands more sophistication. You cannot grow the business by continuously cutting costs, a lesson learned the hard way by observing the activities of Al 'Chainsaw' Dunlap in the 1990s.[1]

Dunlap has a lot to answer for. Even today, senior executives in many major corporations continue to emulate his one-dimensional cost-cutting approach. You may have seen this type of behaviour. It almost always brings on a bout of *anorexia industrialosa*,[2] the excessive desire to be leaner and fitter, leading ultimately to total emaciation and death. In supply chain terms this approach has also encouraged senior executives to engage in endless benchmarking and process re-engineering exercises that go nowhere (witness the early efforts at Six Sigma), and innumerable on-going initiatives in the name of 'continuous improvement'. Cost-cutting, re-engineering, benchmarking and continuous improvement might have a place in the corporate arsenal, but they are not the answer to supply chain complexity. Seldom have these activities had the customer in the frame. In short, there has been a lot of effort and activity for relatively little gain.

What is required is sustained investment in performance-enhancing supply chains. Look no further than a leading organization such as Nokia. It has delivered positive Cash Flow Return on Investment (CFROI) over a long period and therefore the capacity to invest in competitive-building capabilities on a sustained basis.[3] If only we could all achieve this level of performance! Another challenge facing chief executive officers (CEOs) is the fact that so many people working in businesses think that systems technology is the one-stop shop for supply chain solutions. It is a mindset that started in the run up to the year 2000. No doubt you remember that phenomenon. Resources were poured into new information technology, affecting all areas of the enterprise, but for limited returns, and the world did not come to an end as some predicted. The same mindset is now saying information systems will be the saviour of the supply chain – especially in this new age of terrorism, where the hope is that technology will magically make your business secure and manageable. Beware such prophets!

It's the people, stupid

In 1997, Australia's largest processed food manufacturer, Goodman Fielder Ltd, had a rare opportunity to achieve a major transformation of its conglomerate-like business. It had businesses in breakfast cereals, oils and margarine, poultry, ingredients and milling and baking. David Hearn, the new Managing Director, had arrived from United Biscuits in the United Kingdom and was intent on boosting the financial performance of the company. He chose to start by transforming the logistics arrangements, which were messy and duplicated across several business units.[4] A new corporate strategy was devised and ready for implementation by mid-1997, but it never happened. In effect, David Hearn was overpowered by the managing directors of the business units, and the transformation simply limped along for a while before eventually fizzling out. Suffice to say, the financial performance of the company went the same way. This was a very powerful example of how internal resistance can slow down, or worse, stop, what should have been a very successful change for the good. A great opportunity was lost and the company has since struggled through ownership changes, privatization and, most recently, an attempt to list on the stock exchange again. In the meantime, the world has moved on from logistics to supply chains.

What do you think is the key ingredient in modern supply chains? The technology and the trucks? Or the people who design and run them? Supply chains may seem like uncontrollable, inanimate beasts, but they are in fact living systems propelled by humans and human behaviour. It seems as though light might be dawning at last, in some quarters at least. *Harvard Business Review* convened an elite panel in 2003 to discuss future supply chain challenges and one member aptly concluded that '... despite years of process breakthroughs and elegant technology solutions, an agile, adaptive supply chain remains an elusive goal. Maybe it's the people who are getting in the way.'[5] Indeed. But what we are interested in is not how they get in the way, but how they bring the supply chain to life.

We can see the potent presence of human behaviour both inside and outside the enterprise. Customers, suppliers and third-party providers are driving the supply chain from the outside, while staff, managers and board members are seeking to manage and respond from the inside. If you can understand and correctly apply a more enlightened approach to managing this 'human factor' in the supply chain, you'll discover a primary source of performance improvement in the foreseeable future. It's all there for the taking.

It is best to stop thinking of supply chains as a 50/50 mix of infrastructure and information systems technology. Start thinking of the ideal mix as more like 45/45/10[6] – human behaviour, systems technology and asset infrastructure. Whether we accept it or not, we are already shifting from Newtonian-like thinking to a more organic model. Once we accept this fact, a new world of performance improvement beckons, at every intra- and inter-organizational interface along our supply chains. Some more enlightened executives in adjacent fields have been on this wavelength for some time. David Smith, Head of Knowledge Management at Unilever, commenting in the *Financial Times* in 1998, mused that '...[organiza-tional] alignment is 50 per cent of the game. Processes are 30 per cent. IT is no more than 20.'[7] He was referring to what goes on at the intersection between knowledge management and supply chains.

If you need any more reasons, consider that during the next decade it will become progressively more difficult for enterprises to stand alone and compete successfully in their respective marketplaces. What we will see, and are already seeing, is the formation of supply chains made up of par-ties that consciously choose to work together in a preferred alliance (on either the supply or user side), competing with other similar supply chain alliances. In this world, you'll need to find and acquire completely new capabilities simply to stay competitive.

Talent will be at a premium. So too will be the ability to select and manage new alliances and relationships with parties who bring specialized capabilities to help us 're-align' with customers, fast. At the same time, we will need to transform in other ways by embracing completely new busi-ness models.

Writer Thomas Friedman brings us some helpful insights in his recent book, *The World is Flat*.[8] He says that the 'connectivity' resulting from con-vergence of communications technology, computer technology, and the explosion of software has led to the levelling of the global playing field, or a 'flat' world. And he cites what he calls 'supply-chaining' as one of the ten flattening forces that have caused this new phenomenon over the last decade. But even Friedman hardly acknowledges the underlying human forces at work in this massive transformation. He seems to be more concerned with all the **effects** rather than looking more deeply into what is driving them.

Where did this transformation start?

To understand the current transformation of the supply chain, it's helpful to go back and see where it all began. Despite seminal articles by acade-mics Robert Neuschel and John Stolle some 40 years ago, nothing immediate happened. Neuschel was one of the first to recognize that distri-bution activities stretched across a 'no man's land between functions' in organizations. He argued that any effort to reduce costs in logistics needed to be balanced with reaching the desired level of customer service and product.[9] Stolle observed that physical distribution was easier to analyze than to manage.[10] Logistics costs could be readily calculated; however, activities and tasks were scattered throughout the business and often under the control of divergent departments. The result? A fragmented approach to distribution – not unlike what a lot of companies have even today.

Businesses in those days focused primarily on managing finished product as it came off manufacturing lines. The production function of the enterprise was all-powerful. Product was stored in various places and then transported through a limited number of channels to the consumer. At the time, with customers just starting to feel their buying power, it became obvious that the greater levels of service being demanded could not be sustained unless more was known about the in-bound side of logistics. By the early 1980s, the customer and supply ends of the organization had been connected and the logistics function formally established. Initially logistics was structured only as a coordinating role, but often other managers in the enterprise saw this development as a grab for power by the new function. Unhappily, even to this day, many senior executives are still confused about the distinction between 'control' and 'coordination'.

By the late 1980s, three important subsystems were clearly emerging in the enterprise. At the upstream end was the in-bound logistics subsystem, consisting of procurement, in-bound transportation, inventory management, materials handling, facilities management and corresponding information systems. Downstream from production was the finished goods (or out-bound logistics) subsystem. This was a mirror image of the in-bound side, consisting of facilities management (including depots, warehouses and distribution centres), transportation links, inventory management, materials handling and information systems.

Where was production in all of this? It was caught firmly in the middle. While the production subsystem held out for an independent existence, it would gradually disappear in many enterprises over the ensuing decades. Indeed, these days production is effectively an integral part of the overall logistics effort in most forward-thinking enterprises. The combination of in-bound/out-bound logistics and production is sometimes called 'operations'. Meanwhile, service organizations had not even begun to think about any of these definitional matters; they were still mostly in the Dark Ages.

So for the enterprise to perform well, all three subsystems in this 'bow tie' organization structure have to be in synch. Once any one of them gets out of synch, the outcome is very predictable at any time – either stock-outs or overstocks.

By the 1990s, events conspired to cause a great leap forward, like some accidental chemistry experiment. The 'discovery' of the Internet opened endless channels for humans to communicate one-to-one. Coincidentally, a plethora of user-friendly software suites arrived on the scene. Now we could move forward from the previous preoccupation with internal integration and begin to link with parties upstream and downstream in a genuine network of supply chains. In almost a single stroke of genius (or good fortune), we had moved from talking about the concept of supply chain management to operationalizing supply chains, as depicted in Figure 1.1.

Let us consider what we mean by supply chain management, as it's a term bandied about today to cover all sorts of things. Supply chain management involves parties upstream and downstream agreeing to work together by joining their respective 'logistics' systems together. Simple? In concept, yes. But working together in complex chains, or networks, is difficult to achieve in practice.

In supply chain management, 'logistics networks' are a subset of supply chains, the key difference being the crucial interfaces between each supplier–buyer combination. Value is either created or destroyed through the management of these interfaces along the 'chain' or network. Given that a supply chain is the combination of multiple logistics networks, the potential to improve performance is much greater than within a single logistics system. In practice, all product, service and public sector enterprises have multiple supply chains running through them in a complex three-dimensional array.[11]

Another key difference in old and new ways of thinking is the approach to managing supply chains. We used to think of logistics as largely infrastructures and operations-based, which led to an operational excellence mentality. So management focused on cost and logistics was regarded as a cost centre. Not too exciting for those who worked in it! We now understand that managing *extended* supply chains involves far more than keeping costs in check (or working to reduce them). Managing supply chains actually involves understanding the interaction between human behaviour, information technology and infrastructure. Unfortunately, this is the antithesis of what happens in business today.

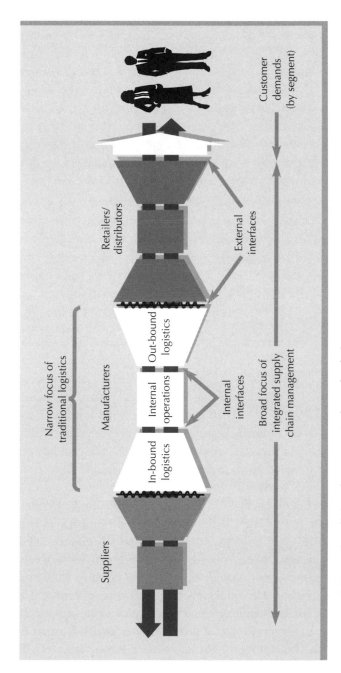

FIGURE 1.1 ◆ Operationalizing the concept of supply chains

Since all types of enterprises have supply chains of various configurations running through them, you can see the extent of the oversight. How can we expect to start solving operational problems without first recognizing that the primary driver of goods and services moving through the supply chain pipeline is people? So far, there is only a small body of knowledge that goes beyond the hard assets of the supply chain – systems, infrastructure and equipment – to get to what really drives performance: the soft intangible assets of human behaviour and knowledge.

Watch the customer not the competitor

Management thinker Michael E. Porter caught everyone's attention in the late 1970s when he launched his quest for 'competitive strategy';[12] and he is still saying that '... every organization must have a clearly defined strategy to deliver superior profits'.[13] Competitive analysis and strategy are obviously critical to success, but we should not get things out of perspective. We know now that there is much more involved.

Do you not think it's time that companies should start understanding what is going on inside their own businesses first? Porter's philosophy seems to have transfixed generations of managers into watching their competitors. The result? They haven't developed the same degree of sensitivity towards internal resources and the internal dynamics of their own firm. They are even less aware of the interactions at the edges of their business. A myopic focus on competitors and the external environment can only limit understanding of internal cultural capability, which is so critical to executing strategy. With such a focus, it's not surprising there has been such a mismatch between strategy and implementation.

Organizations can inflict much more harm on themselves by the very way they behave internally than any external competitor is capable of inflicting. Maybe it would be more appropriate to adopt Maria Sharapova's philosophy in winning the 2004 Wimbledon tennis championship: 'I like winning. I love competition. But I try to be myself. I worry about what I want to achieve. Not what everyone else does.'[14] This is also a winning formula for business, because it avoids overemphasizing external factors at the expense of internal factors. It has certainly worked for Maria Sharapova – she was ranked World No. 1 in women's tennis in August 2005.

If more enterprises were prepared to 'zero base' rather than 'copy cat' their strategies we would surely see fewer failures. It would also put a stop to the endless progression of new initiatives being rolled out in search of the next 'silver bullet'. Rob Murray, the incoming CEO of Lion Nathan, one of the largest brewers in Asia Pacific, expresses a similar philosophy: 'Right now, we're focused on trying to drive our own economic model and trying to make our own business work. You often end up losing if you obsess about what your competitors are doing. So I don't really care much what they are doing.'[15]

Can you see why we need to watch the customers, consumers and end-users of our products and services first and foremost? Unless all our energies and resources are focused on improving the 'alignment' between our business and customers (and suppliers too), then we are most likely wasting everyone's time and debilitating the company in the process. If we are sensitive to customer needs and buying preferences, it will be obvious what we have to do, and, like Sharapova, we won't have to worry so much about our competitors – they'll be worrying about us. The relevance of these insights to the design and operation of supply chains will become obvious in later chapters when we explain the inexorable principles that link an enterprise (internal cultural capability and leadership) with its marketplace, through operational strategy. All of these parameters interact in a multidisciplinary way, yet we continue to separate them into silos in the false hope that it will simplify our management task. The paradox is that we're only adding further layers of complexity.

Internal 'forces of darkness'

Strategy is, in effect, just a set of *intentions*, written on a piece of paper at a point in time, which acts as a *bridge* between the enterprise and its market-place. Until these words are brought to life and executed in the form of actions, there is little difference between 'good' and 'bad' strategy. In fact, some would argue that an 'ordinary' strategy well implemented is better than a 'brilliant' strategy poorly executed. We can continue to debate this point, but we know from experience that 40 to 60 per cent of the original intentions specified in business plans are dissipated or lost before ever being executed. While some of this loss is clearly a result of changing market conditions, competitor actions and the influence of government regulations, the biggest factor in the failure to execute best laid plans is the cultural resistance inside the enterprise itself. How often have we been in meetings where strategies have been presented by leaders on the assumption that their vision and its accompanying instructions will be automatically followed? Yet it's obvious that deep down some people, while appearing to agree with a plan to implement strategies, are often quietly making up their minds to resist and sometimes opt out entirely. This is the insidious side of culture at work inside the enterprise. The forces of darkness can undermine perfectly good strategies because particular people have different values to those needed to put the strategies into action.

Organization design is the key

How can we anticipate and stymie negative and unwanted responses? Well, apart from the very useful list quoted above, we need to consider the two factors that have perhaps most inhibited the development of business logistics and supply chain management as commercial disciplines over the past 40 years. The first is confusion around terminology. Terminology is still an issue, as new terms are introduced on an almost daily basis. But we can at least be reassured by the fact that managers are becoming better educated and are more likely to understand what is really involved in moving goods and services, irrespective of the labels used. The second is inappropriate organization design. We cannot dismiss its pervasive negative impact so easily.

The fact is that functional organization designs, which have served us so well for so long, together with matrix and partnership variants, are being rapidly marginalized. This is happening as increasing competitive intensity in many industry–market combinations drives customers towards more aggressive and demanding buying behaviours. The result is that as enterprises cling to these outmoded designs while markets move away, the degree of 'mis-alignment' is inexorably increasing. Worse still, it seems as if few enterprises have found ways of staying in *dynamic alignment* with their marketplace. New organizational configurations are now urgently required to work in parallel with existing formats.

The four principles for designing more effective organization structures proposed by Lowell Bryan and Claudia Joyce provide a useful guide for future organizations.[16] In essence, they suggested that organizations need a 'portfolio' of coexistent structures that mirror the mix of dominant buying behaviours found in the marketplace. This means that successful organizations will blend all their disciplines in different configurations to match their various groups of customers. Spanish fashion retailer Zara, for instance, does this perfectly. They form teams across functions for a product category such as children's wear, combining the efforts of the traditional areas of design, logistics, production, sales operations and marketing. The result is a cluster that can respond in real time, in a cross-organizational way, to a specific customer group, globally. Such customer-focused and more flexible configurations are actually fundamental components of different supply chains. We are foreshadowing a new understanding of the way enterprises will work in future.

Looking beyond conventional wisdom

To reach a new understanding of supply chains, we have to first leap ahead of another quest popular in the world of 'logistics', and that is the determination of academics, consultants and practitioners of the 1990s to extract the full potential of *internal integration*. Despite advances in technology that saw the introduction of Enterprise Resource Planning (ERP) systems, integration was always going to be a mirage. Why? No one during this period confronted the real blockage: the predominantly functional organization designs adopted by most enterprises. Such structures set people to work in a straitjacket environment and offered little or no prospect of ever aligning with customers.

Indeed, the conventional functional style of organization design is still used by most enterprises in the world today, even though it is at least 90 degrees out of phase with the way customers want to buy. It was not until the mid-1990s, when the Internet arrived, that things moved forward again. The convergence of the Internet as a communications medium, and the coincidental development of a myriad of new software applications, brushed aside many of the internal and external obstacles to integration. This effectively operationalized the supply chain for the first time. However, there was still something missing – an understanding of how the 'people factor' played out in all this.

In search of *dynamic alignment*

As long ago as 1989 it occurred to me that 'logistics' as a field of management science lacked any substantive theoretical underpinning. Without such a theoretical base, it offered little prospect of further breakthrough developments, at least in the short to medium term. It seemed that we had hit a type of 'knowledge ceiling'. In response, I set out in search of ideas **beyond** the boundaries of conventional logistics thinking, in adjacent fields of management science. This proved to be an inspired move as it ultimately opened rich new avenues of thought that helped to inform us better about the workings of modern logistics networks and supply chains. What was started in 1989, and continues to be developed to this day, is a holistic view of how enterprises function, a type of 'new integrated theory of the firm'. The logic that underpins this approach was that casting a wide net could potentially produce new insights into how enterprises, and therefore *enterprise supply chains*, worked. And so it proved to be.

Alignment is not a new idea. In fact it has quite ancient origins. One of the earliest forms of alignment occurred in nature – the flight of wild geese.[17] Remarkably, a flock of geese flying in V-formation can fly five times further than a single goose on its own, so powerful is the aerodynamic effect in formation. A more contemporary example is the Australian 4,000 metre men's pursuit cycling team winning the Olympic gold medal in Athens, with all four riders in line, wheels millimetres apart, chasing around the oval race track at high speed.[18]

By applying the term alignment to the supply chain, I am seeking to emphasize the dynamism involved – the type of movement we can see and measure when it comes to a flock of geese or an Olympic cycling team. Alignment is a living (rather than static) concept that applies to the enterprise as a whole. We want to capture the underlying mechanisms in supply chains, which themselves are integral to all enterprises. We call this overarching concept *dynamic alignment*, because it holds true under **changing** conditions, and for the first time gives us an opportunity to design and operate supply chains that stay abreast of customers and consumers as they evolve over time.

The economist R.H. Coase,[19] in his 1937 essay 'The Nature of the Firm', introduced the notion of 'moving equilibrium', where internal components interacted in such a way as to cause the firm to either expand or contract in size. It is very likely that Coase was primarily thinking of economic components and did not consider the behavioural dimension, but this concept is very relevant to supply chains. Some 60 years later, Labovitz and Rosansky went part of the way towards redressing this apparent oversight with their dual concepts of vertical alignment (linking strategy and people inside the organization) and horizontal alignment (linking processes and customers).[20] They also introduced the notion of the self-aligning organization, but their work was mainly based on anecdotal evidence, and as such lacked predictive capability.

Perhaps the first indication that strategy and culture in an enterprise could be systematically linked came from Norman Chorn's doctoral research in 1987.[21] Subsequently, Chorn, myself and co-workers in our consulting firm[22] set out to study the leadership styles of individual executives. This led us to Carl Jung's seminal work on personality types[23] and ultimately to Ichak Adizes[24] and Gerard Faust,[25] who developed the 'P-A-E-I' coding system to categorize different management styles, encompassing 'Producer-Administrator-Entrepreneur-Integrators'.

Our collaboration during this period proved to be fortuitous, as we were able to combine this important research on leadership and personality types with my earlier work in customer segmentation and vision development. It led directly to the first genuine multidisciplinary *dynamic alignment* framework that linked marketplace and strategy, with internal cultural capability and leadership styles in the enterprise. The seminal framework is depicted in Figure 1.2.

We realized that the P-A-E-I behavioural coding methodology (or 'logics' as we called them) developed by Adizes and Faust to describe different management styles of individual managers applied equally well at the aggregate level – this was the step jump in logic we made at the time. In other words, *groups* of people inside enterprises with similar values could be identified and described as *subcultures*. Similarly, groups of people on the outside who shared similar dominant buying values for specific product or service categories could be identified and described as *behavioural segments* (otherwise known as *external subcultures*).

We had indeed found the 'missing link', which turned out to be a behavioural metric (or logic) that could be used to describe (and measure) what was happening at all four levels of the emerging *dynamic alignment* model.

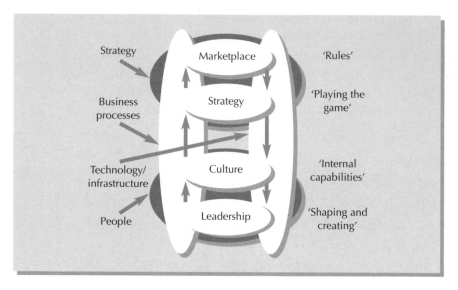

FIGURE 1.2 ◆ Elements of the *dynamic alignment* framework

Source Adapted from Figure I.2 in Gattorna (2003), p. xiii; also Gattorna (1998), p. 5

This new behavioural metric is indeed the DNA of business and enterprise supply chains, a topic we will explore in more depth in Chapter 3. Just as important, this new coding regime facilitated comparative analyses of all four levels of our model in search of potential 'mis-alignments'. As engineers well know, you cannot make meaningful comparisons unless a common metric is involved. We had found that unique metric – something that had evaded previous researchers – mainly because no one had been looking across all the fields of management science, concurrently.

Behavioural forces at work in supply chains

The behavioural coding system that we developed forms the foundation of the new insights on supply chains that I describe in later chapters. The roots of this system are firmly embedded in Carl Jung's theory of psychological types, which states that all conscious mental activity occurs in two perceptual processes: sensing and intuition; and two judgement processes: thinking and feeling. Adizes and Faust resolved and simplified Jung's original framework and identified four key behavioural types or 'logic sets' that might exhibit a dominant tendency. These are best represented as two pairs of countervailing (behavioural) forces, which are always in *dynamic tension*, and are present in all human interactions, as depicted in Figure 1.3.

In the context of supply chains, we are particularly interested in the specific interaction between buyers and sellers. Adizes and Faust originally labelled these behavioural forces as P-A-E-I as described above, but we later relabelled 'E' to 'D' and defined them as follows:

P (**Producer**): the force for action, results, speed and focus.

A (**Administrator**): the opposing force to D, and represents stability, control, reliability, measurement, logic and efficiency.

D (**Developer**): the force for creativity, change, innovation and flexibility (originally labelled 'E' for Entrepreneurial by Adizes and Faust).

I (**Integrator**): the opposing force to P, and represents cooperation, cohesion, participation and harmony.

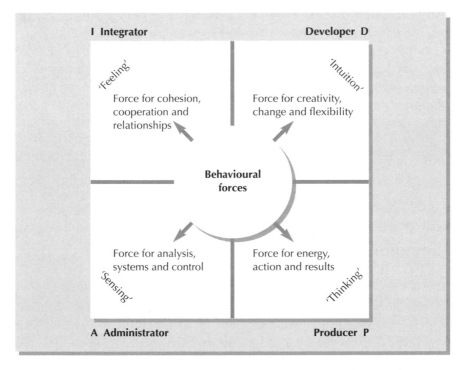

FIGURE 1.3 ◆ **General characteristics of the four dominant behavioural forces or logics**

Source Adapted from Figure 29.1 in Gattorna (1998), p. 474

The four elements of the P-A-D-I logic come together in different ways to produce 16 possible combinations, all of which are in *dynamic equilibrium*; each dominant logic combination has a different 'centre of gravity'. For example, if we are describing a particular buying style we may discern an overriding preference for speed, results and performance to specifications (P logic), and a lesser preference for reliability, consistency and price (A logic). There may also be some preference expressed for flexibility (D logic) and cohesion (I logic). So the overall summary of this particular buying behaviour can be represented by the shorthand code Pa, as depicted in Figure 1.4. Note that we have opted only to use 'primary' and 'secondary' parameters to describe the 'dominant logic', whereas Adizes originally used all four parameters in his coding of management styles. Our more abbreviated coding regime doesn't lessen the value of the approach, but has the advantage of making it simpler to use in practice.

The important insight to take on board here is that all customers have hierarchies of values. We are seeking to bring **the most dominant buying values to the surface** as these will ultimately drive behaviour and therefore are the values we need to align our responses with.

In the example in Figure 1.4, although the centre of gravity is in the P quadrant, and there is a secondary tendency towards the A quadrant, some overlap into the D and I quadrants suggests that there is also an influence of each coming into play. However, these forces are significantly less than the primary P logic and secondary A logic that defines the dominant centre of gravity. Horizontal and vertical logics can be combined (e.g., DI, or Di, Ia or IA, etc.) but it is impossible to combine diagonal logics, i.e., I and P

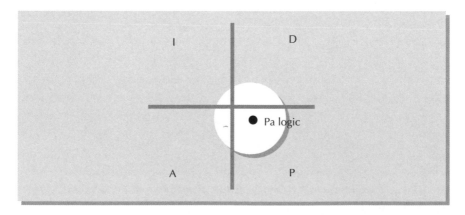

FIGURE 1.4 ◆ **Example of how 'dominant buying logics' may be represented – 'Pa' logic**

logics or D and A logics, as they are at the opposite ends of a continuum. This is because the more a buyer moves along the diagonal towards one end of the continuum, the less the influence of the opposing logic.

The four elements of *dynamic alignment*

So let us consider the logic of our model and see what impact it has on our thinking. The key driver in the marketplace is the dominant buying behaviour or natural preference exhibited by customers for a particular product or service category in a particular competitive environment. This is Level 1 in the *dynamic alignment* framework, as depicted in Figure 1.5.

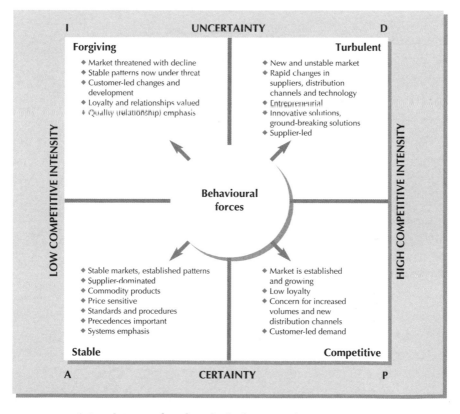

FIGURE 1.5 ◆ **Level 1 – marketplace logic framework**

Source Adapted from Figure 29.2 in Gattorna (1998), p. 474

Level 2 is the strategy element. This is the bridge that links the enterprise's internal cultural capabilities with the external marketplace, as shown in Figure 1.6.

Having an aligned set of subcultures (sitting on top of a set of enterprise-wide shared values, otherwise known as corporate culture) is crucial to the successful implementation of operating strategy. Figure 1.7 shows this third level in the *dynamic alignment* framework.

Finally, Level 4. Effective leaders understand the aggregate values of their enterprise, and can mould from these the appropriate subcultures to align with the preferences being expressed by customers in the marketplace. There are four primary leadership styles identified: Visionary (D); Company Baron (P); Traditionalist (A); and Coach (I). These different leadership styles are depicted in Figure 1.8 (see p. 22).

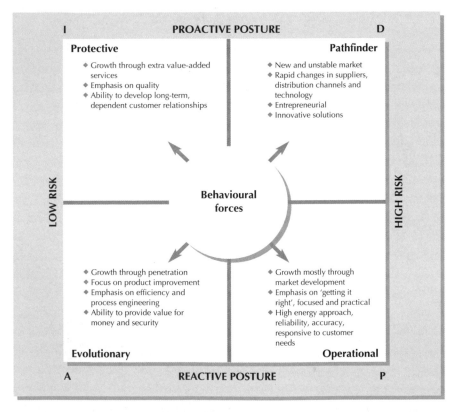

FIGURE 1.6 ◆ Level 2 – strategy logic framework

Source Adapted from Figure 29.3 in Gattorna (1998), p. 476

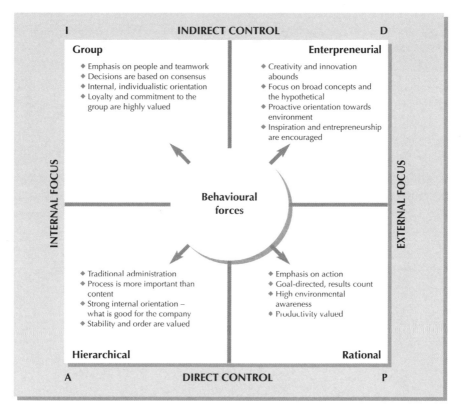

FIGURE 1.7 ◆ Level 3 – culture logic framework

Source Adapted from Figure 29.4 in Gattorna (1998), p. 477

Have a look at the 'quick' *dynamic alignment* diagnostic in Appendix 1A. It is designed to enable you to assess rapidly the overall degree of alignment (or mis-alignment) of your enterprise in a particular marketplace.[26]

Time to re-invent the enterprise

Let us consider the need for organizations to adapt to new market conditions and the integral role that supply chains play in the change process. In 1996, Levi Strauss & Co. undertook what at the time was heralded as the most dramatic change programme in American business.[27] Despite solid growth in revenue and profits, Levi's management felt their

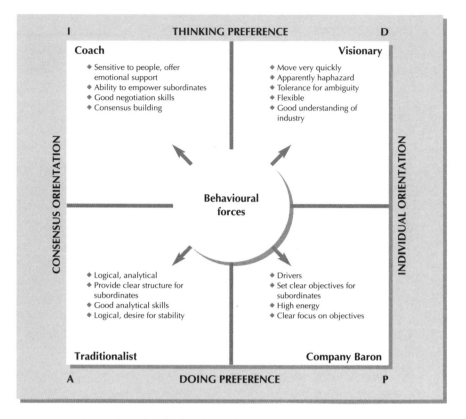

FIGURE 1.8 ◆ Level 4 – leadership logic framework

Source Adapted from Figure 29.5 in Gattorna (1998), p. 478

customers were telling them they should change – and they were listening. As the project unfolded it became very clear to team leader Thomas Kasten that Levi's customer service problems were deep-rooted and they involved the entire supply chain, from concept to end consumer. The resulting transformation was timely for Levi's because it set up the company for strong growth for another decade. How many enterprises are as sensitive to the need for change as Levi's? But how many either wait until the last moment or get lost in the change process itself?

The *dynamic alignment* model can make a difference. The model provides both a *map* and a *tool* to help you achieve superior performance across your corporate supply chains. It is a map to help you navigate your way through the increasingly complex network of supply chains out there today. And it's a tool because it helps to pinpoint how to align specific supply chains to customer behaviours. This is why it's such an important breakthrough for management thinking in general, and for the design and operation of supply chains in particular. It explains for the first time how the softer science of human behaviour can be integrated with the more tangible – and generally better understood – world of infrastructure and technology.

The underlying logic of the *dynamic alignment* framework is that an enterprise needs to be aligned with its customers or markets in the context of the prevailing operating environment. The power of this framework lies in its ability to reveal the interaction between customers' needs, helping to formulate appropriate response strategies, and to successfully execute those strategies through the shaping of internal cultural capabilities by appropriate relevant leadership. The essential starting point for successful *dynamic alignment* is a comprehensive understanding of customers' fundamental needs and matching dominant buying behaviours. This particular subject will be explored in more detail in Chapter 2. However, it is not difficult to observe the difference between successful and unsuccessful enterprises as measured in terms of organizational effectiveness metrics, revenue and CFROI performance.

Successful organizations generally have leadership that is clearly in close touch with, and empathetic to, their customers and market conditions. Empathetic leaders tend to formulate the relevant strategies and shape the most appropriate cultural capabilities to underpin and drive these strategies into their marketplace. Tesco, IKEA, Cessna, Nokia, Nestlé, Caterpillar and Dell are just a few examples of successful *dynamic alignment* in their respective marketplaces. And the way Lord Coe and his bidding team dramatically won the 2012 Olympic Games for London is another example of superior *dynamic alignment*, beautifully conceived and executed to perfection. There is no real size limitation on the application and usefulness of *dynamic alignment* – it applies equally well to large and small enterprises. An example of the latter is the nine-strong chain or 'charm bracelet' (as Belinda Seper refers to the store group) of fashion retail stores developed by Belinda Seper in Sydney under her 'Belinda' branding. While there is clearly a common theme across all stores, each is different in its own way. Each store has its own personality in response to the lifestyle needs of women in each store's catchment area.[28]

Less successful enterprises, on the other hand, fall at the first hurdle. Their leadership appears to lose touch with customers and corresponding market conditions, and the strategies and underpinning cultural capabilities put in place become progressively more mis-aligned, until finally the responsible board is forced to move to replace the leadership and start the process all over again – often resulting in huge expenses to the business with an accompanying negative impact on the share price. We saw clear evidence of this when IBM got into trouble in the early 1990s, and more recently with the much publicized demise of Carly Fiorina at Hewlett-Packard. Other examples of significant mis-alignment include such high-profile names such as Enron, Marks & Spencer, AMP, Parmalat and J. Sainsbury. All of these organizations are endeavouring to regain their former glory through radical initiatives designed to overcome serious mis-alignments with their customers which resulted in progressively worsening operating and financial performance.

This phenomenon occurs in all types of organizations, from religious to political and from public to private businesses. They all have one thing in common: people and their behaviour. Indeed, taking a leadership position these days is far riskier than in yesteryear, because there is little or no time allowed for them to learn on the job. In many ways it is akin to what is known in aeronautical circles as 'fly-by-wire'.[29] We have to accept that the enterprise will be in a state of 'dynamic instability' all or most of the time, and therefore it is vital to learn fast how to manage under these trying conditions. Aeronautical engineers learned to work with this 'dynamic instability' in aircraft as flight speeds increased exponentially. It is now up to managers in commerce and industry to do the same and increase the speed of their decision cycles. We will consider this further in Chapter 7 when we discuss *agile* supply chains.

Responsiveness at last

We did not set out to solve every problem in the world faced by enterprises, but it's increasingly obvious that little or no progress can be made to improve performance unless we take a more eclectic approach than is in vogue at the moment. By going well beyond the accepted boundaries of conventional management theory and practice, we can practise and embrace a new approach to the art of supply chains. And they are still something of an art form. Fortunately, the more holistic *whole-of-enterprise* perspective offered by the *dynamic alignment* framework gives us a new way forward. A fertile new world awaits if we pursue this line of thinking, a world where more value can be released and higher performance achieved, on a sustained basis.

Indeed, logistics networks and supply chains (comprising multiple organizations in 3-D arrays) are largely driven by people power, either in customer or employee capacities. Systems are the next most critical area because these deliver information to people for decision-making, such as 'make or buy or act' in some way in the enterprise. So it appears that the whole concept of *dynamic alignment*, when applied to logistics systems and supply chains, is simply another way of expressing optimal cost–service effectiveness. This is the realm where customers are serviced appropriately, no more, no less, eliminating over- and under-servicing for ever. At last we have a way around the service problem that confronts every manager every working day, epitomized by the words, 'We know we are over-servicing some customers and under-servicing others, but we don't know which is which.'[30]

Dynamic alignment principles bring with them a paradigm shift, away from conventional thinking which suggests that as service levels are progressively increased, cost-to-serve increases at a faster rate, approaching infinity at very high levels of service. This does not necessarily follow if resources are subtly re-allocated to align better with and more accurately reflect customer buying behaviours. Armed with a clearer understanding of the implications of improved alignment between an enterprise and its marketplace, the potential exists to move to a *best-of-both-worlds* strategy, where improved service comes at a lower overall cost-to-serve, at least up to a point, as shown in Figure 1.9.

Building more responsive supply chains means building more responsive enterprises overall, because service means different things to different people, and customers do not split hairs between functions inside the enterprise. Figure 1.10 illustrates in more detail the four primary customer service logics that result in at least 16 possible combinations; some types are more often observed than others, but they all exist in practice.

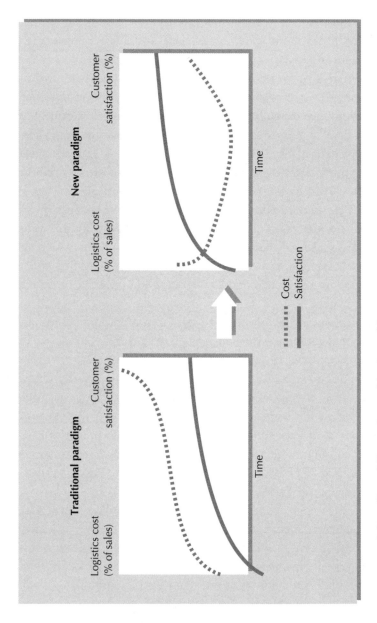

FIGURE 1.9 ◆ Paradigm shift to a best-of-both-worlds strategy

Source Adapted from Figure 1.1.1 in Gattorna (2003), p. 4

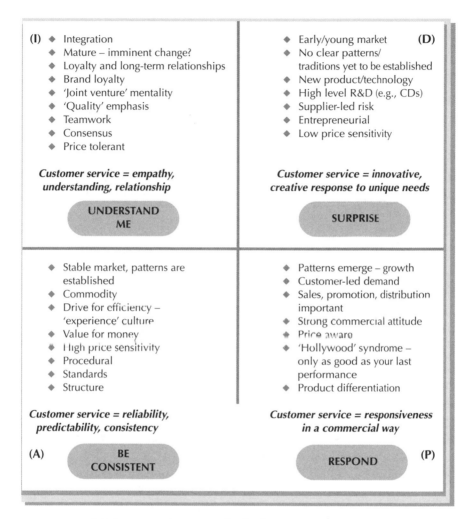

(I)
- ◆ Integration
- ◆ Mature – imminent change?
- ◆ Loyalty and long-term relationships
- ◆ Brand loyalty
- ◆ 'Joint venture' mentality
- ◆ 'Quality' emphasis
- ◆ Teamwork
- ◆ Consensus
- ◆ Price tolerant

Customer service = empathy,
understanding, relationship

UNDERSTAND ME

(D)
- ◆ Early/young market
- ◆ No clear patterns/ traditions yet to be established
- ◆ New product/technology
- ◆ High level R&D (e.g., CDs)
- ◆ Supplier-led risk
- ◆ Entrepreneurial
- ◆ Low price sensitivity

Customer service = innovative,
creative response to unique needs

SURPRISE

- ◆ Stable market, patterns are established
- ◆ Commodity
- ◆ Drive for efficiency – 'experience' culture
- ◆ Value for money
- ◆ High price sensitivity
- ◆ Procedural
- ◆ Standards
- ◆ Structure

Customer service = reliability,
predictability, consistency

(A)   **BE CONSISTENT**

- ◆ Patterns emerge – growth
- ◆ Customer-led demand
- ◆ Sales, promotion, distribution important
- ◆ Strong commercial attitude
- ◆ Price aware
- ◆ 'Hollywood' syndrome – only as good as your last performance
- ◆ Product differentiation

Customer service = responsiveness
in a commercial way

RESPOND   **(P)**

FIGURE 1.10 ◆ Primary customer service logics

Source Adapted from Figure 2.4 in Gattorna and Walters (1996), p. 31

For one class of customer, good service means surprising them with an innovative, creative response to meet their unique needs, at speed. This is a D logic. For another class of customers with a different mindset, good customer service means delivering a reliable, predictable service, on a consistent basis. For this type of customer, consistency is essential. This is the A logic. For yet another class of customer, good service means being responsive to their demanding requirements in a commercial way. For them, straight out responsiveness and timeliness is paramount. This is the P logic. Finally for another group of customers, the opposite is true, as they seek service that is empathetic and understanding, generally delivered in a quietly consistent way. For them the crucial ingredient is having suppliers understand their special need for a close and sharing relationship, which ensures they are not taken out of their comfort zone. This is the I logic.

Following these logics leads us to conclude that the concepts of 'responsiveness' and 'flexibility' (much sought after by all supply chain participants) are not about doing one thing well after all, but rather having the capability to do several things well, often concurrently. We will explore this theme further in Chapter 2.

If you have any doubt about the importance of managing modern supply chains look no further than the example of some leading companies that I mentioned earlier. Why is it that one national icon, Marks & Spencer, could lose its way, while another, Nestlé, could move from strength to strength? Both had secure positions in their respective markets, enjoying a strong brand and loyal customer following. But one misunderstood its customers and made the wrong decisions about its supply chains; the other was in touch with its customers and was unfazed by supply chain complexity. Nestlé knows what *dynamic alignment* means.

And why is it that retailer J. Sainsbury was rudderless in the changing world of supply chain and globalization, while Tesco expanded its business to capture the advantages offered by the changing times? Sainsbury acted like a large steamer moving slowly through the market waters. It lost market share due to huge stocks-outs, high costs and lower margins. But Tesco navigated through changing times, expanding from food into other categories such as petrol and insurance. It secured its position through strong leadership and clear supply chain strategy. Again, one company could capture the benefits of smart supply chain management, while another was overcome by supply chain complexity. But things can change!

Trying to navigate your way through the spaghetti bowl of today's supply chains is not easy for any enterprise, regardless of their age, market penetration or financial resources. Some do it better than others and reap the rewards. Successful organizations understand that building more responsive, customer-focused supply chains is the key to the future. *Dynamic alignment* of supply chains means being able to see the life within those supply chains, capturing the energy and opportunity, and lining that up with the demands of customers. In the coming decade, little else is going to happen in an enterprise outside the domain of its supply chains. Supply chains **are** the business, and you better believe it!

Living lessons

1 Take a more liberal view of the scope of supply chains – you will be well rewarded. We are talking about the central nervous system of all business.

2 You cannot afford to let your market move away from you.

3 Building more responsive supply chains means building more responsive enterprises overall.

CHAPTER 2

Customer conversations

All pathways lead to customers

We have all been seeking the Holy Grail of improved operational and financial performance. The problem is we have been looking in the wrong places. The secret of designing a superior supply chain is to start by re-segmenting customers along buying behaviour lines and then reverse engineering from there. We need to shape specific value propositions and underpin these with appropriate organization structures, processes, technology and other building blocks.[1] Indeed, something that we have known for some time – but have been denying – is that customers are the ultimate frame of reference. Mattias Holweg and Fritz Pil were adamant about this when they promoted the use of Built-to-Order (BTO) strategies.[2] We believe introducing such a customer focus is critical to a breakthrough in supply chain thinking.

We shouldn't blame senior managers for failing to emphasize customers sufficiently because outdated organizational designs have not helped. Hierarchical, rigid structures have often fragmented knowledge and responsibility into silos, leading to little information on customers ever filtering through to the people in back-office positions. What's more, most organizations have adopted erroneous and mostly irrelevant customer segmentation regimes. These include segmentation using Standard Industrial Classifications (SIC, which are now being re-defined and upgraded), industry sectors, geography, size, profitability, product type and an assortment of institutional parameters around which sales forces and logistics operations are mobilized. Thomas Davenport and his colleagues were right when they concluded that 'a firm needs more than transactional data to gain (customer) insight'.[3] Successful companies agree that the person **behind** the transaction must also be considered. We can better understand and predict customer behaviour by examining behavioural data along with the corresponding transactional data.[4] Indeed, this is where knowledge management intersects with our interest in customer buying behaviours. Unfortunately, companies are relying too much on technology-driven transactional data, which leaves big gaps in their knowledge about customers. Something else is needed to fill these gaps.

Confusion around segmentation

The segmentation of customers, together with product differentiation, are perhaps the two most fundamental concepts in marketing. *Product differentiation* is reasonably straightforward, but confusion is rife when it comes to the concept of *segmentation* and how it is operationalized. Essentially, the idea is simple: we need to group customers with shared features together so that we can match service strategies to their unique needs. Each segment must be distinct, accessible and economically viable in size. Based on these guidelines your ability to dissect a market is only limited by the breadth of your imagination. But therein lies the problem.

One of the earliest forms of segmentation used by enterprises was the classic *one-size-fits-all* approach. This attempt to standardize all products and services was born out of a misguided drive to simplify internal processes for the sake of managerial convenience. A pity about the poor customers; alignment was not even on managers' radar! However, increasingly sophisticated customers soon forced big-brand companies to look for solutions that were more accommodating to what they wanted. Unfortunately, some suppliers went to the other extreme and fell into the *over-customization trap*, where every customer was treated as unique. In turn, this led to further complexity and even higher cost-to-serve. In reality, the compromise (or '*80 per cent' solution*) lies somewhere in the middle of these two extremes: creating three or possibly four substantive behavioural segments rather than one or many.

How do your sales and marketing people target your customers? Generally, sales and marketing managers have developed a myriad of ways to divide their markets and allocate resources, or in particular, to organize their sales forces and logistics functions. They have paid little or no attention to the impact on the back-of-shop operations. Indeed, a real 'disconnect' continues between the way market-facing personnel view customers and the information they communicate back to non-market-facing personnel. And yet it's fundamental that everyone inside the enterprise who contributes to serving customers, either directly or indirectly, should be on the same wavelength. Despite advances in technology, we do not seem to have achieved this most basic level of common understanding. And while the search goes on at the front-end of organizations to find ever more subtle ways of understanding what customers want,[5] little or no work appears to be taking place to link this ever evolving understanding to back-office fulfillment operations. Sound familiar?

Most enterprises will ultimately adopt a segmentation method to guide the design and operation of their supply chains. In many cases, unfortunately, you pay your money and get what you deserve! We have compelling evidence from many research and consultancy projects during the last two decades that there is really only one 'right' and cost-effective way to group customers, and that's on the basis of their dominant buying preferences/behaviours, i.e., behavioural segmentation. This approach goes to the very heart of customer values and expectations. We don't need to distinguish between the way we serve customers in a sales sense and the way we serve them logistically. It would be quite incorrect to do so, because we now understand that customers themselves do not make these artificial distinctions. It is all the same to them. Customers have a holistic set of expectations (or 'buying values') that are manifested in a hierarchy of attributes including, among others, price, speed, brand, innovation, supply continuity, particular specifications, quality and support.

Perhaps one of the best recent attempts at arguing the case for behavioural segmentation (for the purposes of channel design) was undertaken by US strategic change researchers Phil Nunes and Frank Cespedes.[6] They argue that customers have 'escaped' from conventional channels, and this is certainly true. But then again, we need to find faster and better ways of keeping abreast of the evolving, learning customer. They identified four kinds of buyers, not unlike the 'straw man' I will present later in this chapter. However, in some respects they go overboard in attempting to describe how the buying behaviours of the four kinds of buyers vary across the five stages of a typical purchasing process. Of course, this can (and does) occur in practice, but their approach introduces an unnecessary layer of complexity, which paradoxically makes it more difficult to adopt in practice. Indeed, any new method of segmentation should be user-friendly, and this one is not. We agree with the notion that 'unfettered customer behaviour is inevitable',[7] but this is not necessarily bad, or something we should openly resist. Quite the contrary. The solution is to accept that knowledge-rich customers will inevitably find ways to access products and services by selecting from the increasing number of pathways or channels on offer. We can achieve true alignment if the customers are satisfied with this process. But to get to this point, we must first develop a much deeper understanding of the internal cultural implications on the organizations of all the parties along these channels and supply chains.

Moving away from one-dimensional solutions

Consider the supply chains that exist in your industry. How difficult would it be to shift towards using multiple supply chains to serve your different customer segments? And how effective? Where would you start? Let's look at several approaches investigated by academics and commentators since the mid-1990s.

Marshall L. Fisher was one of the first to define and explore the idea of multiple supply chains.[8] He proposed classifying products based on their demand patterns and devised two main product categories – functional and innovative – each requiring distinctly different supply chains. He concluded that '...the root cause of the problems plaguing many supply chains is a mismatch between the type of product and the type of supply chain'.[9] He suggested a matrix where functional products, such as staples with predictable demand, should be handled by an 'efficient' supply chain; and more innovative products, such as fashion apparel and electronic high-technology goods, would require what he termed a 'responsive' supply chain. In his estimation, problems arose when innovative products were processed via an 'efficient' supply chain configuration.[10] Does this thinking ring true for your organization?

We believe there are some weaknesses in Fisher's framework. Fisher assumes the demand patterns for so-called staple products will stay constant under all market conditions. But demand for any product or service can be unstable, so it is incorrect to imply that supply chains can be designed around particular product categories. Changing market conditions can and do influence demand patterns and effectively change so-called staple products into different types of 'products'. For example, under normal circumstances, Fisher might classify petrol as a staple product, exhibiting relatively predictable demand patterns among consumers. However, if there is even the sniff of a refinery strike, or an accident interrupts supply, consumers are likely to rush to petrol stations and pay whatever price is being asked at the pump. In such a situation, the supplying oil company has to manage the unpredicted spike in demand differently from everyday demand for petrol. The Coca-Cola Company is another example. Coca-Cola exhibits different demand patterns when sold in volume through a supermarket outlet compared to when sold in smaller quantities via the corner shop or a vending machine; and the corresponding supply chains for each channel are configured differently too. So focusing solely on the product and its 'typical demand characteristics' is not the answer.

Hau Lee, the well-known Stanford University professor, attempted to develop Marshall Fisher's work in his paper, 'Aligning Supply Chain Strategies with Product Uncertainties'.[11] He proposed four types of supply chain strategies, which look very much like my own taxonomy of four supply chain types, namely efficient supply chains (equivalent to my *lean*), risk-hedging supply chains (equivalent to my *fully flexible*), responsive supply chains and agile supply chains (which taken together appear to be equivalent to my *agile*). He does not suggest anything equivalent to my *continuous replenishment* supply chain type; some of these characteristics are probably buried in his efficient supply chain type.

The framework he uses to develop his categorization of four supply chains involves matching supply uncertainty and demand uncertainty. This is a useful development, but in the end it proves to be inadequate. Why? Because it is based on categorizing products as either functional or innovative – this is meant to characterize whether they are of low or high demand uncertainty. This is the weakness in the framework because we have already concluded that products and services can be subject to different customer buying behaviours, which in turn will change their demand and supply situation.

Lee's model lacks the all-important dynamic capability that we will discuss in more detail later in this chapter. It is more of a static representation at a point in time, which although an approximation of reality is not close enough when product-market situations are changing ever more rapidly. As an example, a small washer on a piece of equipment may be categorized as a staple by Lee, but it could become critical if it fails, thereby causing the machine to fail. In that circumstance, a customer's buying behaviour for the humble washer would surely move (albeit temporarily) from staple product (involving an efficient/lean type supply chain) to emergency requirement (involving a *fully flexible* type supply chain) – extreme opposites. Lee seems to recognize the requirement for a dynamic approach when he says that '... because of shorter and shorter product life cycles, the pressure for dynamically adjusting and adapting a company's supply chain is mounting'.[12] Perhaps this will be achieved, but in a somewhat different way to that which he originally envisaged.

IBM also has a view on this vexed topic of multiple supply chains. Bill Gilmour, IBM's global consumer product industry leader, argues that fast-moving consumer goods (FMCG) manufacturers need two supply chains to service their retail customers,[13] i.e., mass production push (equivalent to my *lean*) and something at the other end of the spectrum to handle unpredictable (pull) demand (equivalent to my *agile*). He does not suggest how this might work. But there is no shortage of viewpoints on the topic.

Another consultancy, Booz Allen Hamilton, proposes what it has termed 'tailored business streams' as its contribution to the debate on multiple supply chains that continues to converge.[14] Its view that '... the challenge for companies is not achieving a single point of focus. It is harmonizing multiple points of focus,'[15] is well made. Its research found that what it called 'Smart Customizers', that is companies that aligned their market-facing and fulfillment operations with customers, exhibited a 2:1 performance gap over those that did not. This is a significant finding and should accelerate the movement towards multiple supply chain alignment that I am proposing in this book.

A third academic to offer insights into this topic is Jonathan Byrnes of MIT; he acknowledges that three or more supply chains may co-exist in and between enterprises.[16] Companies such as Wal-Mart, P&G and Target are typical of those taking advantage of new supply chain information technologies, which are 'becoming more capable of dynamic management, assigning the right product to the right supply chain at the right time'.[17] His insights appear to be similar to those expressed by Fisher. But here too we should scrutinize where he places the most focus, and in this case Byrnes emphasizes what he calls '... an intelligent, precise supply chain IT system'.[18]

Like other commentators before him, Byrnes is close, but not quite close enough. He too is skirting the more fundamental issue of *who* is actually *pulling* and *pushing* products through supply chains in the first place. If we factor this dimension into the equation we will have the ability to explain a lot more about how modern supply chains operate and how they should be designed for peak performance. Byrnes is right about one thing though, that 'sooner or later, competitive pressures will force companies to employ dynamic, differentiated supply chains, and there are compelling first-mover advantages. The supply chain managers who start to create these systems now will lead their industries for a generation to come.'[19] This said, we are still left wondering about the underlying mechanisms that will bring about this most desirable outcome!

A fifth framework is provided by A.T. Kearney, which offers a '... how-to approach for developing strategies that appropriately align with each supply chain'.[20] Their 2004 paper, 'How many supply chains do you need?', uses a combination of customer-related and product-related variables to segment supply chains. Unfortunately, any early promise is unfulfilled as they follow a similar path to that taken by Fisher by categorizing the type of supply chain by product category. As discussed, this works some but not all of the time because buying situations inevitably change for most if not all products and services. The secret is to segment customers by their dominant buying behaviour and **then** consider what this means for the design and operation of the corresponding supply chains, rather than think in terms of segmenting supply chains from the inside out. A subtle but important distinction.

Perhaps the most recent word on the topic of 'aligned supply chains' comes from Janet Godsell, a researcher at Cranfield.[21] Godsell introduces the notion of 'demand chain strategy' that links demand fulfillment (otherwise known as supply chain) with demand definition and creation (otherwise known as marketing). She sees demand chain management as 'the crucial missing link between business unit, market, and supply chain strategy – that creates alignment around a common set of demand chain objectives to ensure that the demand chain meets the needs of customers and shareholders alike in the most efficient and effective way'.[22] I am not too keen on the new terminology, but that aside, Godsell proposes a useful process for developing demand chain strategy, as follows:

1 Set demand chain objectives.

2 This will drive market strategy, comprising a) relevant segmentation and b) customer value segmentation.

3 This sets up the supply chain process strategy, comprising a) supply chain drivers and b) differentiated supply chain process strategy.

4 It also sets up process enablers, such as organization design, performance management, and systems.

This then feeds back into the demand chain objectives in an on-going interactive process. This model, is a useful introduction for approaching the alignment model, with a few caveats; Godsell is primarily linking the market with the supply chain processes. I am proposing that there's more – culture and leadership must be addressed as well if we are to align with our customers. More grist for the supply chain 'alignment' mill.

Disappointingly, none of the above perspectives seems to address the underlying influence and power of organizational culture in either supporting or resisting 'best laid plans'. In my view culture is the real 'missing link' in our understanding of how supply chains work in practice, and it is exactly this gap in current knowledge that we are addressing in this book.

Fittingly, Dave Anderson, a former colleague at Accenture and now retired, has the last word on the subject in his paper on 'Quick-Change Supply Chains'.[23] He acknowledges that 'most of today's supply chains ... are "hard wired"', which means 'they accommodate only standard service offerings and have no ability to meet fast-changing availability or delivery requirements. Yet business success in the 21st Century will increasingly demand quick-change supply chains.'[24] His 'quick-change' supply chains are equivalent to my multiple (aligned) supply chains. The only thing left to do now is agree how this philosophy should be implemented on the ground. In this respect we are not that far away from success, and increasingly harsh trading conditions in many industries will provide the incentive to find a way to jump this last hurdle. In my experience (and research), those parties in supply chains under the most pressure usually either give up or innovate first to survive. If successful, these 'first movers' receive most of the benefits from their innovation, but very often the costs involved flow to the opposite end of the chain, depending of course on the balance of power at that time. This is the world of 'survival of the fittest'.

Adding the missing behavioural dimension to supply chains

At this stage we should remind ourselves of an important point made in Chapter 1: supply chains are not inanimate mechanical structures. Products and services only move from raw materials and production sources to consuming markets because of human intervention. This can come from either outside the enterprise (customers) or inside (company personnel). My experience, gained from consulting assignments around the globe over the past two decades, only reinforces this point of view.

In fact, the empirical evidence we gathered not only confirms the importance of human intervention, but brings to light some entirely new perspectives on customer buying behaviour. The following two pivotal insights have the potential to completely revolutionize the way we do business:

1 Customers always exhibit a small but finite number of dominant buying behaviours for any given product or service category, usually no more than three, but four at most.

2 The preferred dominant buying behaviours of customers can change temporarily under the pressure of changing conditions, such as lifestyle circumstances or the product life cycle. Behaviours usually return to the preferred position when conditions return to 'normal'.

The changeability of dominant buying behaviours is probably the phenomenon that Nunes and Cespedes were attempting to cover using different stages in the purchasing life cycle.[25] But this is not equivalent to the observed phenomenon of changing buyer behaviours under changing market pressures. Interestingly, they appear to agree with my position on this topic with their comment that 'buying behaviour also depends on the shopper's particular circumstances (and) a buyer wears different hats at different times'.[26]

Coupled with these two insights, there are two further observations that can now be made:

1 People often exhibit a mix of preferred dominant buying behaviours depending on the product or service category they have in mind at the time. This means that an individual may display various different buying behaviours for different product and service categories – a fact that has perplexed and confused market researchers and marketers for decades.

2 Customers do not distinguish between the outputs of different internal departments or functions in an organization; they don't say, 'the sales force is good but logistics fulfillment is poor'. Customers are very binary in their outlook and see service as simply good or bad – with little in between.

Can you now see why aligning with customers as they continuously learn and evolve their hierarchy of values is so difficult? Clearly, segmenting supply chains according to customer buying behaviours is a dynamic process. It is like trying to hit a moving target, rather than seeking an all-embracing descriptor of a stagnant customer type, which is where previous approaches have erred.

From this point it is only a small step in logic to the concept and practice of *multiple supply chain alignment*, as depicted in Figure 2.1.

Supply chains with different configurations start to emerge around the most commonly observed types of behavioural segments, shown in Figure 2.2.

Even though there are many combinations and permutations of possible behavioural segments, in my experience the four-segment combination depicted in Figure 2.2 is evident in markets as diverse as petrol, legal services, travel, dairy products, third-party logistics services and financial planning; note the equal emphasis on services as well as products. More examples can be found in Appendix 2A.

It is worth repeating that there are particular types of behavioural groupings where customers naturally reside, but customers can and do switch between all four buying behaviours according to situational pressures. Also, it is not uncommon in large complex organizations to find evidence of more than one buying behaviour present, although mostly in different timeframes, e.g., the different ways Nestlé buys a range of dairy ingredients from its New Zealand supplier, Fonterra. For some product, Nestlé prefers to push on price; for others there is a preference for a particular product specification, at a premium.

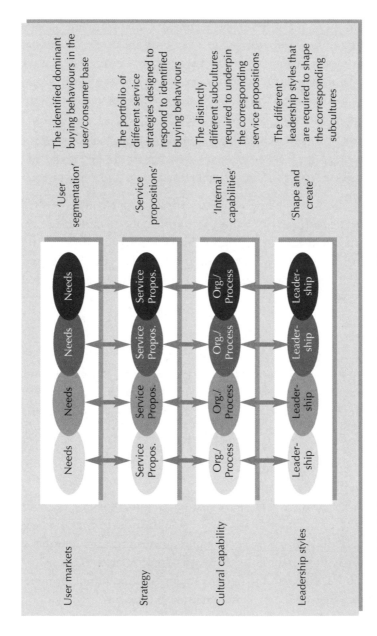

FIGURE 2.1 ◆ Multiple supply chain alignment on the customer side

Source Adapted from Figure 4.3.2 in Gattorna (2003); p. 459

Collaborative	*Efficiency*	*Demanding*	*Innovative solutions*
Close working relationships for mutual gain	Consistent low-cost response to largely predictable demands	Quick response to unpredictable supply and demand conditions	Supplier-led development and delivery of new ideas
Ia	**A**	**Pa**	**Dp**
◆ Mostly predictable ◆ Regular delivery ◆ Mature or augmented products ◆ Primary source of supply ◆ Trusting relationship ◆ Teamwork/partnership ◆ Information sharing ◆ Joint development ◆ Forgiving ◆ Price not an issue	◆ Predictable demand within contract ◆ Regular delivery ◆ Efficiency low-cost focus ◆ Multiple sources of supply ◆ Little sharing of information ◆ More adversarial ◆ Standard processes ◆ Power imposed ◆ Transactional ◆ Very price sensitive	◆ Unpredictable demand ◆ Commodity relationship ◆ Time priority/urgency ◆ Opportunity focus ◆ Ad hoc source of supply ◆ Low loyalty, impersonal ◆ Fewer processes ◆ Outcome oriented ◆ Commercial deals ◆ Based on pragmatism ◆ Price aware	◆ Very unpredictable demand ◆ Higher risk ◆ Flexible delivery response ◆ Innovation focus ◆ Rapid change ◆ Individual decision making ◆ Solutions oriented ◆ Management of IP ◆ Incentives/ego ◆ No price sensitivity

FIGURE 2.2 ◆ **The four most commonly observed dominant buying behaviours**

Source Adapted from Table 1.3.1 in Gattorna (2003), p. 32

At this stage we are in a position to make two more observations:

1   In segmenting customers, geography has little impact on the range of dominant buying behaviours; the only thing that changes is the proportional mix of these same buying behaviours.

2   Similarly for country (or national) cultures, the only change from country to country is again the proportional mix.[27] When you think about this it makes sense, unless of course we are dealing with extra-terrestrials! Too often, too much is read into the potential impact of different national cultures, when really we should be emphasizing the similarities.

From spaghetti bowls to conveyor belts – a *dynamic* perspective

Can you see the result? Four discrete supply chains (or conveyor belts) run through most organizations. Each has a different configuration and operating characteristics, achieved by combining largely standard processes and activities in unique ways. The supply chains themselves may also combine in different ways, e.g., agile with lean, collaborative with agile; but more about these subtleties later. The combination of up to four coexistent supply chains is depicted in Figure 2.3. Obviously, variations around these four 'generic' types can and do exist, but in my experience these are the ones most commonly present and therefore the most deserving of attention.

A note before we go on. As much as possible, I've chosen to label the four generic supply chain types with existing names, e.g., in particular, *lean* and *agile*. Why? The literature already has too much different terminology without my adding further to the confusion. However, having said that, I need to briefly explain where my definitions of these terms vary from existing interpretations:

●   *Continuous replenishment* supply chain: this one is quite straightforward. To work properly, it requires collaboration with customers (pull), as simple as that.

●   *Lean* supply chain: my definition of lean varies from existing usage in that I do not think lean necessarily involves collaboration with customers;

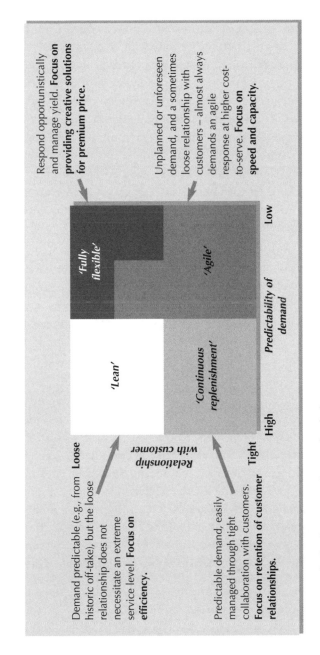

FIGURE 2.3 ◆ The four generic supply chain types

that's why we have *continuous replenishment*. However, it may involve some pull component via collaboration on the supply side. But my definition of lean and the traditional definition both involve push into the marketplace, and a focus on efficiency by removing cost wherever possible. But lean still requires some external view in order to develop and align the appropriate value propositions with customers. However, we should not be trying to convert all customers to a collaborative buying behaviour mindset – that is plain wasteful, and does not work. So the subtlety is that lean is not completely internal in its orientation. Marks & Spencer misguidedly tried to go lean in the late 1990s, but this approach did not align with its customers' value set – so they got it wrong and failed. In fact, adapting to the customer's value set is a key consideration at all times. Lean works well when it fits the value proposition of customers with low cost and efficiency at the front of their mind.

- *Agile* supply chain: this means responsiveness to customers in unpredictable demand situations; it is all about pull. Customer pull. And it can be achieved in various ways. However, the appropriate agile response almost always involves building in redundant capacity along the supply chain – in the form of inventory, labour and production.

- *Fully flexible* supply chain: this is an extreme example of an *agile* supply chain. Indeed, some would argue that this is not a free-standing supply chain type, but rather a 'must have' *competence* that can be brought to bear as and when customers need extreme solutions. Whatever your point of view on this, it is important to have this competence for business continuity in crisis situations – and they do arise from time to time! As such, it might involve a small group of highly skilled and entrepreneurial people being available on a stand-by or emergency basis. GE has its incubator which probably doubles, in part at least, as its *fully flexible* capability. The thing to remember about this type of supply chain is that the supplier always leads the market in search of the most appropriate innovative solutions; customers count on them for this. In every other situation, customers have their say.

Can you see what ability your firm needs for all these supply chains? The abiding challenge facing enterprises of all types is *flex*, i.e., the ability to have each supply chain capability compartmentalized inside the business, and have enough flexibility to change between supply chains with the shifting marketplace, which after all is not very fast. It is a bit like watching grass grow if you are alert to what is happening! So facilitating easy switches between the three mainstream supply chains, with the fourth on stand-by, is the type of dynamic we are suggesting. It's this more dynamic view of how supply chains serve the marketplace that makes this book stand out from other current literature on the supply chain.

Each of the four types of supply chain depicted in Figure 2.3 may be characterized by different 'flow types', shaped by a combination of customer buying behaviours and internal culture-driven behaviour. These flow types are illustrated in Figure 2.4.[28]

The management of complexity will reduce significantly if the behavioural segment-driven regime suggested here is adopted. This is quite the opposite effect to that experienced where so-called standard processes (and standard technology) are implemented across entire organizations. This leads paradoxically to increased complexity and higher cost-to-serve – because of all the exceptions created along the way. If organizations are predominantly designed to deliver one type of value proposition, and the marketplace contains, say, three dominant types of customer buying behaviours, then the degree of alignment will be very limited, and the organization will find itself continually making costly exceptions. The conclusion? Complexity is significantly reduced through superior *dynamic alignment*.

Flexibility is actually increased when alignment conditions are fulfilled. There is a lot said about flexibility and the need for organizations to be more agile and adaptive in the fast-moving world of the third millennium. However, flexibility is not about having one offer, and then creating a myriad of exceptions to achieve fit with customers; that's far too expensive and does not deliver the required service on a sustainable basis.

Genuine flexibility can only be achieved through multiple alignment. The organization must be 'hard-wired' to a limited number of customer segments via a hybrid organizational structure and a unique combination of processes and corresponding technology applications. Then, if customers change their buying behaviours under pressure of new operating conditions in their respective markets, it simply means they move to another of the previously identified dominant buying behaviours for that product or service category. They are thereafter serviced in the predefined way for that segment. This is flexibility without the corresponding cost penalty. In business-to-business (B2B) situations, it is possible that a given customer organization will exhibit all four of the identified buying

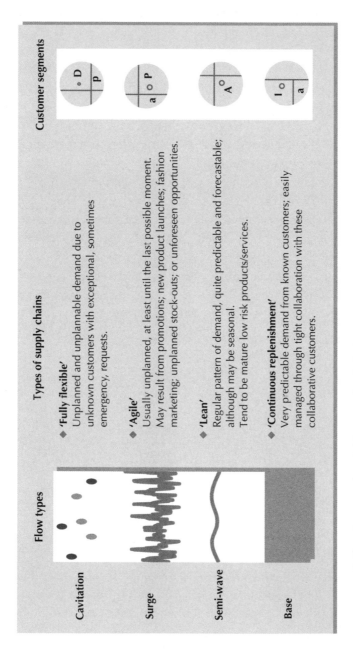

Flow types	Types of supply chains	Customer segments
Cavitation	◆ **'Fully flexible'** Unplanned and unplannable demand due to unknown customers with exceptional, sometimes emergency, requests.	D / p
Surge	◆ **'Agile'** Usually unplanned, at least until the last possible moment. May result from promotions; new product launches; fashion marketing; unplanned stock-outs; or unforeseen opportunities.	a / P
Semi-wave	◆ **'Lean'** Regular pattern of demand, quite predictable and forecastable; although may be seasonal. Tend to be mature low risk products/services.	A / a
Base	◆ **'Continuous replenishment'** Very predictable demand from known customers; easily managed through tight collaboration with these collaborative customers.	I / a

FIGURE 2.4 ◆ Flow types and matching supply chain types

behaviours at different times; this is quite normal and relatively easily managed once understood. Figure 2.5 (see p. 48) shows the details of each combination of supply chain–value proposition–customer buying behaviour.

Alignment of the appropriate value propositions with customers' true needs and expectations significantly improves operating and financial performance for several reasons:

◆ It is easier to focus on consistently fulfilling customer requirements (better service).

◆ It is easier to charge appropriately for 'value added' supply chain services (improved margins).

◆ It allows advanced functional excellence to be brought to bear in high value segments, e.g., collaborative planning within the 'Collaborative' segment.

◆ It also facilitates functional excellence in lower value segments, e.g., reduced cost-to-serve.

◆ It allows better management of opportunistic business in the 'Demanding' and 'Innovative solutions' segments, leading to increased revenue and margins.

◆ It allows the development of new service offerings resulting from continuous innovation across all supply chain types, e.g., increased revenue.

Zara – genuine *dynamic alignment* in practice

It is rare to find a company that demonstrates the benefits of alignment as well as Zara, the Spanish fashion retailer and manufacturer.[29] Zara is a superb example because its business brings almost every facet of alignment and supply chain principles into play. It is a powerful reminder that good performance flows from a combination of many factors. Of course, Zara mainly sells women's, men's and children's fashion apparel, a segment that will always be demanding in behavioural terms. Zara's decision to focus mostly on a segment with a single type of dominant buying behaviour means it has an easier task in designing the appropriate supply chain configuration. And it has done just that with distinction.

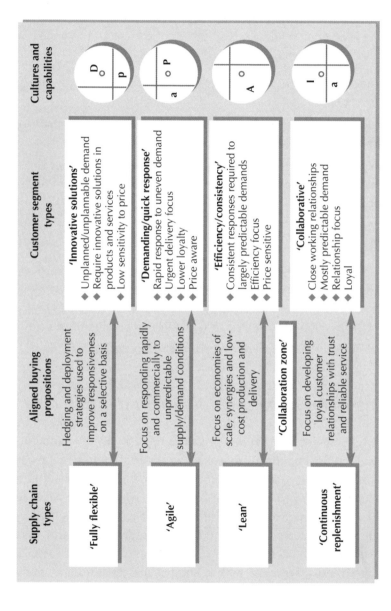

FIGURE 2.5 ◆ **Aligned supply chain 'value propositions'**

Source Adapted from Figure 7 in Christopher and Gattorna (2004), p. 120

Zara's amazing agility could even encourage it to move into adjacent, less fashion-oriented markets for apparel, competing with the likes of British retailer Marks & Spencer. Zara would have an immediate advantage if it did so, as it could easily work inside the current Marks & Spencer cycle time (from design to store shelf), in the process winning more customers for lower-priced, less fashionable apparel. The success of Zara's agility is demonstrated in its ability to move quickly from 'sketch to store' in 15 days, resulting in customers' perception of their stores always having fresh product. In contrast, Marks & Spencer has a more traditional supply chain for textiles and apparel, with cycle times up to a year. Only two major clothing collections are released by Marks & Spencer each year: Spring/Summer and Autumn/Winter, and consumers lie in wait for the inevitable mark-downs and clearance sales.

'Triple-A' supply chains are not here yet

The good news is that the idea of aligning your supply chains with customers, suppliers and third-party logistics providers (3PLs) is intuitively attractive and catching on fast.[30] In fact, we seem to be hearing all the right rhetoric lately. But no one has joined all the dots and fully understood what is involved in engineering an aligned supply chain. We are at best in a world of observation and anecdotes, and still some way from a comprehensive theory to guide us into the future. Hau Lee comments that 'most firms already have the infrastructure in place to create Triple-A supply chains. What they need is a fresh attitude and a new culture to get their supply chains to deliver Triple-A performance.'[31] By 'Triple-A' he is referring to the three qualities – adaptiveness, agility and alignment – that enterprises need to exhibit in their supply chains.

Achieving superior performance is easy to say but difficult to achieve when most organizations still have such a poor understanding of how cultural capability underpins all action on the ground in some way or other. We must work to design and embed the appropriate subcultures in the organization to reflect the customer segments (otherwise called external subcultures) that exist in a particular market. It simply will not happen by chance. The ideal mix is the 45/45/10 we described in Chapter 1 – commit 45 per cent of effort to human behaviour, 45 per cent to systems technology and the remainder to asset infrastructure. Unfortunately, we still seem to be stuck in the 'old' 0/60/40 world, with zero emphasis on human behaviour and 60/40 on technology and infrastructure respectively. Other researchers have taken different routes towards alignment,[32] and some have even tried to use the alignment concept to help anticipate market trends.[33]

Beyond institutional segmentation

One of the most common ways that enterprises segment their markets is along 'institutional' lines, because it is convenient. Data is easily collected on recognizable institutions. Sometimes whole channels are built around specific institutions. For example, a recent re-organization at the Australian brewing business Foster's Australia, part of the Foster's Group, has resulted in the introduction of a new service model.[34] The sales force has been split into dedicated teams servicing 14 different channels, made up of customers grouped into institutions such as hotels, nightclubs, five-star hotels and resorts, restaurants, national retailers and independent liquor stores. This institutional channel model, which is expected to take three to four years to implement, will involve an overall increase in the number of staff serving customers, but is expected to reduce supply chain costs.[35] But will the lower costs necessarily follow? More importantly, will revenue climb faster than incremental costs?

More recently, Foster's has divulged more about its plans.[36] It has signalled to the market its intention to pursue a 'Blue Ocean strategy',[37] which involves making multi-beverage offerings to the 14 institutional segments identified in the Australian market. The better news, however, is that Foster's has gone further and re-organized the 14 into four behavioural segments – *Integrated*, *Destination*, *Local* and *Connect*. On the basis of public information and previous work I've done in the beverage industry, I've interpreted what each of these four new segments might look like. See Figure 2.6 for a summary of their characteristics. The Foster's strategy is truly a breakthrough, with dedicated customer-facing teams focusing on each of the four segments, and those in logistic fulfillment operational roles needing to deliver differentiated service to match. Some method of coding customer behaviour will be required to keep people working in these back-of-shop operations in synch with the responses required.

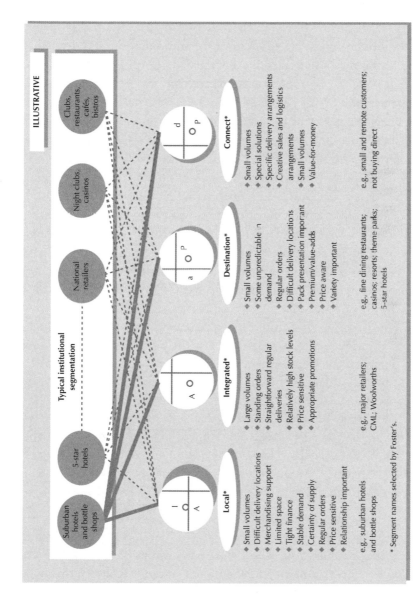

FIGURE 2.6 ◆ **Foster's new behavioural-based segmentation in Australian beverage industry**

Fortunately, this level of management sophistication is well within reach of current technology.

Ultimately it's all a question of 'packaging'. Customers in the different segments are all buying beer, but they are buying it in different ways with different product mixes, pricing, response times, quantities and relationship requirements. What the supplier must do is find correspondingly appropriate ways to align internal resources with these multiple customer requirements via a limited number of cost-effective supply chain configurations. Other examples of this phenomenon are provided in Figures 2.7 and 2.8. In Figure 2.7 we see where the Coca-Cola Company is selling and delivering to three types of customer institutional segment, all with differing service requirements. In terms of the fulfillment part of the operation, the logistics/supply chain infrastructure has to be capable of delivering an array of at least three discretely different responses.

Figure 2.8 shows the customer segments used by a publisher of children's books. Here again, each of the three behavioural segments has distinctive service priorities, requiring correspondingly appropriate supply chain responses. Management must overcome conventional mindsets in order to deliver this multidisciplinary capability.

Two other examples of multiple supply chain alignment in different industries are provided in Appendix 2B. In the health care industry, four types of supply chains were necessary to carry all the supplies consumed in public hospitals. And, as already intimated in Chapter 1, major processed food manufacturer, Goodman Fielder Ltd also needed a similar number of supply chains for its business in Asia Pacific. Unfortunately, this design was never fully implemented because of a combination of internal resistance from business unit executives and subsequent changes in leadership at the top of the organization. So how do you undertake a behavioural segmentation of your customers? There are two main approaches:

● *First, the top–down approach.* This is where your organization taps into its accumulated knowledge of customers to develop a detailed map of customer segments. You would start by conducting a workshop and quickly developing a first approximation. You can then refine the model progressively with other internal audiences and finally validate the findings with external customers. When everyone involved is satisfied with the segment descriptors, another project team can allocate each customer to one of the pre-defined behavioural segments. After that it's

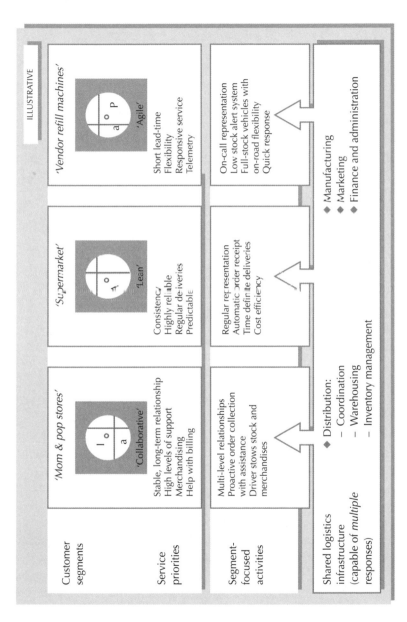

FIGURE 2.7 ◆ The three different supply chains at Coca-Cola, Japan

Source Adapted from Figure 2.14 in Gattorna and Walters (1996), p. 44

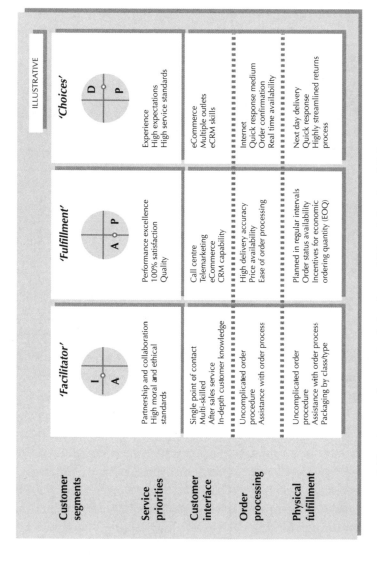

ILLUSTRATIVE

	'Facilitator'	**'Fulfillment'**	**'Choices'**
Customer segments	I · A	A · P	D · P
Service priorities	Partnership and collaboration High moral and ethical standards	Performance excellence 100% satisfaction Quality	Experience High expectations High service standards
Customer interface	Single point of contact Multi-skilled After sales service In-depth customer knowledge	Call centre Telemarketing eCommerce CRM capability	eCommerce Multiple outlets eCRM skills
Order processing	Uncomplicated order procedure Assistance with order process	High delivery accuracy Price availability Ease of order processing	Internet Quick response medium Order confirmation Real time availability
Physical fulfillment	Uncomplicated order procedure Assistance with order process Packaging by class/type	Planned in regular intervals Order status availability Incentives for economic ordering quantity (EOQ)	Next day delivery Quick response Highly streamlined returns process

FIGURE 2.8 ◆ **The three main supply chains for a children's book publisher**

a simple matter to calculate the size of each segment in terms of numbers, volume and revenue.

- *Bottom–up is the second method.* This involves your enterprise individually assessing each customer using the 'Quick' Behavioural Segmentation Diagnostic described in Appendix 2C. Staff would assess and code every customer in P-A-D-I terms and aggregate them into segments based on the similarities of their respective codes. While this bottom–up method can be somewhat time-consuming, the advantage is it provides an in-depth basis for segmentation from the start.

There is a third way, which involves undertaking sophisticated market research in the form of a conjoint analysis. In-depth investigation of the customer will deliver sound, timely and market-based information. However, except in special situations,[38] the additional time and expense is not warranted based on the extra degree of accuracy it produces. Either of the first two methods will provide sufficient accuracy for the initial segmentation. After that, personnel can be trained to continually track and, if necessary, update the experience with customers on a day-to-day basis. This 'continuous improvement' approach will ultimately lead to an accurate picture of your customer base.

Once you finalize a comprehensive re-segmentation of your customer base, it is important to take the opportunity to compare the value propositions and strategies **currently** in play with the 'ideal' strategies indicated by the new segmentation regime. Appendix 2D provides you with a 'quick' diagnostic format for comparing 'current' and 'ideal' strategies; the results of this comparative analysis will surely prove enlightening.

One final word on this topic of customer segmentation, channels and supply chains. Very often suppliers, such as FMCG and pharmaceutical companies, have more than one customer between them and their consumer base. And it is more than likely that these will have different – even opposing – dominant buying behaviours at each level. Schering-Plough, the pharmaceutical company, faced such a problem when it launched an innovative product for hayfever in the mid-1990s. The consumer was attracted to the product through Schering-Plough's advertising and wanted what at the time was a rapid fix. Many retail pharmacists, however, were not prepared to stock the product as they made less margin than on other competitive products. Area health authorities have a similar problem when building and operating hospital facilities. Patients (end-users), nursing staff, administrators, doctors, boards and government all have different 'buying behaviours'. So the task of reconciling all the different mindsets and expectations is a difficult one, even before the operational fulfillment comes into play. We should not lose sight of this other dimension of the alignment problem.

Optimal pathways to customers

So what is your ultimate goal? You need to configure your total logistics network and wider supply chain arrangements so that you have the capacity to deliver an array of supply chain responses that align with the dominant buying behaviours of your customers. And you must do this in an increasingly competitive operating environment. This objective is amply demonstrated by the case of Fletcher Challenge Paper, the major New Zealand based newsprint manufacturer, since acquired by Norske Skogg.

Fletcher Challenge Paper

In 1999, Fletcher Challenge Paper (FCP) was supplying 85 per cent of newsprint to a small number of major newspapers in Australia and New Zealand, and other users in Asia. Indeed, each of these individual customers was a market in its own right, with complicated end requirements. At the time, the company faced the threat of new newsprint capacity coming on-stream in Asia, which was threatening existing pricing arrangements and reducing margins. FCP decided to segment the relatively small number of major users of newsprint along 'buyer value' lines. The output of this buyer values segmentation is shown in Figure 2.9.

FCP also decided to model its entire supply chain network in order to understand the costs involved in servicing its major customers. The company used a sophisticated Network Optimization Modelling tool.[39] It was a complex undertaking which took six months to complete, but the results were beneficial. Figure 2.10 illustrates the complex supply chain model that was in place at FCP, from forest to newsprint user.

Logistics network structure

The company sourced major virgin fibre from a combination of owned, managed and third-party forests, and sourced waste paper from more than 100 domestic suppliers. Production occurred at three paper mills

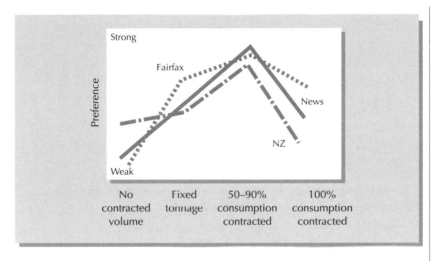

FIGURE 2.9 ◆ **Buyer values segmentation in the Asia-Pacific newsprint industry**

on six machines. Seven major grades of paper were produced – representing more than 500 different stock-keeping units (SKUs) – and distributed through six distribution centres to more than 100 customers.

Business challenge

FCP's front-line challenge was to develop a comprehensive and transportable Decision Support System (DSS) to identify the benefits of supply chain optimization. But it also needed to use the system in conjunction with its buyer value and competitor analysis so that it could develop an optimal supply chain strategy. Why? FCP's ultimate goal was to increase market share and margins in an otherwise mature industry.

Approach

FCP developed an optimization model in sufficient detail that could test the validity and cost of current operating constraints in the supply chain, such as existing supplier and customer agreements and contracts. To cater for the multiple modelling objectives and provide the required detail, the model was designed to enable:

◆ evaluation of alternate sources of supply and supplier yields;

◆ evaluation of benefits from closing specific items of plant;

◆ re-allocation of products to paper machines;

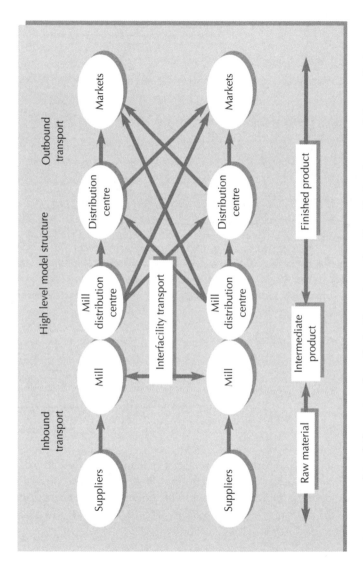

FIGURE 2.10 ◆ Logistics network optimization at a major New Zealand newsprint manufacturer

- evaluation of multiple cutting patterns on paper machines to minimize waste across the network;
- multiple production recipes for similar finished product; and
- alternative customer pricing structures.

Scenarios

The decision support capability of the model was integrated with customer and competitor analysis to model various scenarios, such as:

- major incursion by a competitor;
- new local entrant (i.e., new local mill);
- loss of 100 per cent of major customer business;
- gain of 100 per cent of major customer volume;
- increase in sales of specialties to commercial printers; and
- long-term change in newsprint demand (minus 25 per cent to 10 per cent).

The modelling prompted a range of possible responses. FCP could do nothing; use price as a deterrent; or choose to amend contracts or change capacity. It gained significant new insights into the differences between each major customer/market, which were subtle but important. The company was able to customize its product and service offerings for individual customers. Based on a deeper understanding of the cost of serving different customers/markets, each segment was served more cost effectively. Over- and under-servicing was eliminated. FCP achieved cost savings of around NZ$10 million a year and, just as importantly, improved its margins while enhancing its relationship with customers. Through all the changes, customers felt they were being better served. It was win–win all round.

Network Optimization Models of the type used by Fletcher Challenge Paper are very powerful, especially when linked to buying behaviour segments in the target market. Every enterprise should build one of these models to enhance decision-making quality. Unfortunately, my experience is that relatively few companies understand the value of this type of decision support tool, and fewer still know how to build one. More detailed information on these invaluable tools can be found in John Gattorna (ed.) *Handbook of Supply Chain Management* and John Gattorna (ed.) *Strategic Supply Chain Alignment.*[40]

Reverse alignment

So far, most of my focus has been on the downstream customer side of the supply chain, because that is the fundamental frame of reference or starting point for all supply chain design and operations. The 'reverse' or supply side is the mirror-image of the customer side, and both are depicted in Figure 2.11.

Typically, a small but finite number of distinctly different supply/procurement chains link suppliers' dominant selling behaviours, procurement strategies of the buying organization and the internal cultural capabilities and leadership styles of the buying organization, as depicted in Figure 2.12. This is the mirror-image of Figure 2.1.

The four types of generic procurement chain on the supply side ideally match the four corresponding dominant selling behaviours depicted in Figure 2.13. But they do not have to match exactly; sometimes it is possible to have a mix of procurement and customer supply chains.

And as with the customer side, each procurement chain requires different buying propositions matched against the identified supplier segments, as indicated in Figure 2.14.

The Royal Australian Navy (RAN) and the Logistic Support Agency-Navy within the Defence Materiel Organisation (DMO) are testing 'alignment' principles to guide the purchase of main engines for part of its surface fleet. A pilot project has already been conducted with a major international supplier, with promising results. Indeed, not unexpectedly, the buying behaviours of the Navy/DMO for engines/rotatables, components and spares, and maintenance were quite different in each category. This pointed to a need for different procurement strategies, and corresponding aligned responses from the supplier. So much for the old one-dimensional 'tender' process! It is very refreshing to find a public sector enterprise such as the

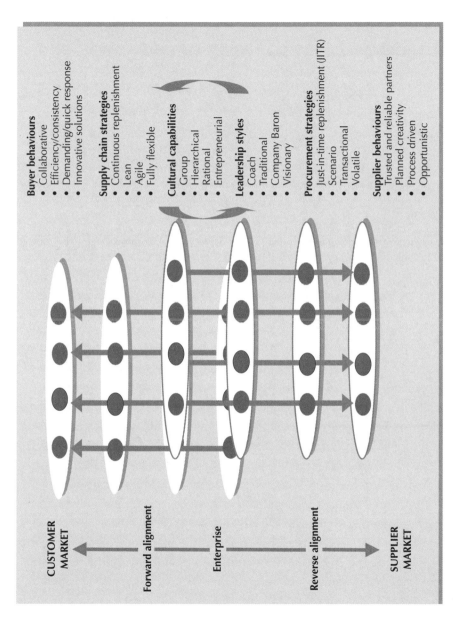

Buyer behaviours
- Collaborative
- Efficiency/consistency
- Demanding/quick response
- Innovative solutions

Supply chain strategies
- Continuous replenishment
- Lean
- Agile
- Fully flexible

Cultural capabilities
- Group
- Hierarchical
- Rational
- Entrepreneurial

Leadership styles
- Coach
- Traditional
- Company Baron
- Visionary

Procurement strategies
- Just-in-time replenishment (JITR)
- Scenario
- Transactional
- Volatile

Supplier behaviours
- Trusted and reliable partners
- Planned creativity
- Process driven
- Opportunistic

CUSTOMER MARKET

Forward alignment

Enterprise

Reverse alignment

SUPPLIER MARKET

FIGURE 2.11 ◆ **Supply side alignment, the mirror-image of the customer side**

Source Adapted from Figure 3.5.2 in Gattorna (2003), p. 346

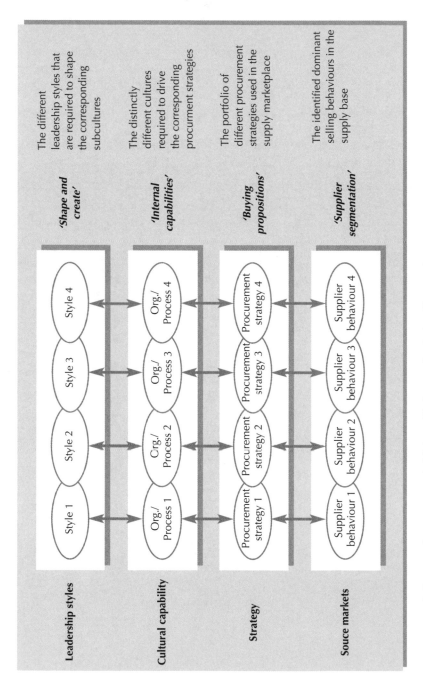

The different leadership styles that are required to shape the corresponding subcultures

The distinctly different cultures required to drive the corresponding procurment strategies

The portfolio of different procurement strategies used in the supply marketplace

The identified dominant selling behaviours in the supply base

'Shape and create'

'Internal capabilities'

'Buying propositions'

'Supplier segmentation'

Leadership styles

| Style 1 | Style 2 | Style 3 | Style 4 |

Cultural capability

| Org./ Process 1 | Org./ Process 2 | Org./ Process 3 | Org./ Process 4 |

Strategy

| Procurement strategy 1 | Procurement strategy 2 | Procurement strategy 3 | Procurement strategy 4 |

Souce markets

| Supplier behaviour 1 | Supplier behaviour 2 | Supplier behaviour 3 | Supplier behaviour 4 |

FIGURE 2.12 ◆ **Reverse (procurement side) multiple supply chain alignment**

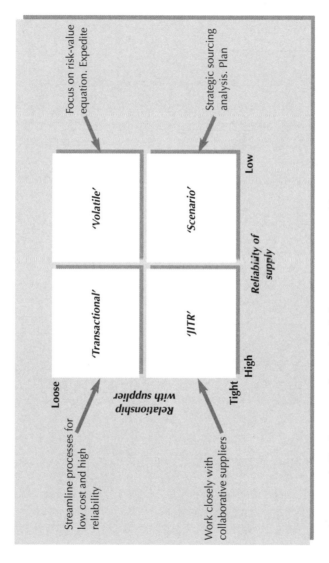

FIGURE 2.13 ◆ The four generic supply chains (procurement side)

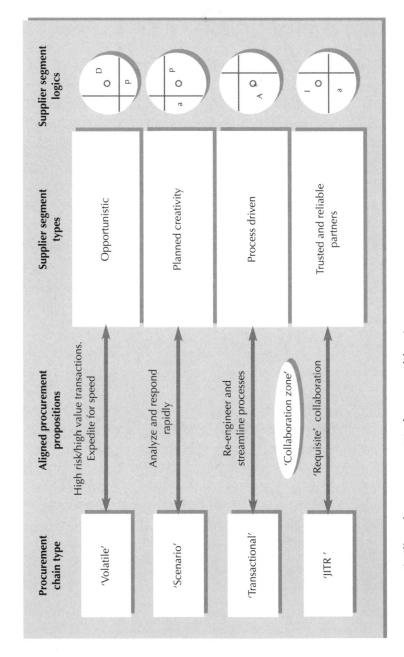

FIGURE 2.14 ◆ Aligned procurement 'value propositions'

Logistic Support Agency-Navy embracing leading-edge thinking and practice. Again, it is all about 'leadership', as we will discuss further in Chapter 4. But it is not always necessary to have a like-with-like match between the supply-side and customer-side supply chains. Indeed, it's possible to have various combinations of these depending on what provides the best alignment with the downstream customer's requirements. We will refer in more detail to mixed supply chain logics in Chapters 5–8; see also Figure 8.4 in Chapter 7 for a diagrammatic representation of mixed procurement-side and demand-side supply chains through to customers.

Now the picture is almost complete

If you take even a cursory look at Figure 2.11, you'll see why *dynamic alignment* of extended supply chains isn't easy to achieve. Clearly, a lot of pieces must be engineered into position if alignment of the various internal and external stakeholders is to occur, leading to the desired boost in performance. However, the good news is that we now know much more about what pieces are necessary for alignment, even if we haven't quite discovered how to orchestrate them to perfection. Chapter 3 will address this knowledge gap and help us move ahead to the implementation of alignment principles on the ground. Significantly, this is the area where most other commentators have not dared go, but it's essential that we tackle implementation and understand more fully the cultural forces at work inside the enterprise. Success will raise our level of understanding several notches, from a descriptive albeit superficial level to a more satisfying explanatory level. Taking that learning journey will give us far more predictive capability and get us closer than ever before to the Holy Grail – *dynamic alignment* of our supply chains.

Living lessons

1 There is only one 'right' and cost-effective way to group or segment customers: according to their dominant buying preferences and behaviours.

2 Supply chain configurations that lack a dynamic capability to 'flex' between different delivery service propositions will inevitably lead to service failures and reduced operational and financial performance.

3 For the best outcome, link behavioural segments at the customer end, and suppliers at the source end, with a network optimization model that allows a clear line of sight on the best pathways through an otherwise complex network.

CHAPTER 3

Implementing a multiple supply chain alignment strategy

Working with people to deliver the required responsiveness

'**W**ho needs competitors when we have colleagues like this to work with?' I will always remember this telling observation in 1972 by my boss at the time, Don Johnson, a Vice-President in FMC Corporation's Petroleum Equipment Group, who was setting up divisional operations in Australia, based in Melbourne. The parent company, FMC Corp., was and still is a major United States based conglomerate, with interests in many industries, from food machinery to defence. We had just come out of another interminable meeting, where very little had been achieved if you take out the politiking. Years later I came to understand what he meant, and unfortunately the same disease has continued to spread at geometric rates in many businesses! Nothing changes. Witness what happened to Carly Fiorina in her early days at Hewlett-Packard when she was trying to win over a skeptical workforce:

Mid-level managers and rank-and-file employees didn't openly attack her new ideas. They just meandered around them. In public forums, Fiorina appeared to win support. Then managers huddled privately to decide whether they liked what they heard. They softened goals, adjusted time-tables, made some exceptions. By the time they had finished, they had gutted whatever it was that Fiorina was trying to achieve. Resistance was so subtle and pervasive that she couldn't accomplish anything by getting angry. There was no obvious opponent. It was just the system.[1]

Sound familiar? Louis Coutts, international management consultant and founder of the Hawthorne Academy in the United Kingdom, expresses much the same sentiments when he exclaims:

> *Whenever I hear the war cry, 'We need to change the culture of this organi-zation,' I cringe. Culture cannot be imposed; it must be discovered. What is frequently overlooked is the fact that the culture of an organization is con-tained in the hearts and minds of the people it employs. It's already there, waiting to be expressed. To the extent that we allow that culture to be expressed, a range of benefits will emerge. If we don't allow that culture to be expressed, an organization will always fall far short of its potential.*[2]

No doubt you are familiar with this cultural war cry. From what I have seen over the last two decades, it seems that most, if not all, enterprises have problems converting stated intentions (otherwise called plans) into actions on the ground. Indeed, it's not unusual for 40–60 per cent of stated intentions and best-laid plans to go unrealized, for any number of reasons. Certainly, the changing operating environment comes into play here and can force a change in plans. But resistance from people within the enterprise can be the biggest factor causing the slippage of intended strategies. As observed in Chapter 1, enterprises can inflict much more damage on themselves than any external competitor will ever do.

The management literature has largely ignored the potential for self-wrought destruction; research normally focuses on competitors as the main source of concern. Most likely, this has been because the role culture plays in driving action inside enterprises is not fully understood. Ironically, if culture is functional, it may be the organization's only key competitive strength because it is the only thing competitors cannot easily copy in the short term.

How often have you heard the same old mantra? Just formulate smart strategies (on paper), and the rump of the organization will automatically implement these into the marketplace, unquestioned and unmodified. Experience tells us something different! What we now know is that while the downward force of strategy on the organization to deliver plans is con-siderable, an even stronger force exists – the upward force exerted by the organization's culture. Quite simply, the resident culture selects those parts of the strategy it is prepared to put into action, and those parts which it chooses to resist – as Carly Fiorina discovered.

You can see why the 'cultures' in an enterprise are a major determinant of what plans get acted upon; together we call this cultural force *cultural capability*. In this book I will refer to the various cultures that I identify as 'subcultures', as they are aspects of the broader organizational culture. These have an ability to get things done within different supply chains. The refusal of managers and staff to deliver on intentions creates a hole which they mostly fill with a disparate array of other activities, often taking the organization off the critical path to high performance. This in turn leads to frustration among the senior executives, who have a primary responsibility to shape the appropriate subcultures to get the job done in the first place. In this sense, the leadership has failed the organization, often because they are out of touch with their marketplace and their people.

Cultural mis-alignment hinders performance

So what is this mysterious phenomenon that has such an impact on the way enterprises perform? *Culture*, as depicted schematically in Figure 3.1, is the intangible human force that sits **below** the surface of the 'performance iceberg'. It represents the organization's values, beliefs and deeply held assumptions that people import into the enterprise over time. Culture represents the 'unwritten' rules about what is expected and valued in the organization. Edgar Schein defines culture as:

> *a pattern of shared basic assumptions that the group learned as it solved its external and internal problems, that has worked well enough to be considered valid and, therefore, to be taught to new members as the correct way to perceive, think, and feel in relation to those problems.*[3]

The four-level alignment framework introduced in Chapter 2 provides an invaluable way to see into the mysterious force of organizational culture. The key is to understand what is happening at the interface between each level, and particularly the **interface** between strategic response (Level 2) and cultural capability (Level 3). How many times have you seen internal culture derail the successful implementation of your plans? In short, the potentially damaging impact of mis-aligned culture is a reality that has long been overlooked. And it's now time to change that oversight.

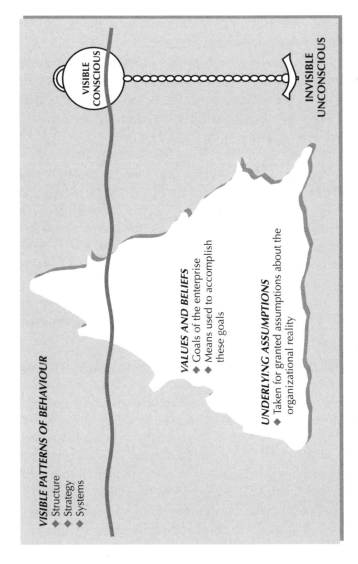

VISIBLE PATTERNS OF BEHAVIOUR
- Structure
- Strategy
- Systems

VISIBLE CONSCIOUS

VALUES AND BELIEFS
- Goals of the enterprise
- Means used to accomplish these goals

UNDERLYING ASSUMPTIONS
- Taken for granted assumptions about the organizational reality

INVISIBLE UNCONSCIOUS

FIGURE 3.1 ◆ The 'performance iceberg'

Source Adapted from Figure 4.3.3 in Gattorna (2003), p. 460

Of course, the invisibility of culture is in stark contrast to the tangible world of hard assets, infrastructure, systems technology and observed behaviour that fills the conscious world. Most people tend to manage what they can see, while either ignoring or remaining oblivious to what they can't see, touch or feel. This is the problem that has plagued not only the design and operation of supply chains, but all forms of human organization endeavour over the centuries.

Expressed simply, *organizational culture* is the way of life within the enterprise's reality or 'the way we do things around here'. Culture at the organizational level involves a shared understanding of how an enterprise perceives and responds to its operating environment. This explains how a company responds to market conditions and different customer demands. Enterprises express this as wanting to achieve a customer-focused culture. Culture also acts as the 'glue' holding the internal mechanisms together, making it capable of accomplishing what an individual alone cannot. Conversely, when culture is dysfunctional, it eventually leads to the demise of the enterprise. There are plenty of 'corporate shipwrecks' to support this latter point.

Pressure today on companies and governments to deliver shareholder value puts too much focus on cutting costs, which then creates inefficiencies in culture. For example, procedures are not documented or kept up to date because there are not enough people to do it, or people have left the organization and have not been replaced. Systems are not upgraded or are in a constant state of change. Employees avoid communicating with their manager as it usually means more work, adding to an already heavy workload. Customer service eventually suffers.

While there are common *corporate values* that apply across the entire enterprise, often referred to as *corporate culture*, other values can exist, forming subordinate cultures, sometimes termed subcultures. These are essential to ensure different response strategies are there to meet different customer demands in the marketplace. The dominant logics that shape these subcultures are the same logics that shape and drive the dominant buying behaviours of customers because, in both cases, humans and human behaviour are the common denominator.

It is also important to clearly distinguish *climate* from *culture*, to avoid confusion and misreading organizational culture. Climate is how the enterprise *feels* about itself, its mood, morale and the level of employee satisfaction at a given point in time. This is equivalent to external customer perceptions of the organization, which are expressed as opinions of the relative performance of various suppliers. Both the internal climate and external customer perceptions are subject to rapid change, whereas culture and the dominant buying behaviours of customers are permanent features and cannot be easily changed.

Can you see then, the pivotal role culture plays in implementing strategy, achieving superior performance in single enterprises and delivering performance along supply chains of linked enterprises? We need to achieve *dynamic alignment* between the internal culture and the expectations of external customers. Not an easy feat!

We learned in Chapter 2 that there are various combinations of the four primary subcultures present in all enterprises, and these are described in Figures 3.2 and 3.3.

The opposing cultural forces are P-I and A-D. The overall culture of an enterprise is the net outcome of the pull of the four forces and is ultimately represented as the dominant force, with a supporting secondary force.

Each of these four subcultures (and their various combinations) has particular strengths and limitations. This has to be factored into any change programme that seeks to improve alignment between an enterprise, its strategies and the marketplace, since the four subcultures require very specific actions to shape and mould them.

Mapping internal values and cultures

Culture mapping is a way of profiling an enterprise in quantitative terms; it makes visible what is invisible. A culture mapping questionnaire is distributed to all staff. The responses – which are usually a high proportion of the original number sent out – are sorted and mapped in any number of ways, e.g., by level, department, business unit, division, overall organization, etc.

A typical array of output maps are provided in Appendix 3A. The *current culture* is represented by the black dot or centre of gravity; it provides a picture of employee views on current behaviours, beliefs and values. The *preferred culture*, indicated by the open square, is where people would naturally like to be if there were no constraints on them or the business.

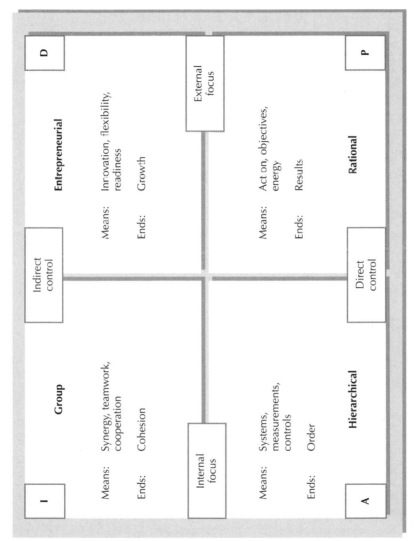

FIGURE 3.2 ◆ The four generic enterprise subcultures

Source Adapted from Figure 4.3.5 in Gattorna (2003), p. 461

| **I** | **Group culture** | **Entrepreneurial culture** | **D** |

Emphasis on cohesion, teamwork, synergy and consensus

- Closed informal communication which is shared by way of cliques and membership of an 'inner circle'
- Control achieved by commitment to common values
- Management support emphasizes the *internal* climate and environment
- Individuals' tasks are negotiated by consensus
- Rewards are based on informal standards and the ability to maintain internal cohesion – good team players
- Deviant behaviour is tolerated – provided it adheres to consensus values

Emphasis on individualism, creativity and fast response

- Open informal communication which is shared with whoever happens to be around at the time
- Control achieved by commitment to a common vision
- Management support emphasizes leading and inspiring
- Individuals are empowered to perform their roles
- Rewards are based on creativity and entrepreneurial behaviour
- Deviant behaviour is tolerated – provided it is goal directed

Emphasis on order, stability, information and control

- Closed, formal communication which is shared only on a 'need to know' basis
- Control achieved by focus on processes
- Management support emphasizes procedures
- Individuals' tasks are established by precedence
- Rewards are based on formal standards and the ability to maintain internal cohesion – good administration
- No deviation from approved processes

Emphasis on analysis, guidelines and sustained high levels of activity

- Open formal communication by way of committees and memoranda
- Control achieved by focus on results
- Management support emphasizes planning
- Individuals are given structural authority to perform their roles
- Rewards are based on formal standards and relevant results – analysis and action
- No deviation from plans or performance standards

| **A** | **Hierarchical culture** | **Rational culture** | **P** |

FIGURE 3.3 ◆ **Details of each subculture**

Finally, to complete the picture, the *ideal culture* is superimposed over the two previous plots, and represents the predominant behavioural segments present in the target marketplace. By comparing all three plots we are able to identify important 'mis-alignment' and decide what specific initiatives to take (if any) to improve alignment between the enterprise, its marketplace and current strategies. The comparative analysis gives us the ability to identify mis-alignments in great detail.

The subcultures present in an enterprise are the collective set of values and beliefs held by staff and management; they influence the thinking and action of the organization as already indicated. Techniques as described above have been developed to map multiple cultural dimensions by measuring the values present in relation to people's beliefs about the enterprise where they work.

Below is a list of ten cultural dimensions, any combination of which may be used in cultural mapping. However, experience suggests that a minimum of five are required to produce usable results. The components of each of these dimensions are described in more detail in Appendix 3B. Note: the same P-A-D-I logics apply in each of the four quadrants of these factors. The ten dimensions are:

Autonomy/decision making: indicates the extent to which individuals feel they are able to take initiative and make decisions.

Change tolerance: measures employee assumptions about the enterprise's capability and willingness to change.

Communications: measures the nature and degree of information sharing going on inside the enterprise.

Conflict: assesses how and why conflict arises in the enterprise, and how it is resolved.

Control: measures the way in which organizational effort is monitored and coordinated.

External coping:	assesses the values which influence the enterprise's ability to cope with external operating environment conditions.
Identity:	employee assumptions about the enterprise's effectiveness in the marketplace, and the extent to which they identify with this.
Internal organizing:	assesses the values which affect the way in which work is allocated, integrated and organized.
Long *vs* short term:	this dimension (identified in Geert Hofstede's cross-cultural work) represents employees' emphasis on the future in the case of those with a long-term orientation (e.g., savings and persistence); and the past or present for those with a short-term orientation (e.g., respect for tradition and status quo).[4]
Performance reward:	measures employee assumptions about what constitutes 'good' performance.

These ten cultural dimensions represent the way an enterprise's culture can be dissected and analyzed to understand better what is happening within the organization. Ultimately they help us to determine which dimensions we need to focus on to improve alignment between strategy and primary customer segments. It is much more precise than the seemingly brutal approaches used in the past, and that alone makes it infinitely more effective.

How does this help us? Through culture mapping, we can identify more accurately the most appropriate levers to use in the change process, thereby eliminating much of the guesswork that has previously plagued change management initiatives. Of course, the result of pulling any of these levers never occurs as fast as expected, but managers can now at least persevere with certain actions in the knowledge that they are on the right track, and therefore the action being taken should have the desired effect when the wheels stop spinning – and real traction is achieved.

In this process, the culture's appropriateness or inappropriateness, strengths and dysfunctional aspects are highlighted vis-à-vis the 'ideal' cultures identified through the array of customer behavioural segments. Managers are therefore in a much better position to understand how to communicate to staff, and predict how staff members are likely to handle and resolve conflict, change and cope with external pressures.

The most appropriate performance and reward system can then be more readily identified, and the recruitment process can be fine-tuned to attract people who not only have the necessary technical qualifications, but also bring with them into the enterprise a mindset that reinforces the desired culture and corresponding strategies. Culture mapping also helps managers to improve individual and team performance. A 'quick' culture diagnostic which can be used to assess the current culture of your organization is contained in Appendix 3C. This should be overlaid with the market segments identified in the 'quick' behavioural segmentation diagnostic, and any mis-alignments noted; see also Appendix 2C.

Climate factors

The influence of the more transient climate factors at work in an organization should not be under-rated, because they provide a measure of the level of stress in the organization. This is depicted by the gap between the *current* and *preferred* cultures as defined earlier. The bigger the gap, the more the stress. So, in conjunction with undertaking a culture map, it is also important to gain some insight into the issues concerning employees about their work environment. The factors considered in assessing the climate or the *mood* of the organization are:

Physical environment: employee perceptions about the physical and aesthetic aspects of their workplace.

Job stressors:	those factors which have a negative effect on employee performance.
Job motivators:	those factors which stimulate individual performance.
Job rewards:	employee perceptions about tangible and intangible aspects of reward and performance.
Corporate self-esteem:	the extent to which employees believe the organization is successful.
Communication:	employee perceptions about the style of delivery and the content and process of information sharing in the organization.

For the best results, climate and culture information should be analyzed together. Climate will signal the problem, and the clue to the root of this problem will be found in the culture data. For example, people may complain about poor communications inside the company. The culture map may reveal a predominantly A type (or logic) communication style, which means that information is only shared on a 'need to know' basis. In effect, this means that information is being withheld from people, leaving them with the feeling that communication is poor.

In summary, *culture* is the internal reality of the organization, while *climate* is the mood. *Culture* drives strategic capability, while *climate* reveals whether or not employees are satisfied or dissatisfied. *Culture* is a long-term capability embedded in the enterprise, and difficult to change rapidly. *Climate* is a short-term issue because it involves perception, and as such can be changed relatively easily. Ultimately, *culture* is the key to internal capability, and it informs *climate*.

Inducing change in organizations

For successful change to happen in an organization, four critical elements are essential, as depicted in Figure 3.4.

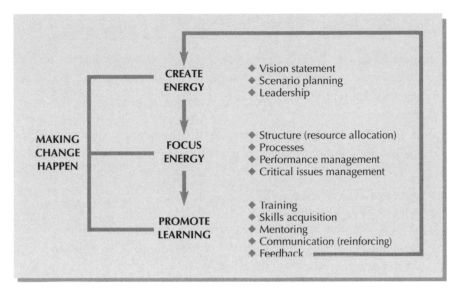

FIGURE 3.4 ◆ Inducing change in organizations

1 **Pressure for change:** change only occurs when there is pressure on the enterprise; this can come from internal or external sources. The pressure for change needs to be articulated and communicated throughout the enterprise.

2 **Create energy:** the preferred future scenario must be clearly communicated so that all employees share a clear vision of the enterprise's future direction. Visible leadership at all levels is essential to drive and communicate this vision throughout the enterprise and to seek and gain employee commitment.

3 **Focus energy:** the enterprise's new direction must be underpinned by the appropriate structure and processes to ensure it can implement the vision. Critical Issues Analysis (CIA) will ensure that the organization remains on track towards its stated goals and resources are allocated accordingly. Performance management is extremely effective, not only in overcoming inertia, but also in reinforcing the proposed change programme.

4 **Promote learning:** change requires new sets of skills acquired through extensive training, coaching and mentoring, or through outsourcing. To ensure change is effective, two-way communication is essential for all employees to remain committed to the new direction and to provide input to the process. This in turn leads to continuous learning and feedback that facilitates the on-going change process.

Framework for achieving organizational change

Successful change therefore requires the simultaneous presence of four key ingredients, i.e., pressure for change, a clear shared vision, capacity for change and actionable first steps. These four ingredients are depicted in Figure 3.5.

As you will have already experienced, the pressure for change is necessary to get the whole process moving. Without pressure, it's unlikely that much will happen, irrespective of the rhetoric. Fortunately, most industries and enterprises are feeling enough pressure these days to seriously begin to engage in genuine change initiatives. Once the pressure is established, it is vital that the leadership develops and communicates a clear vision of where they want to take the enterprise and the position being sought in the target market. This vision statement[5] provides the organization with some necessary boundaries to work within, and creates the energy from within, as depicted earlier in Figure 3.4. Of course, it is possible to describe each type of supply chain in 'visionary' terms, such as:

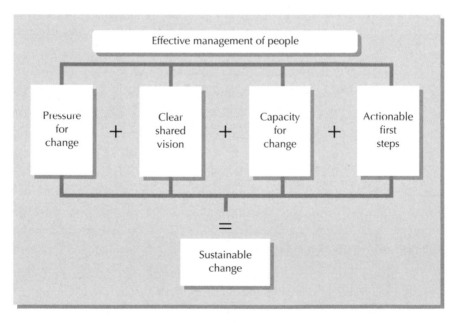

FIGURE 3.5 ◆ A framework for fast and effective management of change

Source Adapted from Figure 28.1 in Gattorna (1998), p. 447

Continuous replenishment:	'bringing customers and suppliers together for mutual benefit...'
Lean:	'most efficient, reliable, low cost...'
Agile:	'most responsive, competitive, quick turnaround...'
Fully flexible:	'new, innovative supply chain solutions...'

However, all this will come to nothing unless the enterprise possesses the capacity to change through a systematic set of actions, based on a clear understanding of what is the 'gap' and how this gap can be bridged. This is where prior work in identifying the main behavioural segments in the marketplace and undertaking an internal programme to map existing subcultures are vital pre-requisites.

Finally, with the above three steps successfully completed, it's important to start the actual change programme with actions that are credible in the eyes of staff and management, and once some initial small successes are achieved, to accelerate the whole process.

Interestingly, experience has shown that implementation of proposed changes should not be too drawn out, because this can provide personnel with the opportunity to galvanize forces inside the company to resist and repel the change programme in part, or in full. Indeed, there is evidence to suggest that the faster the actual implementation is carried out, the greater the chance of achieving the desired outcome. This conclusion is based on the analysis of numerous business cases for the implementation of new systems technology and the implementation of proposed new logistics network configurations. Obviously, common sense should prevail, because absolute speed without the application of appropriate resources and/or communications with internal staff and external suppliers and customers can be disastrous.[6] But in spite of the problems that have been encountered with fast implementations, there is enough evidence to reverse the myth that slow is better, because we now have a better understanding of the pivotal role of culture.

Country cultures

The seminal work of Geert Hofstede[7] on cross-cultural management has helped immeasurably in understanding more about the differences in country cultures, and how these can modify the way individuals and organizations behave in certain situations.

As depicted in Figures 3.6 and 3.7, Hofstede's original work identified four major dimensions on which country cultures differ. He labelled these power distance, uncertainty avoidance, individualism and masculinity. Later research added the dimension of short- versus long-term orientation. Brief descriptions of Hofstede's five dimensions are described by Nadeem Firoz *et al.* overleaf:[8]

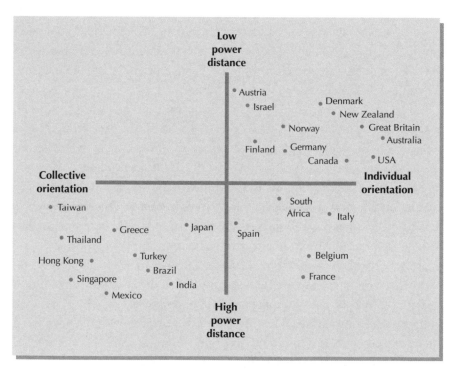

FIGURE 3.6 ◆ Country values

Source Adapted from data taken from Figure 7.1 in Hofstede (1980), p. 318

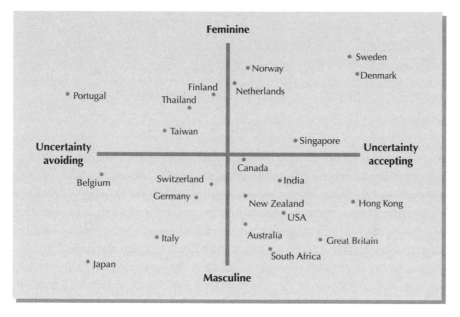

FIGURE 3.7 ◆ **Country values**

Source Adapted from data taken from Figure 7.1 in Hofstede (1980), p. 318

Power distance:	the extent to which less powerful members of society accept that power can be distributed unequally.
Uncertainty avoidance:	the extent to which people try to avoid situations where expectations and outcomes are unclear.
Individualism:	the relationship between an individual and the group to which that person belongs.
Masculinity/femininity:	the 'masculinity' dimension describes societies where there is a polarization of the traits displayed by males and females. In a masculine society, traits such as assertiveness, strength and focus on material success are primarily considered male, while women are supposed to exhibit tenderness and a concern with

	quality of life. A 'feminine' society is one where both men and women exhibit traits of tenderness, modesty, etc., and there is less of a polarization between the sexes.[9]
Long-term orientation:	the extent to which people within a culture have a long- versus short-term outlook on life.

So, the country cultures exhibiting different combinations of the above dimensions will have a pervasive influence on the way business is done in general, and on how supply chains operate in particular, across all source and consumption markets. Given that many of the world's major companies are now global in reach, this is a factor that requires more understanding and sensitivity as the search for ever higher performance continues.

Based on our own empirical work and the work of Hofstede, we can say that country cultures do **not** throw up previously unknown dominant buying behaviours in similar product and service marketplaces around the world, nor do they reveal unknown subcultures and patterns of behaviour inside organizations across the global terrain. The key insight here is that the prevailing values (or cultures) in a given country appear only to have a modifying influence on the 'mix' of previously identified dominant buying behaviours for a particular product/service.

We were able to confirm this observation while undertaking a behavioural segmentation across global markets for the dairy ingredients division of New Zealand manufacturer Fonterra, involving 3,300 international B2B customers located in more than 100 countries.[10] This is an important observation because it means that multiple supply chain alignment is a phenomenon which is valid in all countries or markets, and all the supplying enterprise has to recognize is the varying mix of previously identified dominant buying behaviours from country to country.

Dominant subcultures in the four generic supply chains

In Chapter 2 we identified the four most common types of supply chains that have been observed during the course of many projects during the last two decades; their corresponding P-A-D-I codes are shown in brackets:

Continuous replenishment supply chains (Ia)

Lean supply chains (A)

Agile supply chains (Pa)

Fully flexible supply chains (Dp and Di variants)

Other configurations have been observed – for example, the *fair deal* supply chain (Ai), which is a close variant of the *continuous replenishment* supply chain type – but the four types listed above are clearly the most common.

For the designer/operator of an array of supply chains, the important thing to know is the particular mix of the four most dominant types of buyer behaviour evident in the marketplace, **and** the current prevailing culture inside the enterprise which is powering management's strategies into these behavioural segments. These are the two 'end conditions' that must be known at the start of any transformation programme. Perhaps this gives a clue as to why so many change programmes have failed in the past. Executive leadership has not understood that both of these end conditions must be known, and acted upon, in order successfully to implement change initiatives.

Core roles within the supply chain function

Apart from the subcultures that must be present across the enterprise's multiple disciplines to drive the appropriate strategies towards the identified customer segments, the supply chain function has to develop particular subcultures to support the multiple roles it is expected to play. These are summarized in Figure 3.8 as *core technology, building infrastructure* and *interface management*. The P-A-D-I logics that define each of these roles are also detailed in this diagram.

Changing the enterprise to improve alignment

Figure 3.9 provides a quick insight into where the emphasis must be placed if the four generic types of subcultures (P, A, D, I) exist in the first place. Particular combinations of these subcultures must be present in

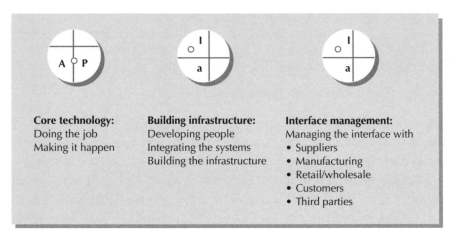

FIGURE 3.8 ◆ Supply chain functional subcultures

Source Adapted from Figure 4.3.10 in Gattorna (2003), p. 467

order to underpin the four generic types of supply chains identified via our extensive fieldwork, i.e., Ia, A, Pa and Dp/Di (there are actually two variants of the *fully flexible* supply chain).

Change programmes in the past have failed because of the lack of understanding about enterprise cultures, and the implications this has for the strategies being pursued at the time. This in turn has led to agitated staff and frustrated management, all for very little benefit. This phenomenon has been aptly named the *Canary syndrome*.[11] In this scenario, executives bang the cage every few years and keep the canaries (or staff) in a state of high agitation, without really achieving anything. The good news is that we no longer have to put up with this treatment. We understand what levers are available to create successful change, and more importantly, we know the combinations to use them. It is very similar to using X-rays to identify problems inside the human body. As long as the person conducting the analysis has an appropriate frame of reference, be it medical knowledge or as in this case an understanding of the mix of behavioural segments in the marketplace, it is possible to plot a systematic course of action to close any identified gaps. Behavioural segmentation techniques have emerged to provide the essential external market frame of reference. And new techniques to map the internal culture(s) inside

I

Emphasis on teamwork, consensus, participation, cohesion, strategy

- Define 'what we stand for' statement
- Emphasize teamwork
- Consensus decision making
- Define common values
- Joint-peer job design
- Informal standards for performance assessment of teams based on cohesion
- Reward team effort, loyalty and commitment
- Cash based rewards for team (gain-sharing)
- Training emphasizes personal interaction and team building
- Recruit 'I' people

D

Emphasis on individualism, creativity, entrepreneurial behaviour

- Define 'our future potential' statement
- Allow people to work on their own to fulfil their potential
- Make individuals accountable for their decisions
- Formulate vision
- Job design to increase autonomy
- Informal standards of performance assessment for individuals based on creativity, flexibility
- Reward creativity of solutions, ideas, experimentation, lateral thinking
- Incentives for individuals, e.g., learning experience
- Open, informal communication for whoever is around at the time
- Training in creative thinking; creative problem solving
- Recruit 'D' people

A

Emphasis on stability, order, systems, control

- Define 'how we do things' statement
- Centralize decision making, especially for cost control measures
- Change guidelines to rules
- Define jobs by method
- Formulate policy and procedure manuals
- Set efficiency/productivity objectives
- Measure and reward conformance to systems and procedures
- Provide cash rewards based on productivity, 'sticking to the rules'
- Establish a formal, regular, structured, systematic communication process on 'need to know only' basis
- Training programmes which emphasize planning, measuring, controlling and 'use of systems'
- Recruit 'A' people

P

Emphasis on results, urgency, high levels of activity

- Define 'what we are fighting for' statement
- Decentralize decision making; encourage staff to solve problems
- Specify clear guidelines, not rules
- Job design based on results, outputs
- Formalize position descriptions; individual performance objectives
- Measure performance against objectives
- Provide regular feedback on performance
- Reward achievement of objectives; speed of response.
- Provide incentives/merit-pay, based on results for *individuals*
- Establish a regular, structured communication process
- Training programmes which emphasize optimum use of time and resources
- Monitor competitor information and market conditions
- Recruit 'P' people

FIGURE 3.9 ◆ **The embedded emphasis of the four generic subcultures** enterprises have coincidentally been developed over the last decade. It is now just a matter of comparing the two to gauge the degree of mis-alignment.

Change programmes are either 'evolutionary' or 'revolutionary'. Evolutionary change occurs when change to the culture is incremental, and as such does not require an immediate alteration to the enterprise's 'subconscious'. Such change may be planned, but often occurs 'naturally', as the organization adapts to its changing marketplace.

There are distinct modifications (but not radical change) to strategies, organizational structures and management processes, such as expanding sales territories, changing product portfolios and new channels of distribution. Some logistics examples of this would include the move from hard-wired electronic data interchange (EDI) systems to web-based communications, the use of network optimization models to rationalize the supply chain and strategic sourcing through the prioritization of suppliers.

Revolutionary change occurs when there are fundamental changes to underlying assumptions, values and beliefs, causing a significant change to manifested strategic behaviour. It is usually planned, and often occurs when the enterprise is a 'victim' of rapid changes occurring in its own operating environment. Revolutionary change is almost always enterprise-wide, with radical shifts in strategy that may impact on the vision, organization structures, decision-making protocols, power distribution and status among the executive leadership. It is almost always accompanied by the import of new executives from outside the enterprise.

The suite of diagrams in Figure 3.10 defines the eight main *change pathways* that have been identified, four *evolutionary* and four *revolutionary*. In each case the so-called ideal culture has to align with the target market segment. Given that we have previously identified at least four types of predominant behavioural segments in most product/service markets, what are the implications? Well, it means that the executive leadership has to retain some parts of the current culture, while splitting off other parts and taking finely tuned initiatives to align with two or three other buyer behaviour segments to achieve the desired multiple alignment. As the marketplace fragments, we have to reflect an equivalent fragmentation in the internal culture of the enterprise, albeit in ways that still make the enterprise manageable.

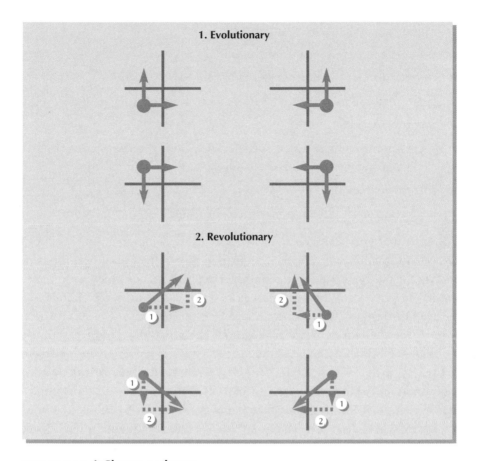

FIGURE 3.10 ◆ **Change pathways**

Source Adapted from Figure 4.3.6 in Gattorna (2003), p. 463

See also Appendix 3D for more detail on how *evolutionary* and *revolutionary* change is achieved.

In general terms, there are a limited number of change levers or *DNA building blocks* that can be used. For example:

◆ organization structure, reporting relationships and decision rights;

◆ job design (and positioning personnel in the most appropriate organization slots);

◆ processes;

◆ IT systems;

◆ methods of internal communication;

◆ training and development initiatives;

◆ key performance indicators (KPIs)/performance metrics;

◆ corresponding incentive schemes or motivators;

◆ planning systems;

◆ recruitment from external sources with both the required technical skills and appropriate mindset to support planned initiatives;

◆ role modelling; and

◆ leadership style of the top management team.

Manage these critical building blocks with precision and you inevitably move towards *dynamic alignment* – bringing sustained high performance across the business and throughout the supply chains in which your enterprise participates. While the moves to achieve *evolutionary* change are either horizontal or vertical (i.e., A to P, P to D, D to I, I to A, and vice versa), *revolutionary* change is diagonal, but must also go through both vertical and horizontal moves along the way; you can't simply move diagonally! In other words, while the strategic thrust and ideal culture definition may shift from, say, A to D, P to I, and vice versa, actual implementation must follow a two-stage pathway, as shown by the dotted lines in Figure 3.10. Clearly, *revolutionary* change will take longer to bed down than *evolutionary* change, particularly if thousands of staff members are involved. For example, an enterprise with 10,000 staff can easily take three to four years to fully re-align with its marketplace, unless of course an accelerated approach is adopted as described in Chapter 9.

If I were pressed to choose what were the two most powerful building blocks for change in the list above I would not hesitate to go for leadership followed by organization structure. So, if in doubt, start with these. If you think about it, all the recorded cases of successful change have started with the CEO as the prime mover and shaker. Jack Welch at GE comes to mind. As does Edward Zander at Motorola. He joined Motorola early in 2004 determined to bridge the gap with main competitor, Nokia. His vision was to 'reinvent Motorola as a nimble, unified technology company', and his primary focus was on dismantling 'Motorola's debilitating bureaucracy and a culture of internecine rivalries [that were] so intense that Motorola's own employees refer to its business units as warring tribes'.[12] Have you heard that all before? Well, you will hear the same story and the same pattern repeated many times in the years to come, unless of course senior managers in corporations adopt similar measures to Welch and Zander.

Caterpillar is another organization whose *organizational DNA* became increasingly mis-aligned over its first 50 years of history, from the 1930s until its very existence was threatened in the early 1980s. Disaster was only averted by strong leadership on the part of CEO George Schaefer who took over in 1985 and instituted a radical transformation programme to turn Caterpillar into a more resilient and aligned enterprise. Caterpillar went from major loss in 1992 to sustained profits during the next decade.[13] The biggest factor in the transformation was the new organization structure, a decentralized and accountable business unit model introduced overnight on 29 January 1990. This changed everything once and for all, and put Caterpillar back in touch with its dealers and loyal users. The rest is history. So the combination of inspired leadership, knowing where to start and what to do is invaluable in today's corporations. We need more of this special ingredient, especially in those enterprises where the business is synonymous with the supply chain itself.

Crucial influence of organization design and process

Among the levers for change mentioned above, leadership style of the top management team is thought to have the most impact, but if this is true, then the actual organization design is not far behind. The performance management system, which measures and rewards the new behaviours, is the next most powerful lever for change.

Organization design refers to the way resources are configured inside an organization. It focuses the effort of the organization, as depicted in Figure 3.4, and plays a major role in shaping the cultural capability of the enterprise. The functional capability of each major type of organizational design will be further examined in Chapters 5–8, but it is important to flag the importance of this key factor in organization performance when discussing culture and implementation. In the scheme of things, **organization design** is so powerful because it is the springboard for strategies formulated by the business and deals directly with resource allocation and configuration issues. On the other hand, **processes** that underpin each type of supply chain are more focused on ways of doing things. Ultimately, although both these powerful factors play pivotal roles in shaping cultural capability, organization design is a more powerful influence than process.

Organization design must always follow an understanding of both the marketplace and corresponding strategy formulation (in that order), not the other way around. This point was made a long time ago by the Roman Centurian Petronius when he said:

> We trained hard, but it seemed that every time we were beginning to form up into teams, we would be reorganized. Later in life I was to learn that we tend to meet any new situation by reorganizing, and a wonderful method it can be for creating the illusion of progress while producing confusion, inefficiency and demoralization.[14]

Avoid the temptation to build the organization around individuals, and above all beware of embracing generalized principles, such as flatten the organization, empower people, decentralize controls, form autonomous work teams or set market-focused objectives. There is nothing intrinsically wrong with any of these, but it is unlikely there is any single solution for a C21 enterprise. Similarly, it is too simplistic to say that 'what we need around here is a common culture', or 'we need a standard set of management practices'. These simplistic statements contain little value at best, and are downright misleading at worst.

Perhaps one of the most effective organization designs is that of a cricket team, so well known throughout the former British Empire. In a cricket team, there is the team objective of winning a Test Series of five matches or indeed just one Test Match. Each match takes five days to play! Within the team of 11 players, there are specialized roles that are played with individual flair. However, if the situation of the game changes it may be necessary to subdue individual expression and play more defensively. So, the cricket team has a nice blend of loose and tight roles that are played by individuals, but the overall good of the team is never subjugated to individual goals.

Changing the culture – now faster than ever

In 1991, in the early development days of our new *dynamic alignment* model, we worked with new CEO Bob Scott at General Accident (UK) in Perth, Scotland. This 10,000-strong company had just suffered an appalling financial loss, and Scott, a New Zealander, was appointed to turn things around. Over the subsequent two years we systematically worked our way through all the levels of the *dynamic alignment* model: reviewing the competitive environment for GA's General and Life Insurance businesses in Britain; introducing a direct channel to consumers and rationalizing the domestic branch network; mapping and working on ways to change the legacy culture; and bringing new blood into the leadership team at all levels. It was a hard grind, but by the third year the results were beginning to show a substantial improvement in profit.

As it became clear that his strategy was winning I remember asking Bob Scott what he would do differently if he were to do it all over again, and his answer: 'I would go much faster.' Changing the culture of a company the size of General Accident (UK)[15] in three years seemed a fair result, but we now know a decade later that it is both possible and preferable to move faster when transforming an enterprise. Kurt Swogger, Research Director of the Polyolefins & Elastomers business at Dow Chemical Company, did it simply by choosing the right people and putting them in the right roles to find and launch innovative products at speed.[16] He grew a 'starter' culture that had key personnel working on concepts that potentially added value for customers, and he put 'finishers' in 'finisher' roles to ensure these were delivered as promised. In the process Swogger improved the degree of fit between a member of staff's personality and their roles from 29 per cent in 1991 to 79 per cent in 1995.[17] In addition, he worked on the building block of recruitment and consciously hired the most appropriate people. In so doing, he increased the Myers-Briggs Type Indicator (MBTI®) based Creativity Index in his research and development (R&D) group (made up of both scientists and managers) from around 200 in 1991 to 260 by 1995, well above the national average of 235. His work showed that it is indeed possible to change the dominant culture in large organizations in a relatively short time through a deep understanding of the 'genetic nature of individual personalities and group cultures'.[18]

The same could be said for the more operational cultures commonly found in many corporate logistics and supply chain functions these days. It has always bothered me why a company like Philips, with such an impeccable pedigree for innovation and creativity in consumer and electronics products in particular, cannot seem to lift itself to the same creative levels when designing and operating its vital logistics networks and global supply chains. Why? Maybe it's high time Philips switched some of its product R&D people to the task of thinking about new supply chain business models! The results are likely to be impressive if not unexpected. There is certainly one chief executive intent on re-shaping the culture. Ken MacKenzie, the incoming CEO of the ailing packaging group Amcor, is determined to tear down what he calls 'a silo mentality that is festering throughout the company and is hampering returns'.[19] So the message of the power of culture, for good and evil, is getting through to the highest levels at last. Let's hope that top management teams everywhere embrace the power of this hidden force and take advice on how it can be turned to the benefit of all stakeholders of the enterprise.

Living lessons

1 It is the underlying cultural values which determine what gets done in organizations – not what you write down in business plans.

2 Now that it is possible to map *current, ideal* and *preferred* cultures in an organization, change management initiatives can be carried out with more precision and with greater probability of success.

3 The leadership group in an enterprise must take responsibility for shaping the various subcultures necessary to underpin and drive proposed strategies into the marketplace – there is no escaping this responsibility.

CHAPTER 4

Leading from the front

Converting customer insight into successful implementation

How do you judge a good leader? Many of us can recognize good leadership when we see it, but it's harder to define. My experience tells me that successful leadership is not necessarily transferable from one organization to another – nor is one style necessarily right for a particular organization *through time*. Leaders and leadership styles need to be just as dynamic as the people they lead and the customers they seek to satisfy. Effective leaders will be able to shape the subcultures and implement the strategy needed in a complex supply chain environment. As John Kotter put it, 'institutionalizing a leadership-centered culture is the ultimate act of leadership'.[1] Kotter in fact was one of the first management writers to recognize that 'aligning' people around a vision, and its related strategies, involved far more than simply organizing and staffing.[2] Leadership and management are 'two distinct and complementary systems of action. Each has its own function and characteristic activities. Both are necessary for success in an increasingly complex and volatile business environment.'[3]

Politics gives us some telling examples of how different leadership styles are needed for different situations or challenges. Sir Winston Churchill was a strong and decisive leader as British Prime Minister throughout World War II, but he was unsuccessful during the ensuing peace time and was soon replaced. A more recent example is New York's Mayor, Rudolph Giuliani, who was heavily criticized before the 11 September terrorist strike for his stance on race relations and civil liberties. But post 9/11, attitudes to Giuliani changed, even if his style did not. The Mayor's strong, energetic and hands-on style sent a consistent message to the city that he was in control and the 'right person' for the job. The point is that good leaders are rarely cardboard cut-outs. Leadership is about *authenticity*, and the best leaders have the unique qualities of a genuine sense of self and the ability to inspire. According to Mike Hanley, 'in leadership circles, authenticity means "being yourself"'.[4] Look at the likes of Jack Welch (GE); Richard Branson (Virgin), Terry Leahy (Tesco), Gerry Harvey (Harvey Norman) and Michael Hawker (IAG); all share a certain quality. Bob Goffee, the London Business School professor, claims that 'truly inspirational leaders are able to be themselves with great skill'.[5]

Unsuccessful leadership can be demonstrated in a myriad of ways and results in either the collapse of an organization or poor performance. Can you think of some recent dramatic examples? The leadership triad at Enron produced an unhealthy 'group think' culture that ultimately led to the company's demise: Ken Lay (former Chairman and CEO), Jeff Skilling (CEO for six months after Lay retired) and Andrew Fastow (their Chief Financial Officer, CFO). In Italy, the Italian dairy company Paramalat SpA almost collapsed after its former CEO Calisto Tanzi defrauded the company of more than €500 million. He is now in jail. Paramalat SpA's new CEO Enzo Bondi is working to restore the company, repay investors their lost funds and re-establish the firm's credibility within the financial community. An early step along that long path was taken on 6 October 2005, when the company stock was re-instated on the Milan Stock Exchange.

You might have also come across some of the poor leaders in large corporations that are now being characterized as 'workplace psychopaths'.[6] Exhibiting the same ruthlessness and narcissism of a criminal psychopath, these leaders somehow manage to stay under the radar as they rise to senior levels in organizations. They cunningly manage upwards, while behaving vindictively towards their subordinates and creating a culture of mistrust. These are the worst kind of leaders because they leave a trail of destruction, the effects of which are often felt for a considerable time after they have either departed or been unmasked. John Clarke quotes one such example in his book *Working with Monsters*:

> *David worked for a large insurance company, and had a variety of techniques and devious strategies that helped him get promoted. Among other things, he would steal co-workers projects so he looked better than they*

did, and would spread false rumors about his boss. He lied to clients to make sure he got the contract, and then passed the work on to someone else who would get the blame when services were not delivered as he had promised. David was an up-and-coming star in the company. Most people had no idea that he had ruthlessly achieved his numerous promotions at the expense of the people around him.[7]

However we judge them, it is fair to say that today's C-level executives face several paradoxical situations of which their predecessors were probably not even aware. 'Chip' Goodyear, the CEO of mining and resources giant BHP Billiton, summed up the predicament of today's leaders by saying, 'there are only two types of CEO, those that have been fired, and those that will be fired in the future'.[8] It's tough at the top, but the job has to be done and done well for the sake of all stakeholders.

This challenge is being taken up by boards and CEOs around the globe. Sony, for instance, has taken the radical step of appointing Howard Stringer, a Welsh-born American, to the top job in an attempt to boost its flagging fortunes. Jeff Bezos is still driving Amazon.com towards the promised profitability in a business that looks more like a logistics fulfillment operation every day. Sir Richard Branson's entrepreneurial and unconventional leadership style is helping him create one of the world's great brands in Virgin, while a series of changes at the top of the once-great UK retailer, Marks & Spencer, have so far failed to reverse its fortunes. Strong and successful leadership! The nirvana for many, but how do we identify, encourage and sustain good leaders?

And yet more complexities are coming the chief executive's way. Since the collapse of several high-profile companies around the world during the past five years, stringent new guidelines on corporate governance have been introduced by major corporations. Martin Hilb's paper, 'New corporate governance: from good guidelines to great practice', is the definitive work on this subject.[9] Boards and CEOs cannot afford to get this vital part of their corporate responsibility wrong in the future.

Identifying leadership styles

The P-A-D-I logic set introduced in Chapter 1 can provide a useful tool to help you recognize leadership styles and match those styles with particular customer groups. If you recall, in Figure 1.8 I introduced the notion of four distinct leadership styles: P (*Company Baron*); A (*Traditionalist*); D (*Visionary*); and I (*Coach*). We identified these four primary leadership styles and up to 16 variants, all of which can be measured using the Myers-Briggs Type Indicator (MBTI®) or a similar instrument to measure preferred behaviour.[10] I suggest that you update your preferred 'Type' by undertaking the full-length assessment with a properly accredited MBTI® agency. To complete the puzzle you should then refer to Figure 4.1 to translate your MBTI® into P-A-D-I terms, thereby facilitating comparisons with the other three levels of the alignment framework.

Figure 4.2 describes each of the four pure leadership styles, and demonstrates how each has both an upside and a downside. No single leadership style will be universally ideal in a multi-segment market, where the shaping of an equivalent array of matching subcultures is essential to achieve overall alignment.

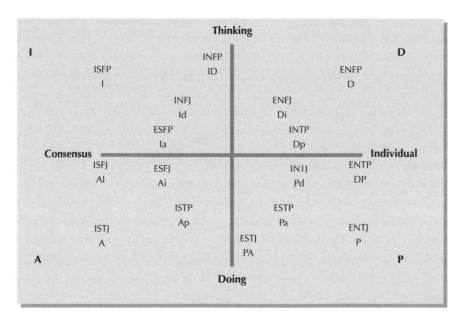

FIGURE 4.1 ◆ MBTI® overlay on P-A-D-I framework

Source Adapted from Figure 29.6 in Gattorna (1998), p. 480

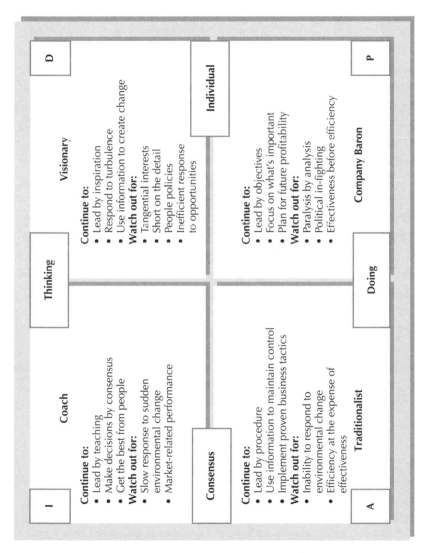

Coach

Continue to:
- Lead by teaching
- Make decisions by consensus
- Get the best from people

Watch out for:
- Slow response to sudden environmental change
- Market-related performance

Consensus

Traditionalist

Continue to:
- Lead by procedure
- Use information to maintain control
- Implement proven business tactics

Watch out for:
- Inability to respond to environmental change
- Efficiency at the expense of effectiveness

Visionary

Continue to:
- Lead by inspiration
- Respond to turbulence
- Use information to create change

Watch out for:
- Tangential interests
- Short on the detail
- People policies
- Inefficient response to opportunities

Individual

Company Baron

Continue to:
- Lead by objectives
- Focus on what's important
- Plan for future profitability

Watch out for:
- Paralysis by analysis
- Political in-fighting
- Effectiveness before efficiency

I

D

Thinking

Doing

A

P

FIGURE 4.2 ◆ **Leadership styles**

Each primary leadership style will now be further explored on two levels, both personal and management. Personal is an individual's behaviour exhibited in personal settings, whereas management is the same person's behaviour in a corporate setting. A *coach*, for instance, is a person who is personally conscientious, respected for their principles and inspires people through the clarity and strength of their convictions. At a management level, these same attributes mean they like to develop the potential of their staff, they dislike change that could threaten the unity of the group and they prefer consensus-based rather than autocratic decision-making.

Traditionalist (A)

Personal:	Serious, quiet, achieves success by concentration and thoroughness. Practical, orderly, matter of fact, logical, realistic, dependable. Like to be well organized. Make up their minds as to what should be accomplished, and work steadily towards this objective, regardless of protests or distractions.
Management:	Likes to maintain superior/subordinate distance. Prefers clear standards and requirements for jobs. Comfortable with the supervision of well-structured tasks. Uses routines and procedures for getting things done. Prefers infrequent changes in work patterns or organization structure. Does not like too much discussion about new ideas and what the future might hold.

Coach (I)

Personal:	Success achieved by perseverance, originality and the desire to do whatever is needed or wanted. Puts best efforts into work and job. Conscientious, concerned for others, quietly forceful. Respected for their firm principles. Often followed because of their clear convictions as to how to achieve for the common good.

Management:	Likes to help develop the human potential among direct reports.
	Prefers consensus-based decision-making.
	Comfortable with changes in work patterns and flexible working hours.
	Dislikes major changes that threaten the unity of the group.
	Does not like autocratic patterns of decision-making.
	Prefers to argue for changes in resource allocation.

Company Baron (P)

Personal:	Matter-of-fact, energetic, enjoys whatever comes along.
	Tends to like mechanical things and sports.
	May be a little blunt or insensitive.
	Does not like long explanations by others.
	Good with tangible things that can be worked, handled, taken apart or assembled
Management:	Comfortable with established procedures and rules.
	Likes to work for change within the existing systems and structures.
	Good at finding compromises.
	Skilled at manoeuvering for increased personal power.
	Uncomfortable with displays of warmth and openness by others.
	Not always keen to put into practice ideas and policies that are considered new, unpopular or risky.

Visionary (D)

Personal:	Enthusiastic, high spirited, ingenious and imaginative.
	Able to do almost anything that interests them.
	Quick with a solution for deficiencies and generally prepared to help people with problems.
	Often rely on ability to improvise instead of preparing in advance.

	Can usually find compelling reasons for whatever they want. Sometimes impatient.
Management:	Likes to use personal influencing skills. Comfortable with criticism, confrontation and conflict. Good at working in poorly structured situations. Good change agent. Uncomfortable with details and routine. Does not like constraints and established procedures. Does not like to maintain group cohesion for its own sake. Does not like lengthy decision-making procedures.

Leadership in large enterprises means leadership at all levels, not just the top management team, so everything being said here applies to all levels. Clearly, in a large enterprise, the task of shaping the necessary subcultures can be allocated to different members of the management team. In a small to medium-sized enterprise (SME), this is usually not possible, and the task inevitably falls to just a few executives. Either way, it is a complex task, and one that is best undertaken by executives that have a preferred leadership style aligned to the organizational unit that they have been allocated and its required subculture.

Ultimately, it falls to boards of enterprises to bear the responsibility for choosing the most appropriate CEO for the particular 'season' that an organization is in, and there are many examples of boards doing just that over the past few decades. Perhaps the most striking contemporary example is Hewlett-Packard. Carly Fiorina arrived as CEO in 1999 and set out a vision to rebuild the image of the flagging organization by trying to 'inspire employees with pleas to help her re-capture HP's lost glory'.[11]

In our P-A-D-I language, Fiorina represented a bit of a dichotomy. On the one hand she pushed hard for innovation (D logic) at the same time as she was seeking synergies (A logic) via an integrated sales force. This is a difficult combination to execute because of the opposing subcultures these two strategic philosophies represent, and in the end she paid the price. As *Business Week* commented, 'She's playing CEO, visionary, and COO, and that's too hard to do.'[12] Prior to her tenure at HP the culture had been characterized by teamwork and consensus. Her entrepreneurial, customer-focused, results-driven leadership style caused confusion and attracted progressively increasing resistance. Ultimately, she was replaced because the board said it wanted more focus on execution.[13] Fiorina's successor, Mark Hurd, appointed in March 2005, is now opting for the more compatible logics of focus by separating the printer and PC divisions (P logic), while pursuing overall cost-saving efficiencies via a dramatic programme to reduce staff across the company (A logic).

Change needs to be *led* not managed

How can real change be driven through an organization? Can you see the different potential and the different roles of leaders and managers? We believe that just as an army must be led rather than managed into battle, so enterprises also have to be led first and foremost, and then managed. Leaders will produce useful change while managers will focus on controlling complexity. Both are essential but very different capacities when it comes to change. Leaders will motivate, inspire and energize people; managers will develop the organization's capacity to deliver through organizing and staffing – they plan and budget. The differences between the two are significant and can be seen in Figure 4.3.

LEADERS	MANAGERS
PRODUCE USEFUL CHANGE	*CONTROL COMPLEXITY*
◆ **Make** the **change** occur	◆ Bring **order** and **consistency** – work within the current system
◆ **Set** the **direction** for constructive change	◆ Manage by **planning** and **budgeting**
◆ Relate to **what** the events and decisions mean to the people involved	◆ Relate to **how** things get done
◆ Focus on **aligning people** – communicate the direction – achieve common understanding of the vision – commitment to achieving the vision	◆ Develop capacity to achieve through **organizing** and **staffing**
◆ Influence people to achieve **goals** and **objectives**	◆ Responsible for **performance** and **productivity**
◆ **Motivate, inspire and energize** – keep people moving in the right direction, despite obstacles to change	◆ Ensure plans are accomplished by **controlling and problem-solving** – rely on **systems** and **structures**

FIGURE 4.3 ◆ **Leading versus managing**

To put a finer point on the art of leading enterprises, various dominant coalitions within the top management team can be engineered to ensure the required cultural biases and corresponding cultural capabilities are embedded in the organization. These coalitions will ultimately be a mixture of the four generic leadership styles expressed in P-A-D-I terms in Figure 4.2. Details of the characteristics of each type in the top management team are provided in Figures 4.4a and 4.4b.

I. REVITALIZERS AND INTEGRATORS	D. CREATORS AND BUILDERS
Shared values	**Shared values**
◆ Participation, cohesion	◆ Creativity, innovation
◆ Change	◆ Rapid response
Team style	**Team style**
◆ Sensitive to people	◆ Move very quickly
◆ Offer emotional support – have the ability to empower subordinates	◆ Apparently haphazard – guided by shared vision
Individual aptitudes	**Individual aptitudes**
◆ Consensus building	◆ Individualism, vision
◆ Good negotiation skills	◆ Flexibility
◆ Good conceptual ability	◆ Tolerance for ambiguity
Individual knowledge	**Individual knowledge**
◆ Group dynamics	◆ Technical
◆ Communications	◆ R&D
Conditions	**Conditions**
◆ Stable, traditional	◆ Turbulent, uncertain
◆ About to change	◆ Rapidly changing
Strategy	**Strategy**
◆ Developing long-term relations with customer	◆ Creation of a market
◆ About to change strategic direction	◆ New product development

FIGURE 4.4A ◆ **Characteristics of top management team (TMT) dominant coalitions**

Source Adapted from Figure 2.9 in Gattorna and Walters (1996), p. 40

A. PRODUCTIVITY AND MANAGERS	P. BUILDING AND GROWTH MANAGERS
Shared values	**Shared values**
◆ Control	◆ Objectivity, facts
◆ Analysis	◆ Results
Team style	**Team style**
◆ Logical, analytical	◆ Drivers
◆ Provide clear structure for their subordinates	◆ Set clear objectives for their subordinates
Individual aptitudes	**Individual aptitudes**
◆ Good analytical skills	◆ High energy
◆ Logical	◆ Clear focus on objectives
◆ Desire for stability	◆ Desire for clarity
Individual knowledge	**Individual knowledge**
◆ Accounting	◆ Marketing
◆ Production	◆ Sales
Conditions	**Conditions**
◆ Established, mature	◆ Settled down
◆ Margins under pressure	◆ Highly competitive
Strategy	**Strategy**
◆ Consolidation, fine tuning	◆ Gaining market share
◆ Improving profits, productivity	◆ Customer focus

FIGURE 4.4B ◆ Characteristics of top management team (TMT) dominant coalitions

Source Adapted from Figure 2.9 in Gattorna and Walters (1996), p. 40

Have you ever seen a universally ideal leadership or management style? Not surprisingly, no single 'ideal' style exists. Instead, as with other elements of the *dynamic alignment* model, multiple styles have to be formed and sustained, sometimes in spite of the natural conflict brought about by having several styles coexisting. As expected, the natural style and value system of the CEO is vital. This is certainly the case at JetBlue, perhaps the leading low-cost airline in the United States. Here the founder and

CEO, David Neeleman, and his executive are consciously trying to preserve the airline's distinctive culture as it grows rapidly from a small to a big company.[14]

However, perhaps the most outstanding example of contemporary leadership is to be found at Li & Fung, where Victor Fung and his brother have transformed what was a small, Hong Kong-based trading company into perhaps the world's first genuine global supply chain company, using all the techniques and technologies you would expect of such a leading company. In many ways, Li & Fung epitomizes the concept of *dynamic alignment* in practice, because it has managed to remain aligned and attuned to its customers and suppliers for nearly a century. Why? Leadership! Significantly, it therefore comes as no surprise that Li & Fung have overcome one of the biggest hurdles to sustained performance by adopting an organization structure which involves specialist teams of 40–50 multidisciplinary personnel dedicated to each of its major retail customers. Surely there are some lessons in here for other corporations?

As you can imagine, if the mix of leadership styles and cultures is inappropriate, as so often happens, then damaging mis-alignments can occur, which ultimately will hamper performance. So what do you have to look out for? The respective flaws of different types of leaders are revealed in Figures 4.5a and 4.5b. Most likely you will recognize some of these: leaders who are inflexible, risk averse or fail to share the corporate vision. No wonder they are constraining growth at best, or worst, wreaking havoc!

Achieving multiple alignment through superior leadership

So where does this leave the corporation? The task of the senior executive is to select the top management team, identifying the natural leadership styles and selecting the necessary technical disciplines. This has to be done in such a way that the embedded imbalance reflects the imbalance in the behavioural segments in the outside market. This same imbalance or bias has to be embedded into the subcultures on the inside of the company so as to either consolidate or further improve alignment. Remember our goal? It's *dynamic alignment* in the supply chain. Through leadership we can also achieve multiple alignment with our customers.

'I' culture	'D' culture
The 'D' manager	**The 'I' manager**
◆ Failure to share vision	◆ Failure to achieve objectives
◆ Seen as maverick	◆ Protects subordinates from reality
The 'P' manager	**The 'P' manager**
◆ Insensitive to group norms	◆ Risk averse
◆ Desire for more internal control	◆ Misses the 'big picture'
	◆ Subdues initiative
The 'A' manager	
◆ Distance from 'real' decisions	**The 'A' manager**
◆ Development of conflicting subcultures	◆ Unnecessary controls
	◆ Inflexible decisions
	◆ Dismisses new ideas

FIGURE 4.5A ◆ **Culture and leadership style – what to watch out for**

'A' culture	'P' culture
The 'I' manager	**The 'I' manager**
◆ Undermines political forms	◆ Inefficient resource allocation
◆ Poor risk tolerance	◆ Climate of frustration
The 'D' manager	**The 'D' manager**
◆ Creates insecurity	◆ Loss of output control
◆ Leaves the rest behind	◆ Loss of strategic focus
The 'P' manager	**The 'A' manager**
◆ Systemic resistance to change	◆ System becomes an end in itself
◆ Mis-translation of objectives	◆ Lose sight of external change

FIGURE 4.5B ◆ **Culture and leadership style – what to watch out for**

Given the four generic supply chains identified in Chapter 2, enterprises have to decide how many of these they are prepared to support. The *continuous replenishment* supply chain requires a leadership that is empathetic and consistent in the way it manages customer relationships. The *lean* supply chain requires a more conventional albeit steady style, with the emphasis on efficiency and reliability, and no particular emphasis on external relationships. The *agile* supply chain must be driven by a leadership style which is predominantly results-oriented with an eye to responsiveness. Finally, the *fully flexible* supply chain requires a leadership style that is predominantly visionary, tinged with the reality that any creativity or innovation introduced must solve a particular problem for a customer.

You will see that we have come full circle since Chapter 1. Superior alignment, leading to superior sustained performance in the enterprise, always starts with the executive leadership being close to the market. The executive has to be close enough to customers to read and interpret *all* the signals being sent their way. Think again of Lord Coe, the Chairman of London's winning bid for the 2012 Olympics. Such was his deep understanding of all stakeholder interests, he led a reversal of fortunes in the 18 months leading up to the International Olympic Committee's decision to choose London.

When leaders and their key customers and consumers are aligned, there is more than an even chance that the most appropriate strategies will be formulated, and that the underpinning subcultures necessary to drive these into the marketplace will also be taking shape under the guidance of the same management team. Lord Coe and his bidding team still have to deliver on this last part. Look for yourself and run a test on your own enterprise using the diagnostics already introduced in this and earlier chapters; success always follows superior alignment. Since supply chains permeate all enterprises, achieving multiple alignment across an array of supply chains embedded in the business is essential if significantly higher operating and financial performance is to become a reality.

Let us consider again the thoughts of management academic Hau Lee. When he described his idea of a Triple-A supply chain, he argued that several enterprises had achieved agility, adaptability and alignment to various degrees.[15] They were Lucent, Wal-Mart, Dell, Zara, Nokia, Cisco and Toyota, and especially Seven-Eleven Japan. But the closing comment in his article is most revealing: '...most firms already have the infrastructure in place to create Triple-A supply chains. What they need is a fresh attitude and a new culture to get their supply chains to deliver Triple-A performance.'[16] This is easy to say but very difficult to achieve in practice, because we are dealing with the unseen cultural forces described in

Chapter 3: the powerful force of human behaviour that lies beneath the surface of the *performance iceberg*.

We have sought to improve our understanding of the mechanisms at work here through the new *dynamic alignment* framework and the diagnostics that we have outlined to measure the mis-alignments that could occur inside and between the organizations along complex supply chains. We are now in a position not only to describe the visible outcomes of mis-alignment, as does the Triple-A article, but also to identify where the mis-alignments are, predict their likely impact and design precise counter-measures. At last some control over our destiny, and now is the time to discard the *mentality of denial*, which has plagued so many enterprises to date. We need to confront and harness the human behavioural forces inside our own enterprises, because this is where the seeds of success lie.

Leadership, vision and values

How clearly have you seen leaders articulate their vision and values? I believe great leaders invariably articulate a vision for their enterprise and then visibly live this vision day-to-day as an example to staff. This vision sets boundaries for everyone in the enterprise and helps to galvanize and focus the energy of the company on key customers, suppliers and other important stakeholders. And if you agree with my assertion in Chapter 1 that *supply chains* are *the business*, then it's vital that enterprises should clearly define the role that supply chains play in delivering the overall corporate vision. If you don't develop such a vision, then the old Hungarian proverb probably applies: 'If you are always trying to be like someone else, who's going to be you?' I believe vision formulation is so important that I've developed a four-part formula for constructing a meaningful statement to guide every level of the enterprise in its daily actions. You will find this in Appendix 4A, along with two examples of operating vision statements developed for large Asia-Pacific enterprises. You can also find a more detailed treatment of this topic in my 2003 handbook on the supply chain.[17]

But how do we bring the vision to life? All companies need to draw up a corresponding set of *values* to underpin the words in the vision statement. These are the corporate values that everyone in the enterprise must sign up to. If they don't, it's highly likely they will become part of the 'internal resistance' movement in the enterprise. It is good to see that increasingly companies are making these all-important values explicit. Xerox is a good example. Xerox CEO Ann Mulcahy attributes the articulating of corporate values, and living these values, as helping her to bring the company through some tough times.[18]

Leadership, vision, values ... they are all critical to success in business, and because supply chains permeate every business, we need to have these qualities present in equal measure, embedded in the supply chain organization.

Peter Drucker, who died in November 2005, was a giant among management thinkers. Indeed, he was arguably the greatest management thinker of the twentieth century – his ideas were always years, and sometimes decades, ahead of their time. Let's hope the legacy of insight and foresight he leaves us in an otherwise thin terrain will be used to the full by future leaders to improve the performance of their enterprises and supply chains – for the benefit of all stakeholders.

Drucker once famously said that 'there are no more advantages to big business, only disadvantage'. Why? He continues that, 'once a company rises above a certain size, the head of the organization has to rely on subordinates for what is going on – who only tell him what they want him to know'.[19] He clearly understood how difficult leadership of major enterprises was.

Living lessons

1   Leadership in and of organizations must be multidimensional and contain 'biases' that truly reflect the 'biases' in customer buying behaviours.

2   When leading collaborative initiatives, certain elements of the top management team who are charged with implementing this strategy should be prepared for other parts of the organization to be pursing opposite strategies – it's called 'ambiguity'.

3   Quite simply, great business leaders intuitively understand their marketplace and the internal cultural environment of their organizations – and have an uncanny knack of getting them to align!

CHAPTER 5

Continuous replenishment supply chains

Where relationships matter most

C an you spot a *continuous replenishment* supply chain at 100 metres? It is the type of supply chain where customers are loyal and, in return, expect a high level of commitment and service. The *continuous replenishment* supply chain has its highs and lows when it comes to demand, but all members of the supply chain seek to satisfy demand in the most effective way. Possibly the most distinctive characteristic of the *continuous replenishment* supply chain is that customers are truly collaborative in their buying behaviour. You know you're in a *continuous replenishment* supply chain when all parties, including third-party providers, collaborate to lower costs, meet demand and continuously improve their delivery times and service. A happy end-customer for one is a happy customer for all!

Are we dreaming? No. Take a look at the Campbell Soup Company, which was one of the early innovators when it conceived and implemented its continuous product replenishment (CPR) programme in the early 1990s.[1] Working with its main retail and wholesale customers, Campbell's worked to reduce the impact of demand fluctuations caused by its retailers' forward buying for promotional purposes. Such buying led to inefficiencies in Campbell's production and logistics processes and inflated the retailers' own costs for storage and handling. A later version of this programme, CPR2, recognized that market conditions required a combination of *continuous replenishment* (low-cost production) and *agile* (promotional) supply chains, and the programme was implemented mainly through changing pricing policies. We'll talk more about mixing supply chains later.

A more contemporary example can be found at Joe White Maltsters, a division of Adelaide-based ABB Grain, one of Australia's leading grain trading and handling companies. Every year, Joe White locks in more than 55 per cent of its production of 450,000 tonnes at the start of the year. Over time it has developed very collaborative relationships with six major Asian breweries, which take on average 50,000 tonnes of malt each per year, at negotiated prices, locked-in via firm contracts for up to four years ahead. These breweries provide updated forecasts three months in advance and set shipping schedules every two weeks. As a result, Joe White knows exactly what to produce when, and ships a steady stream of malt in grain form by container to a regular, pre-agreed shipping schedule each year. Thousands of them! These are dream customers, and a superb example of a *continuous replenishment* supply chain in action.[2]

Customers are forgiving – up to a point!

First, let's look at the customers in the *continuous replenishment* market in more detail. They are largely predictable in their buying behaviour; they demand the regular delivery of mostly mature products and services. The customers normally like to buy from one or two suppliers, and loyalty is taken very seriously. This is not a market that easily embraces risk-taking, by either customers or suppliers. Trust is uppermost in the supply chain relationship. Members of the *continuous replenishment* supply chain readily enter into partnerships and joint-development projects, and freely share information that will help the common cause of improved performance. Collaborative buying behaviours also tend to be very forgiving, and customers with this mindset will put up with a lot, including being ignored. But they will only do so for a limited time, after which they are likely to go to the opposite type of behaviour and become adversarial and demanding.

How can you capture the potential of these customers? The most important thing is to discover which of your customers are truly 'collaborative' and then look after them. Unfortunately, that is easier said than done. Companies rarely get a second chance to restore their relationships in a *continuous replenishment* supply chain without spending a tremendous amount of time and money. Enterprises are often poor at differentiating which customers deserve their priority attention, and as a result, have lost some of their best long-term customer relationships. Some don't even realize it at the time. Leading credit card companies such as American Express and Diners Club are prime examples of this phenomenon. They don't appear to follow up customers and ask them why they are no longer using their card or other services. It seems extraordinary that this should happen, but it's not actually that surprising. Companies lose their focus on collaborative customers because these customers are not overly concerned about price, their cost-to-serve is relatively low and margins are generally good. In other words, they are easy to take for granted! All that these customers crave is recognition, and preferential treatment based on strong personal relationships. They are prepared to trade off other service parameters to achieve this. But ignore them at your peril.

Why else do you think companies lose their focus on important 'collaborative' customers? It's not only that these customers are easily overlooked. It's because enterprises become preoccupied with the other customers, particularly those who are especially demanding and time consuming. You could call these customers the Exocets of the commercial world, because they suddenly appear from 'out of the blue' and are highly destructive on contact. We will talk more about their behaviour in Chapter 7, but suffice it to say that companies seeking to avoid an Exocet strike often will provide erratic over- and under-servicing of these difficult customers. However, the result is often deteriorating performance for customers overall. Unfortunately, suppliers respond inappropriately to customers every day. The trick is to recognize who are the most important customers and who deserves the most attention.

Fonterra

In 2001, when global dairy ingredients company Fonterra segmented its 3,300 business customers across 100+ countries along behavioral lines, it found that 25 per cent of its customers by number, and 40 per cent by volume, were exhibiting collaborative buying behaviour tendencies. But no one at Fonterra was aware of this, and the revelation came as a shock. Consequently, many of its best and most loyal customers were not being given the appropriate attention, and previously good business relationships were souring.

You want what, when?

Of course, leading companies sometimes don't mind being asked to deliver on challenging requests. Demanding customers can stretch their performance and create new standards – for the better. But you have to know when and at what point the extra response is justified. The characteristics of *continuous replenishment* supply chains (or base flow, as defined in Chapter 2) are the mirror image of customers' 'collaborative' buying behaviours; it's as simple as that. The whole emphasis is on gradually building deep and sustainable relationships with customers that exhibit genuine collaborative values. Reliability and trustworthiness are essential ingredients for success in this type of supply chain, because customers greatly value these qualities. You need to respond in a requisite way: not too much or too little, but just enough. I call this *requisite collaboration*.

The customers see value in entering into long-term strategic partnerships because they can secure the certainty and stability for which they've been yearning. Information is freely exchanged in both directions when this relationship is established. The customers provide forecasts of specific requirements, well into the future, and update these on a rolling monthly basis. It's important that staff you select to serve these customers share their values and their commitment to a common goal. Without shared values, you are likely to lose these customers and their future revenue streams. A company that appears to have all the appropriate characteristics for collaboration is vehicle parts manufacturer Unipart, which has enjoyed a 21-year relationship with Jaguar worldwide. These two companies act as one. Unipart participates in every facet of Jaguar's business, from the design of the car and the manufacture of its component parts, through to worldwide distribution. It's a uniquely successful relationship that has endured the test of time.

Jaguar and Unipart are truly in the 'zone of collaboration'. Has your company ever been in this zone? Would you be able to recognize it if you were? I suggest the only way you can come close to such an intense partnership is by only collaborating with the enterprises who really want to collaborate and exhibit genuinely collaborative values. Unilever's former CEO, Anthony Burgmans, made this point strongly when he said, 'if retail customers want to collaborate, we will collaborate with them. But if they want to fight we are ready to give them a good fight too.'[3] This is an important distinction because it provides guidance on the priority for allocating scarce resources. For some, servicing customers has become an art form in that both collaborative and adversarial behaviours are practised in the same marketplace. CEO of Woolworths (Australia), Roger Corbett, puts it plainly – if you 'get too cozy with your suppliers ... you're in trouble'.[4] Corbett is constantly spilling the trading arrangements he has with suppliers. Yet independent field research has found that a small number of key suppliers are collaborating intensely with Woolworths, so why fracture the relationship? Upon reflection this double game makes sense, because true collaboration is very relationship-intensive and, therefore, can only be practised on a selective basis. Corbett's approach may appear to send mixed signals to the supply base, but in reality it's a cunning strategy based on the idea that it is best to collaborate only with those parties who are really vital to your business. The rest simply have to take their chances.

But collaborative responses do not happen by accident. Companies will need to carefully design and manage the operations that underpin this special form of 'alignment' between suppliers and their customers. Certain conditions must be present inside supplying companies for this to occur.

It's all about culture

Perhaps the most definitive research to date in the vexed area of collaboration was undertaken by Mark Barratt, now at Arizona State University.[5] He found the existence of 83 *enablers* of supply chain relationships in coffee supply chains between a manufacturer and a leading retailer in the UK grocery industry. On inspection, most, if not all, of these enablers are related to culture and have underlying values that are clearly *collaborative*, such as commitment, mutual benefit, openness, jointly defined processes and the timely exchange of information.[6] The 34 *inhibitors* to supply chain relationships that Barratt observed also showed a bias towards culture-related factors.[7] Interestingly, both the *enablers* and *inhibitors* were evident at strategic, tactical and operational levels within the manufacturer and retailer organizations participating in the research. The majority of *enablers* and *inhibitors* appeared to occupy the inter-organizational space in the supply chain **between** the supply chain parties.

This is a significant finding given the current efforts by suppliers and retailers in the fast-moving consumer goods (FMCG) industry, globally, to achieve collaboration and make it a source of competitive advantage. Yes, it can be, but only under very specific operating conditions. If these are not present, all the technology in the world won't cause parties in supply chains to act in a genuinely collaborative way towards each other. Barratt's *enablers* and *inhibitors* are detailed in Appendices 5A and 5B respectively.

Of course, this suggests that all parties in supply chains now require a new portfolio of competencies in areas such as customer relationship management, continuous improvement, multi-level communications, management of joint KPIs and many others. But collaboration on its own is not a 'silver bullet' for all occasions.

Getting the subculture right

So how do we attempt to create a subculture to support collaboration? I've heard 'culture' described as trying to hold a fistful of sand: inevitably it defeats you! We found in Chapter 3 that nothing gets done unless the values of the people working in the enterprise support making it happen. Indeed, the fact that so many business plans never materialize is evidence of this phenomenon, although some would argue, quite wrongly, that such slippages are due to the actions of competitors. Actually, both factors impact on implementation, but I'm convinced the insidious resistance that often lurks just beneath the surface is the major reason. On the flip side, the positive force of people's behaviour and beliefs is a critical key to success. Barratt's work on *inhibitors* and *enablers* also supports the idea that 'culture is key'.

Has your business ever sought to generate a particular work culture through change management processes or human resource management? You wouldn't be alone. My experience tells me culture-shaping activities in isolation do not work: there are many factors that can influence and shape a desired subculture in an organization. For *continuous replenishment*, our emphasis needs to be on building a predominantly *group* subculture inside the enterprise. This subculture is characterized by people-focused values such as a commitment to customer relationships, a teamwork style of working that embraces and rewards participation, aversion to risk and the pursuit of synergy through developing cohesive and loyal relationships. A bias towards these values should be evident in all functions that contribute to delivering products and services to collaborative customers. In turn, this means that suppliers and customers need to be open and respectful of each other.

But where do we start? I have chosen ten of the most critical areas that can help you to form a *group* subculture and have described how they are relevant to collaborating in *continuous replenishment* supply chains. None alone is a silver bullet, but putting in place elements of the ten areas listed below will help you to influence the success of your supply chain strategy.

1. Organization design

Let us start with the big picture – the organization's design. Getting a *group* subculture necessary for a *continuous replenishment* supply chain means installing a design that is a matrix of vertical (line) management functions and horizontal account management (staff) functions, as depicted in Figure 5.1. A matrix design is not an easy type of organization to work in because of the conflicts that potentially can, and do, arise at each intersection between the vertical functions, which generally hold the budget, and the horizontal account management functions, which usually deal with the customers. To work collaboratively you need to have an underpinning capability to supply in the first place; if you have that pre-requisite, the collaboration then helps to smooth supply to customers, and everyone benefits.

As one senior executive was heard to say, 'The challenge is not so much to build a matrix structure as it is to create a matrix in the minds of our managers.'[8] The reality is that vertical functional organizations are always going to be 90 degrees 'out of phase' with the way customers wish to buy. While this has been conceded to some extent by the introduction of dual-reporting matrix structures, the fundamentally different objectives of the two types of management groups will always make life interesting – if not complicated.

However, a matrix organizational arrangement works when the people want it to work. In many ways, the task of gaining internal collaboration between different functional groupings mirrors the task of achieving collaboration at the external interfaces with customers. And surely this makes sense. High levels of trust and consensus supported by good

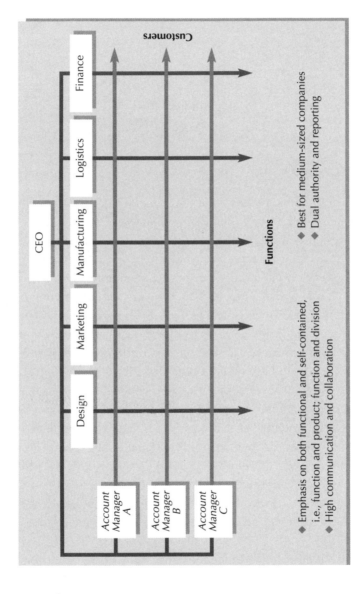

FIGURE 5.1 ◆ 'Functional' and 'matrix' organization designs

internal communications is important to create the right environment for a group subculture to flourish. As a result, staff tend to be long-standing and permanent, but the downside is that small powerful cliques can form that are not necessarily healthy for the business. Most organizations these days are still a mix of functional and/or matrix formats, and this can work well when the market/customer situation is relatively stable and/or collaborative. General Motors has used the matrix style of organization structure to great effect since implementing it in 1998.[9] This replaced a multidivisional organization architecture, which among other things, had almost led to GM's demise.

One of the key challenges in a *continuous replenishment* supply chain is to align customer-facing teams with customer buying values and create 'controlled pull'; and then to optimize the supply side so that it is appropriately 'customized'. This should be possible if you have the right customer information (in a timely fashion) to organize internal resources as simply and effectively as possible.

2. Processes

It is important that the processes followed in the *continuous replenishment* supply chain are participative, internally and externally, and, of course, standard and replicable. Leading companies will put customer account management processes at the forefront, as well as joint-development processes. Everything about these processes is unambiguously focused on the long term. The aim is to maintain and deepen existing relationships with nominated customers in every facet of service; and this is what they expect and demand.

Call centres in the financial services and tourism industries often have technology with caller identification software so that employees can identify the customer and update their information on a real-time basis. When the customer calls, a reference list of facts and preferences is readily available to employees so they can tailor their conversation to put the caller at ease – or feel special. One example of this is the Royal Bank of Scotland in Britain, which operates a number of insurance companies, e.g., Direct Line, Privilege and Churchill. These entities are all aimed at different segments. Incoming calls all go to the same call centre, but the system tells the operators which company the customer is seeking so that they can respond accordingly. A more manual system is used by veterinary surgeons who often refer to pets by their first name and give the pet the owner's last name. They chat about the animal with the owner and ask how things have been going since their last visit. All the information is contained on a card or computer note, but the vet gives the impression of knowing and caring about the much-loved pet.

Whether your system is technologically sophisticated or simple and manual, the fundamental requirement is for the customer to feel important and wanted. The use of empathy and listening skills are important in the process of these interactions. This has been recognized by those companies that tend to hire customer-facing staff with good people skills (e.g., ex-teachers or actors). This type of process is made or broken by the manner of the staff and their ability to exhibit good interpersonal skills – an essential recipe for success in *continuous replenishment* supply chains, supported by technology that will provide adequate information and help in the delivery of the required processes.

3. Systems/information technology[10]

Information technology may not seem like a culture shaper but it is important to get the right systems in place to underpin the required sub-culture. There is no point in seeking collaboration in a *continuous replenishment* supply chain when your IT systems are designed for the opposite effect. IT systems in various combinations provide a 'view' of the business, and this can help you to align your business processes and activities to match the profiles of your customer segments. Point-of-sale systems can provide daily information on the purchasing profiles of your customers. In turn, this information materially assists the replenishment process. Data Warehouses and Business Analytics are vital facilities now readily available to modern enterprises.

In *continuous replenishment* supply chains, transactional intensity is relatively low and systems complexity is likewise low because collaboration flourishes best when the operating environment is relatively predictable and stable. This means Enterprise Resource Planning (ERP) systems are useful but not essential. However, additional systems applications that assist in managing customer relationships are important. The Kanban scheduling mechanism (more commonly associated with lean activities) is useful, as is Vendor Managed Inventory (VMI), although this is usually an in-built capability of most contemporary ERP systems.

Operational environments with more demanding VMI specifications will benefit from the advanced capabilities offered by some of the major supply chain management software vendors, e.g., Manugistics, i2 and Aspentech. The distinction between these providers is that Manugistics and i2 are geared towards more discrete product industries, while Aspentech is a process industry leader. Every Day Lower Prices (EDLP), which is essentially a pricing strategy, is also important in this operating environment, as are Collaborative Demand Planning (CDP), Efficient Consumer Response (ECR) and Collaborative Planning Forecasting and Replenishment (CPFR). There are various other important collaborative design, supply and manufacturing applications, including:

◆ Mechanical Computer Aided Design (MCAD);

◆ Mechanical Computer Aided Manufacturing (MCAM); and

◆ Product Information Management (PIM).

The processes and systems applications for Customer Relationship Management (CRM) are progressively being integrated into a portfolio of systems that combine to jointly service customers, and if used in this way they are extremely valuable in providing access to good customer information to support fulfillment. However, if used in isolation, CRM, while still useful, loses a lot of its potential power. Additional systems on the 'customer end' of the supply chain include support systems such as Point-of-Sale, Radio Frequency Identification (RFID) and the increasingly utilized Global Data Synchronization Network (GSDN).

On the 'supplier side' companies such as the SAS Institute Inc. have designed and produced a whole suite of Supplier Relationship Management (SRM) software applications, e.g., Sourcing Data Quality, Spend Analysis, Procurement Scorecard and Sourcing Strategy.[11] Indeed, SAS proposes a phased approach in using the various individual elements of their SRM suite, as follows:[12]

SAS Sourcing Data Quality:	for commodity coding, supplier normalization, data quality and data gathering.
SAS Spend Analysis:	for spend analysis, ranking, reporting and contract compliance.

SAS Procurement Scorecard:	for KPIs, metrics, enterprise dashboard and performance profiles.
SAS Sourcing Strategy:	supply base optimization, scenarios, demand forecasting and cash flow predictions.

The progression in this suite of four SRM components is from raw data (What happened?), to information (Why did it happen?), to knowledge (What will happen?), and finally, to intelligence (What is the best that can happen? How can I act on this insight?). In this way, hindsight is converted to insight; and performance and return on investment (ROI) are significantly improved. But achieving adequate data quality is an essential starting point. Spend analyses, followed by a procurement scorecard, help to make sense of current performance, and drive the new focus required in the sourcing strategy. From there it is a simple step to e-enable the procurement process with available software packages.

4. Key Performance Indicators (KPIs)

Don't we all love performance measurement? Unfortunately, this important area of management is often poorly understood and misused and abused as a result. Too often companies compile long lists of KPIs across a broad spectrum of functional areas without realizing that specific KPIs apply to each type of supply chain, or combination thereof. Early versions of the balanced scorecard approach developed by Robert Kaplan and David Norton[13] proved both a blessing and a blight; while bringing new disciplines to the monitoring and management of performance in practice the scorecard did not always identify clearly enough the need to align different KPIs with particular customers. Instead, the impression was that an arbitrary list of financial, customer, internal business processes and learning and growth KPIs selected by management applied equally well across **all** customer buying behaviours in the marketplace. This is simply not the case. The oversight has now been partly redressed with Kaplan and Norton's latest insights on balanced scorecards.[14] In any event, we would prefer to use the term 'biased scorecard', meaning that we select *only* those KPIs that are relevant to each type of dominant buying behaviour in a particular marketplace – and for a specific combination or types of supply chains. The mix of these buying behaviours is particularly important, because it will guide us in the selection process and the subsequent allocation of efforts in data specification data collection and monitoring of the selected portfolio of KPIs.

For *continuous replenishment* supply chains, our emphasis should be on measuring customer retention and loyalty, the length of individual customer relationships and our business's percentage of the customer's overall spend. Other measures such as the amount of information sharing and insights to drive customer service improvement are also relevant. Measures such as service reliability, Delivery-In-Full-On-Time-Error-Free (DIFOTEF) and other parameters that reflect the way we are managing the all-important relationship with selected customers are also very useful. In addition, Customer Account Profitability (CAP) measures indicating strong profitability from this customer segment is not unusual. This just reinforces the need to isolate and focus on *collaborative* customers – as a conscious priority.

CRM systems are often used in implementing KPIs that focus on the relational measures commonly used in call centres, health insurance and financial services, and brand-oriented companies. In addition to customer retention rates, cost of customer retention, as well as the 'cost effectiveness' of the tactics used to achieve high rates of customer retention, is monitored, e.g., Toyota measures a range of KPIs that track customer loyalty and retention.

Without a doubt, KPIs are a major shaper of culture in organizations, because people tend to do what is measured, irrespective of whether it is the correct or the most appropriate thing to do in the circumstances. The world is full of examples where particular KPIs set in place inside the enterprise are driving behaviours that are quite clearly dysfunctional. This could be an urban myth, but I once heard of a US airline that ostensibly found a 'motivator' for its pilots to reduce fuel wastage and so encourage more energy efficient flying practices. Pilot bonuses were linked to the reduction of fuel use. This was a very effective motivator for a behaviour change and resulted in considerable reductions in the use of fuel. It also lost them customers! The pilots were turning off the air conditioning while waiting for take-off clearance on the tarmac, which saved fuel, yet in the tropics the passengers were sweltering in the heat.

Call centres modify their KPIs according to the type of calls – inbound or out-bound – and whether they are seeking to gather information, generate sales or build a relationship. Compare the likely KPIs used for a crisis counselling centre with those for a directory assistance service at a telephone company. Both services are provided by telephone, but the type and level of service is very different indeed. An extreme example maybe, but it illustrates the point. In call centres today, the time taken on a call is less important if the operator is trying to transform the caller into a customer. However, the duration and number of calls per day are still important when the aim is simply to deliver information, and not necessarily establish a relationship.

5. Incentives

Incentives are useful in encouraging staff to do what the organization wants them to do, and they go hand-in-hand with KPIs. In the case of *continuous replenishment* supply chains, we need incentives that encourage participative and team processes and behaviours. For a *group* subculture, any schemes that recognize performance in a public way are appropriate, e.g., honour boards, team rewards such as dinner out or bonuses. These types of incentives need to carry a real level of achievement with them and not be something that is inappropriate or seen as irrelevant – otherwise they don't work.

Examples of incentives in this category reflect a participatory emphasis. Until the 1990s, McDonald's used honour boards to acknowledge excellent customer service and exceptional levels of staff performance. Symbols were put on employees' name badges to indicate the level of customer service they had achieved. IKEA, on the other hand, uses departmental sales targets rather than individual ones, encouraging their sales staff to perform as a team rather than compete for customers.

6. Job design

Job design and job descriptions in *continuous replenishment* supply chains need to focus on teamwork and cooperation to satisfy customers. Ideally, any activities involving authority, autonomy or control should be decentralized and negotiated by consensus. Getting the line and customer-facing staff to agree on 'who will do what' in serving customers is especially effective, as it emphasizes how best to manage the relationship.

The type of job design that supports this situation is descriptive rather than prescriptive. If employees are given both responsibility and authority commensurate with the level of their duties it tends to empower them to make more relationship-based decisions. However, this should occur under the guidance of a coach who uses meetings to discuss scenarios and their possible resolutions.

7. Internal communications

Internal communications are a critical factor in shaping the required responses to customers from inside organizations. But this importance has not been fully realized. Suffice it to say that a *group* subculture tends to flourish in an environment where internal communications are highly consultative, and the underlying theme is 'we care'. Fortunately, this type of communication works well in a relatively slow-moving, stable operating environment, which is what the collaborative buying behaviour is all about. However, as will be seen in later chapters, this style of internal communications does not suit a fast-moving world characterized by high levels of uncertainty and unpredictable demand.

The best vehicle for good internal communications in the *group* subculture is team-based, face-to-face, and hence, meetings-based. However, this can be slow and cumbersome and can sometimes become cliquey – in which case certain individuals and groups purposely withhold information from other individuals and groups. But the strength of the team approach is that staff turnover is relatively low, otherwise the 'culture' is lost.

8. Training and development

Training and development efforts are too often unfocused and undifferentiated, and as a result much of the budget provided for this purpose is wasted. It is not essential to train **all** personnel in **all** skill areas. In order to foster a *group* subculture, training and development activities should focus on team-building, and emphasize the value of relationships and the synergy that is derived from them if applied appropriately, both inside and outside the enterprise.

The most effective vehicles for promoting the rapport so necessary to this type of subculture are small 'work groups' and a 'hands on' style.

Fact-based negotiation skills and a thorough understanding of group dynamics are also important. The *group* subculture is supported very strongly by the 'buddy' system, as used in many businesses that adopt project teams. In this case, the responsibility for a person's own work and the development of another person becomes the norm, and results in successful team-building, e.g., consulting teams comprising a combination of senior members, consultants with a medium level of experience and a few junior associates. The junior associates work in quite directed environments, while still learning the culture of the organization.

9. Recruitment

Too often, personnel are recruited into organizations and selected for positions solely on the basis of a combination of their technical qualifications and previous work experience. Little if any consideration is given to the *micro-culture* that they bring to the organization and the impact this could have on their performance. Indeed, if only it were recognized how this particular factor could be used to 'genetically engineer' organizational subcultures, we would see correspondingly more effective implementation of intended strategic plans, across the board.

What we are seeking to grow is a subculture which is personal, has people with good relationship skills, is team-oriented and empathetic, and above all, is focused on delivering personalized service to key customers – on a continuing basis.

10. Leadership style

We now turn our attention to the most vital factor of all in shaping subcultures in organizations – leadership style. You only have to look at the myriad of examples of successful and unsuccessful organizations over the last few decades to realize the impact that particular leadership style can have on their ultimate fortunes. The case clearing houses in Europe and the United States are full of salient examples. The reality is that successful organizations tend to display an array of leadership styles consistent with the mix of dominant buying behaviours in their marketplace. This is a fundamental requirement for success in today's world.

In turn, the top management team in successful organizations tends to formulate strategies that are appropriately aligned to the needs of their customers or markets. They then develop and manage a corresponding array of subcultures inside the organization to drive these strategies into the marketplace. The key is this 'alignment' with customers, but it all starts from the leadership team recognizing their customers' buying behaviours. Such recognition sets up the conditions for ultimate success. Without it, there is little chance of sustained alignment with customers (and suppliers) and corresponding superior operational and financial performance.

So the real conundrum facing today's top management teams is how to develop and (coincidentally) maintain a mix of diverse subcultures inside the organization tasked with under-pinning particular strategies – especially when some of these subcultures have fundamentally opposing values. Few enterprises have yet found a solution to this problem.

In the case of a *group* subculture, it is important to have someone in the management team who has a predominantly *coach* leadership style, and ensures that the values required to form and deliver genuine customer-emphatic strategies are in place. A *coach* leads by example and teaching, is very conscientious and shows genuine concern for others. He or she likes to help, is loyal to subordinates and superiors alike, and remains committed to the vision espoused by the overall leader of the enterprise. The *coach* is also politically astute, seeking to lead by agreement and consensus. In Myers-Briggs terms, this leadership style is epitomized by an ESFJ (or extrovert-sensing-feeling-judging) type. IKEA is a company that has consistently embraced the *coach* style of leadership. This Swedish firm has a very *group*-oriented culture and aims to have a fairly flat organizational structure. Using Geert Hofstede's classification, the country characteristics for Sweden are high individuality, small power distance, low uncertainty avoidance and, like the rest of the Scandinavian countries, highly feminine (i.e., little differentiation between male and female characteristics).

Let's mix it up a bit!

It is important to understand that alignment with customers (and suppliers) does not always work on a linear one-to-one basis. Mixed supply chain logics are sometimes the best solution, but have to be applied skill-fully. An enterprise, for instance, could use collaboration between parties in its supply chain to achieve what is in effect a low-cost or lean result. More often than not, mixed supply chains will be the appropriate solution rather than one of the pure supply chain logics on its own. In terms of the *continuous replenishment* supply chain we are addressing in this chapter, the value of collaboration is to create customer 'pull' to re-align internal supply 'push'. A good supply chain team is able to work at the centre of the bow tie (do you recall Figure 1.1 in Chapter 1?). The trick is to plan and manage supply to balance supply with demand.

Lever Bros (Sunsilk) in Thailand is an example of an organization that is using mixed logics in its supply chains. It has developed a manufactur-ing plant to service two distinct supply chains – one is *lean*, with steady production, and the other *continuous replenishment*, with fluctuating produc-tion. To support this arrangement there is a specific programme to train staff in the competences required for each type of supply chain. Lever Bros aims to have these two supply chains synchronized and integrated through-out its entire business. And it is working. Other examples include automotive companies Toyota and Honda. They have formed remarkable partnerships with their Tier 1 supply base, leading directly to lower-cost components. It's a case of collaboration leading to a lean result.[15]

Another example of the subtle art of cross logics is provided by the Shouldice Hospital in Canada. While the hospital is providing health care, which is not normally associated with the business of supply chains, the way the hospital designs and delivers its service supports our earlier con-tention that supply chains permeate every enterprise and industry. Clearly the hospital has refined and smartly executed its approach to a particular customer segment.

Shouldice Hospital[16]

Shouldice Hospital in Canada has a unique service – it treats only people with inguinal hernias. These patients are in and out of the hospi-tal in three days and back to work in about ten days, compared to the usual hospital stay of seven to ten days, followed by up to six weeks for full recovery. The streamlined approach of this hospital and the focus on one type of operation has resulted in expertise in the preparation of the patient, surgery procedure, recovery programme and rehabilitation – as well as an international reputation attracting 'customers' from all over the globe. Over 95 per cent of hernia patients are male, and Shouldice Hospital has developed its systems to address the needs of this customer category. This is achieved by maximizing the information and control the patient has in the procedure and minimizing time lost from work; which further contributes to the speed of recovery. The shortened time for recovery has decreased the negative impact on both the patient's family and their business.

Patients are admitted in the afternoon and allocated to a group that they are responsible to and for during their stay in the hospital. The group eats their meals together in the equivalent to a hotel dining room (in both quality of food and style). Hospital rooms in Shouldice do not have their own bathroom – instead patients have to get up and walk to the bathroom. At every step the patients are encouraged to return to routine activity. On the first afternoon the groups are taken through a complete explanation of the medical procedure. The next day operations are performed without a general anaesthetic; instead they are given a combination of a local anaesthetic and sedatives (they are semi-conscious). After the procedure is completed the patient is helped to walk back to their bed – in contrast to conventional approaches to hernia recovery, where patients are restricted to complete bed-rest for almost a week after the operation. The same day patients are up and walking (very slowly) in the manicured gardens of the hospital. They are required to walk to meals and exercise with their group. Two days later they are discharged from the hospital after following a programme of increased gentle exercise and instruction on how to continue the healing process. Annually, Shouldice Hospital has sold-out reunions for their patients in a five-star hotel. The venue is packed with more than 1,500 patients who come to rejoin 'their' group to catch up and celebrate.

It is important therefore to understand that alignment with customers does not always have to be on a linear one-to-one basis. Mixed supply chain logics are sometimes more appropriate and can be most effective if applied skillfully. An enterprise, for instance, could use collaboration between parties in its supply chain to achieve what is in effect a low-cost or lean result. So mixed logics in supply chains is often the reality for many businesses. We will discuss this further at the end of Chapter 8.

Real or artificial 'collaboration'

Genuine collaboration appears to occur when the parties in a particular supply chain have similar power, and hence their relationship is by definition more interdependent. Where a power imbalance exists, genuine collaborative behaviour is less likely to occur. Some companies achieve a 'pseudo collaboration' effect through the very power they exert on their suppliers, e.g., Wal-Mart flexing its muscles with its suppliers. Despite these aberrations, the original principle remains true, i.e., seek to collaborate only with those parties in the supply chain who have collaborative values and genuinely wish to collaborate. Only in that way will truly *win–win* experiences be sustained over time. Andrew Humphries and Richard Wilding have developed an evolutionary approach to gaining trust and achieving collaboration, namely cooperation, coordination and finally collaboration.[17]

I have found that strategic relationships between pairs of enterprises, ideally in *continuous replenishment* supply chains, can take two forms:

◆ Supplier–supplier: these are horizontal relationships, which we will refer to as 'alliances'.

◆ Buyer–seller: these are vertical relationships, which we prefer to call 'partnerships'.

Both types of relationship can be explained using the *dynamic alignment* framework introduced in earlier chapters and depicted again in Figure 5.2. Within each of these types there are at least four subcategories of relationships that closely parallel the types of customer behavioral segments that we identified in Chapter 2. These are: *loyalty*-driven relationships (*continuous replenishment*); *cost*-driven relationships (*cost/efficiency*); *performance*-driven relationships (*quick response/demanding*); and *innovation*-driven relationships (*innovation solutions*). However, irrespective of the type of strategic relationship, potential conflict can arise as a result of:

◆ different priorities caused by unclear focus;

◆ incompatible long-term objectives, e.g., cost minimization (supplier) versus profit maximization (distributor);

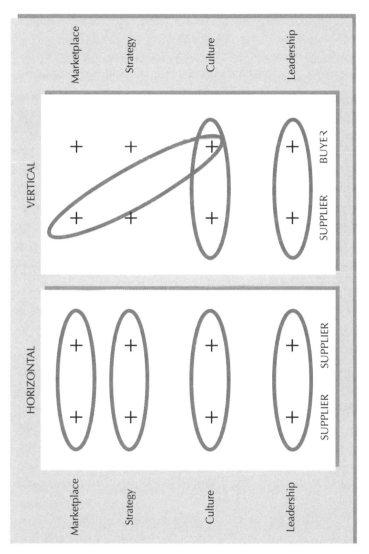

FIGURE 5.2 ◆ Critical interfaces in horizontal and vertical strategic relationships

Source Adapted from Figure 13.1 in Gattorna and Walters (1996), p. 191

- different cultures;
- lack of communications/information;
- traditional 'zero-sum' negotiation strategies; and/or
- incorrect pricing.

Given the experience with conflict as noted above, the priorities for achieving effective strategic relationships must include the following initiatives:

- Develop a common/shared vision.
- Recognize each company's independent objectives, e.g., ROI, budgets, market share.
- Develop common objectives that are as compatible as possible with independent objectives, but which ultimately optimize the mutual benefit to the parties involved.
- Get to know each other's marketplace as this affects the interaction.
- Get to know each other's culture, possibly by placing personnel inside each other's company or by creating strategic project teams with employees from both companies.

Strategic partnering is most relevant to our discussion of *continuous replenishment* supply chains because of the preferred collaborative values present on both sides. Indeed, the ability to select and manage successful partnerships is fast becoming a required competency. The unique *strategic partnering* methodology described in more detail below has been developed and refined through extensive fieldwork; it focuses on fostering growth in trust and shared information, through **joint action**. This in turn naturally leads to the development of joint competitive advantages for members in the same supply chain. The desired outcome is integrated business plans for the collaborating parties and subsequent sustained operating success.

Corporations that have 'collaborative' values and practise *strategic partnering* usually have a number of 'partners'. However, while relationships between partners should be unique, they need not be exclusive. The nature of the strategic relationship forged with one company may be quite different from that forged with another. The essential ingredient for success is that the partners are culturally compatible. Our definition of

Strategic partnering develops enduring corporate relationships based on understanding and shared knowledge. The process gets its name from developing and maintaining a **strategic fit** *between an organization's goals and capabilities and its changing marketing opportunities.*

FEATURES	IMPLICATIONS
Businesses develop a profound understanding of each other's business operations.	The parties develop an approach to business which resembles a 'Good Times, Bad Times' attitudes, allowing for greater flexibility and ultimately control.
Two parties in a given supply chain commit to a unique, though not necessarily exclusive relationship.	Sometimes we work to develop relationships with customers only to lose them just before they start to become ardent supporters, or 'advocates' of our company.
This relationship is mutual and becomes part of the corporate structure.	Conflict is resolved quickly between the parties because they have similar objectives in the partnership.
The intention to commence strategic partnering is initiated at the highest managerial level.	This results in increased commitment to the technique and greater understanding at all levels in the organization.
A 'meeting of minds' is achieved by intra-company communications downwards, and horizontal inter-company communications.	Problems between parties can be pre-empted or solved quickly.
Mutual business plans and shared objectives may be a feature of the partnering.	Companies are in a superior position to their competitors due to their superior knowledge. Gains are achieved by the 'two heads are better than one' maxim.

FIGURE 5.3 ◆ *Strategic partnering* **definition**

strategic partnering is detailed in Figure 5.3, along with the features and implications of this unique relationship type.

Along with others who have worked in this area,[18] we have developed a one-day workshop-driven *strategic partnering* programme, which is fully detailed in Appendix 5C, and is comprised of two stages. In Stage 1, each executive management team attending the event completes the 'quick' *dynamic alignment* diagnostic questionnaire found in Appendix 1A. The primary aim of Stage 1 is to assess the degree of *compatibility* between the cultures and leadership styles of the two parties. In Stage 2, the proprietary workshop-driven *strategic partnering* technique is used. Significant success has been achieved with this accelerated workshop-driven technique, but for best results a preliminary screening process should aim to ensure that only parties with genuine collaborative values (and therefore part of the *continuous replenishment* supply chain) are invited to participate.

The ultimate outcome of the *strategic partnering* workshop is to enable agreement between the two parties on the joint issues they feel need to be resolved. The real-time process in getting to this point creates the required early momentum. However, it is important that before the inaugural meeting breaks up, the senior executives from both buyer and supplier organizations appoint joint project teams to prepare detailed work plans for consideration at a subsequent workshop approximately one month later. On the assumption that the recommendations are accepted all round, implementation of a range of joint initiatives can proceed immediately after that. There is no better communication process than having buyers and sellers working together on joint initiatives for mutual benefit.

After all that, how does your enterprise measure up as a collaborative partner in the various industry supply chains you participate in? In fact do you need to be collaborative at all? Or do you have a mix of collaborative and other types of relationships in your supply chains? Keep an eye out so you can spot the opportunities as they arise.

Living lessons

1   Know who your truly collaborative customers and suppliers are.

2   Only collaborate with those supply chain members who genuinely have collaborative values. Relationships take a lot of time and energy to develop and nurture, so don't squander this effort.

3   Be aware that some situations will require a combination approach, e.g., maybe *lean* on the supply-side with suppliers, and *collaborative* on the customer-side.

CHAPTER 6

Lean supply chains

Focusing on efficiency and lowest cost-to-serve

H ow lean is your business? It's the magic question, as being 'lean' is often seen to be the cure-all approach to lowering costs. It's not so much how low can you go, but how lean can you be? Japanese car manufacturer Toyota got us hot under the collar in the 1980s when it introduced lean manufacturing into its factories. Organizations have been applying lean concepts to corporate logistics systems and the wider domain of supply chain management ever since. However, as so often occurs when new concepts are applied to supply chain thinking, we can start to have unreasonable expectations about the actual benefits. We can also get confused about what we mean by the concept itself. We can probably agree that lean principles are focused on eliminating waste in materials, processes, time and information. But can we expect all of this **plus** creativity, flexibility and adaptability as Kate Vitasek and her colleagues seem to suggest in *Harvard Business Review*?[1]

I want to differentiate between two separate supply chains, *continuous replenishment*, as discussed in Chapter 5, and *lean*. It might seem like splitting hairs, but you cannot simply roll them into one. Not all parties involved in developing *lean* supply chains are going to be collaborative – and that's a fact! In contrast, parties in the *continuous replenishment* supply chain will share information and help each other to eliminate waste; put simply, they collaborate. I see the classic *lean* supply chain as one where low cost is achieved by ensuring customers are not over-serviced. Low costs are achieved by doing the very basic processes, but doing them well. In *continuous replenishment* supply chains it will always be a case of customer 'pull', but in the classic *lean* supply chain, if customers are not willing to share their demand projections, we will naturally have to 'push' product downstream using our best forecasts in what is hopefully a fairly stable environment.

So we are all agreed that lean is basically a 'push' strategy that is underpinned by supply values rather than customer 'pull' as is the case with *continuous replenishment* supply chains. However, to work effectively, *lean* supply chains require collaboration with suppliers on the supply-side. Having said that, it is worthwhile understanding where the original lean concept and practices originated from.

Origins of lean manufacturing

Toyota triggered the quest for lean production when it decided in the early 1950s that American-style mass production would not work in Japan. In the United States, companies were still using the assembly line approach to production that had been so successfully introduced decades earlier by Henry Ford. The mass production of cars was still in vogue, and this required a large market with fairly standardized manufacturing systems – resulting in a limited range of vehicle models.

In contrast, the Japanese market was restricted due to international trade barriers limiting the importation of Japanese cars into Western nations. This market restriction was reinforced by the ban on foreign direct investment (FDI) by the Japanese Ministry of International Trade and Industry (MITI). The ban effectively curtailed the development of any intensively high-capital industry, such as the automobile industry, in a country which, just after World War II, had relatively no available capital. Although the size of Japan's domestic market was small, the demand for variety from the Japanese consumer was very high. The Allied occupation forces also introduced labour unions into Japan, which increased the demand for higher wages and restricted the ability of managers to lay off employees when the economy turned down, as they were accustomed to doing in the past. The Japanese labour market also had no temporary migrants to work in the nation's factories (unlike in the United States, where migrant groups formed the bulk of employees). Consequently, Japan's automotive factories had a higher wage cost compared to that of other nations.

Toyota recognized the impact of these factors and developed the Toyota Production System (TPS), now more commonly known as lean manufacturing. The two major features of lean manufacturing that distinguish it from mass production are: first, increased efficiency through the reduction of errors; and second, reduced carrying costs of inventories achieved by manufacturing in small 'batches'. The key ingredient to these improvements was Japan's highly skilled workforce. In lean manufacturing, skilled workers manage each section of the assembly cycle, which contrasts markedly with mass customization processes. US automotive factories use primarily low-skilled labour on the shop floor and restrict knowledge to a 'need-to-know' basis. The combination of increased human capital in the Japanese workforce, increased individual responsibility, the practice of systematically and consistently tracing problems back to their source and rectifying the cause (thereby eliminating errors and reducing waste – called *muda* in Japanese), along with reduced inventories, has resulted in considerable competitive advantage in the Japanese supply chain.[2]

The relentless customer

You can guess what happened next. The Japanese customer – and customers globally – soon took to the product diversity and lower costs made possible by lean manufacturing. But are all customers lean customers? How do you recognize the customer in what I'm calling the *lean* supply chain? One buying behaviour found in most – if not all – markets to some degree or other is the desire for '*efficiency/consistency*'. In the *lean* market, this behaviour is paramount. While loyalty and service are a premium in the *continuous replenishment* supply chain, in the cost/efficiency segment, it is price and predictability. With such stability in demand, forecasting on the supply-side is both feasible and necessary.

Customers in the *lean* market will often shop around and use multiple businesses in the search for steady supply and lowest price. But in doing so, they can be impersonal or even adversarial, with few if any loyalties developing. This is a very transactional style of marketplace, where information is power and little or no sharing occurs between buyers and sellers. For suppliers, it's a hard relentless market; with customers so price-sensitive that enterprises have virtually no opportunity to differentiate their value proposition. If you are looking to compete in these conditions, you must seek to be the lowest-cost producer, and sustain this advantage over time, using whatever techniques that are available.

Response strategies

The value proposition to customers is that of a 'standard' and reliable service – customers **know** what they are getting. The offering may still have bells and whistles, but the offer is supplied in such a way as to standardize the different components so that it can be done at lowest cost. The notion of innovation is still important here as it is really used to drive manufacturing standardization rather than customer product innovation *per se*. The Zara, Benetton and Toyota stories all demonstrate value-add and clear customer propositions – all managed with innovation to minimize waste, which is where *lean* principles re-emerge.

The best and only way to service the low-cost and reliability-driven marketplace is via a *lean* (or semi-wave flow) configuration of the supply chain. The primary focus is on efficient operations offering high volume and low variety, and mostly producing goods and services to forecast. This is the classic make-to-forecast (MTF) operating environment, compared to the make-to-order (MTO) type of response that we see in *agile* supply chains, explored in more detail in Chapter 7. Customers being serviced by *lean* supply chains are offered the value proposition that: 'you will benefit from low-cost production and logistics achieved by using all available synergies and economies of scale'. The ability to forecast demand more accurately is a big advantage, and the fact that we are usually dealing with mature products with predictable lead-times makes the situation all the more manageable. However, these parameters come at the cost of reduced agility, and are best achieved when system capacity is not under pressure, and production takes place under lower priority schedules.

Getting the culture right

What sort of subculture do you think will work best in a *lean* supply chain? These supply chains need security and predictability to satisfy their customers: nothing too flashy or risky. The relentless cost-driven customers are best served by a *hierarchical* subculture, described in Chapter 3. This is a subculture characterized by policies and procedures, systems, stability and order, control, logic and economy, to name just a few. It is best staffed with people who enjoy working under relatively repetitive conditions. But it can prove frustrating for staff who prefer variety and creativity. Let's look at the various parameters needed to formulate this type of subculture.

1. Organization design

The ideal organization structure for the *hierarchical* subculture is the 'process' design, as depicted in Figure 6.1.

In this type of design, employees are organized around several *core processes* in the enterprise that are replicable on a continuous basis. Teamwork is promoted within the subprocesses, and the overall core process is usually managed by a 'process' manager. As organizations usually have multiple core processes, there are corresponding opportunities for cross-functional teaming. Shared responsibilities and decision making emphasize teamwork in this type of organization and risk-taking is not embraced easily. A good, if novel, example of this situation is the Russian Eye Hospital. Here, operating tables are mounted on a slide arrangement that allows them to move sideways from one operating point to the next. This means that specialists at each station can carry out different steps of the eye operation on each patient.[3] Another striking example of this type of organization design is the phenomenon of the Dabbawallahs of Mumbai in India (see p. 141).

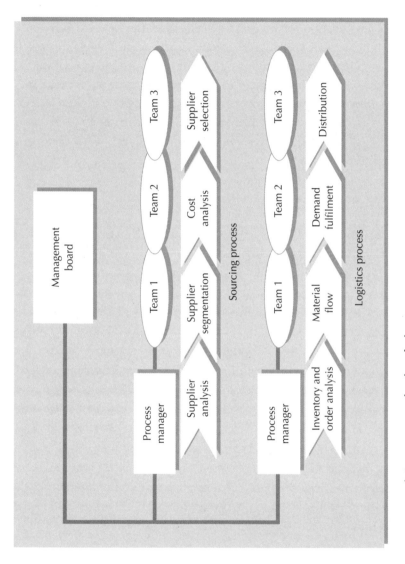

FIGURE 6.1 ◆ **Process organization design**

The Dabbawallahs of Mumbai

Supply chains do not have to be incredibly complex to be efficient, effective and appropriate to the culture. The Dabbawallahs of Mumbai (formerly known as Bombay) are from a particular caste in India who effectively developed a daily delivery service for more than 150,000 home-cooked lunches in a round metal container called a *dabba*. They arranged the successful delivery of lunch from home to work and then the return of the lunch container – all to a level of accuracy far greater than Six Sigma.

In Mumbai, due to cultural traditions from early last century and overcrowding on the public transport system, employees generally do not take their lunch with them to work. However, buying lunch is an effort because workers would have to leave their air-conditioned offices for the crowded, polluted and hot streets of Mumbai, only to buy food of dubious quality. Home-cooked food has until recently been the preference, and an efficient industry has grown up over the past century to resolve the problem of delivery of lunchtime meals from the home to the office, on a daily basis.

The Dabbawallahs have established a network of distribution routes to collect lunches from workers' homes. The *dabbas* are delivered to sorting points at the railway stations, loaded on to dedicated carriages on the normal commuter trains, sent throughout the city, then distributed to offices and ultimately to their owner. One hour later the *dabbas* are collected and returned to the home – following the reverse route taken earlier. This is achieved by a basically illiterate group of people, who have developed a very efficient (albeit manual) system at an incredible level of accuracy – no more than one mistake in every 15 million deliveries![4] In addition to this efficient regular service, the Dabbawallahs will collect a lunch that is not on the agreed weekly route or a late delivery – and deliver for an additional price. But even this foolproof system will fail when heavy rainfall similar to that experienced in July 2005 disabled the train network!

The Dabbawallahs have organized themselves around specific tasks and processes. There is also an element of hierarchy based on age. The more senior/older Dabbawallahs work at the various distribution points where they load and unload the trains. The younger, less experienced Dabbawallahs do all the running around, usually along the pre-defined routes, each and every day.

2. Processes

When certainty and stability – at a low cost – are paramount, transactional-type processes are critical. *Lean* supply chains are all about replicating standardized processes to produce a standardized product. The unerring emphasis is on minimizing cost and achieving optimization in all key production and logistics processes. Most famously, McDonald's led the way in its global application of how to produce and serve a hamburger. Another lesser known but telling example is Domino's Pizza in Australia, which remodelled its business approach for the Australian market.

Domino's Pizza Australia

For Domino's Pizza to successfully compete in Australia where the marketplace is already crowded with individual pizza restaurants and takeaway shops, it had to modify its business model. In North America customers tend to eat fast food in restaurant-style outlets, while Australians usually purchase 'takeaway' food to eat elsewhere; either at home or another venue. This cultural difference, along with some other contributing factors, has resulted in the following changes to the Domino's Pizza model 'down under'.

Labour costs for fast food outlets in Australia are higher than the United States, due to the lack of immigrant labour and a higher minimum wage. The cost of real estate, especially in state capital cities, is also relatively expensive, with few locations available for the typical large fast food restaurants commonly seen throughout the United States. All these factors have an impact on the cost of goods sold. The solution for Australia was to develop shop-front pizza outlets (without dining areas) that used most of the store space for food preparation and the remainder for a comparatively small waiting area for customers. This type of store reduced the level of labour required in the stores, and eliminated the floor space needed for dining rooms (thereby reducing building and land costs), making Domino's a very competitive fast food provider in Australia.

In order to compete well in the low-cost sector of the market, Domino's Pizza follows a strategy of reduced price promotions that 'bundle' the sale of pizza, drinks and extras (e.g., garlic bread). The pizza production processes are all standardized, resulting in a rapidly produced and relatively low-cost product, so although Domino's may 'lose' money during its promotions on individual pizzas it makes money on the 'total' sale. Even with heavily discounted specials it has a policy of 'not reducing the quality or quantity of ingredients used in the pizzas, as customers notice when the pizza doesn't taste as good as the last time'.[5] Domino's also offers the option of extra toppings and changes from the 'basics', although charging more for the service.

Staying on the retail side, Factory Gate Pricing (FGP) trading terms are gathering momentum. Here, instead of the supplier making delivery arrangements, the (retail) customer arranges collection from the supplier. Payment for transport is either by the supplier to customer's carrier, or, by charging the customer a lower price for the goods supplied. It is just another reflection of the imbalance of power that exists today in the FMCG industry – and it is here to stay as there are benefits for large organizations with regular suppliers. However, it is unlikely to provide the same benefits for irregular seasonal categories such as apparel.

3. Systems/IT

The systems that support *lean* supply chains, such as Enterprise Resource Planning (ERP) systems, generally involve significant capital investment. While these systems are essential to underpin low-cost processes, they are also useful as a foundation for all four generic types of supply chain. On top of the ERP system, you can install other non-optimal systems such as Materials Requirements Planning (MRP), Production Planning and Distribution Requirements Planning applications, as depicted in Figure 6.2. It is ideal if you can cap this off by interfacing a free-standing Network Optimization Model (NOM) with the ERP system. This will allow you to test new network and operational scenarios from time to time to ensure that the overall network is meeting agreed service levels, at minimum total (system) cost. More will be said about this important application later in the chapter. The SCOR® model also fits into this section as a useful tool for analysis; but it has its limitations.

In terms of staffing, *lean* supply chains tend to work best with largely permanent staff that are very experienced in their particular roles and enjoy the inherent routine. Labour Management Systems (LMS) may also be used in scheduling staff on shift work, estimating crew size, sorting out change-over of skill-sets as the type of work changes, and mapping skills, all designed to maximize labour resources within given constraints; even constraints as micro as 'employees with fork-lift truck tickets'. In this type of supply chain, point-of-sale (POS) and radio frequency identification (RFID) are very valuable as they are able to automatically trigger re-ordering processes as goods and services are sold (POS) or move 'off-the-shelf' (RFID), in real-time if required.

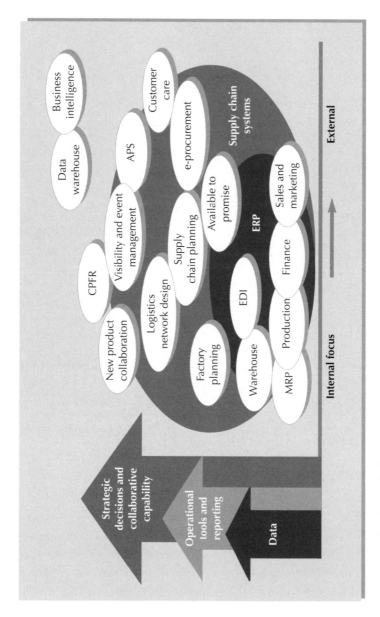

FIGURE 6.2 ◆ A layered view of systems

Source Adapted from Figure 1.1.3 in Gattorna (2003), p. 8

4. Key Performance Indicators

Measurements that track accuracy, quality and predictability are the most relevant metrics for *lean* supply chains. Such metrics include logistics cost per unit, forecast accuracy, forecast/plan variances, utilization factors in storage facilities and transportation modes, Delivery-in-Full-On-Time-Error-Free (DIFOTEF), and variance from established quality standards. These are what really matter. The use of different KPIs in different parts of supply chains and particular types of supply chains is important if desired behaviours are to be reinforced. For instance, in-bound call centre activities usually have KPIs related to customer satisfaction and information management expertise. Call handling rates and speed of response are also important – depending on whether or not the call is a service query or just 'information seeking'. For out-bound activities, the most pertinent performance metrics are those that link sales or referrals to actual business acquisition and/or revenue, and the related costs of these activities.

5. Incentives

The most appropriate incentives in *lean* supply chains are those that encourage behaviours that conform to pre-set policies, procedures and rules. Incentives in this category include a retirement balloon or annuity payments, long-service leave and status symbols such as a large office on the executive floor.

6. Job design

Job design in the *lean* supply chain environment focuses on adherence to process specifications. Authority/autonomy is established by precedent, and control is centralized by way of predefined rules and regulations with which everyone is expected to comply.

7. Internal communications

The style of internal communications is formal, regular and structured to reflect the type of operating environment that is being formed, and the underlying message is that 'we are efficient'. Information is communicated on a 'need to know' basis, and is most often in hard copy format. In any case, communications in this type of subculture are very directive and staff generally react to directions; proactivity is not a quality that is valued. Because 'information is power' in the hierarchical subculture, it is often used as a weapon, which leads to a further lowering of trust in the ranks as individuals feel patronized. But this is not a subculture for individuals anyway, and the prevailing feeling is that there is safety in numbers. Taking any form of risk at the individual level is avoided at all costs.

8. Training and development

The training component of this subculture stresses the use of systems and compliance to rules and procedures. There is a real emphasis on measurement and measurement systems. The style of learning is practical and involves workshops, use of workbooks and the teaching of standard procedures. Competences in analysis, planning, scheduling and communications are mandatory, as are skills in continuous improvement regimes and root cause analysis.

9. Recruitment

To solidify the *hierarchical* subculture, you need to seek out people with deep analytical skills and attention to detail. You should value highly a commitment to accuracy and process organizational skills. Personnel coming into this operating environment should ideally enjoy and indeed thrive on routine. Many organizations already have long-established hierarchical subcultures simply because of their longevity, and there is nothing wrong with that. However, we are observing a distinct shift in customer demand characteristics away from the predictable to the unpredictable, and under these conditions hierarchical subcultures struggle to keep up with the speed of response increasingly demanded by more and more customers.

10. Leadership style

Leaders who thrive in this type of supply chain are *traditional* in that they lead by a combination of consensus and action. They regularly invoke procedures, and tend only to feel comfortable when implementing proven business practices. However, that said, they tend to be very well organized, practical and efficiency focused, although sometimes at the expense of effectiveness. They embrace the values of reliability and productivity, and often use information to control. Their whole life is about maintaining internal company stability and order, a classic ISTJ (introvert-sensor-thinker-judger) in the Myers-Briggs® categorization.

The price driver

I am sure your customers know what a 'special' is. But what about Every Day Low Prices (EDLP)? The idea behind EDLP is simple: retailers promise to pass on discounts to customers so that the supermarket is consistently 'low price'. The aim is deliver a *lower total cost per shopping event for every event* – surely, better than a special! The concept, which gained prominence through the example set by Wal-Mart in the 1990s, is superbly tailored for the *lean* supply chain. *Lean* supply chains are primarily about delivering efficiency across their length and breadth. This is made easier if the products are standardized and have relatively long life cycles. At every stage, *price drives costs* rather than *costs drive price* in *lean* supply chains. Companies will need economies of scale, considerable experience and relatively smooth demand so that capacity utilization can remain high most of the time. At the same time, suppliers are selected primarily on a price basis, on occasions with an eye to value, which we will define as 'quality at a price', but contrary to the conventional definition of *lean*, there is little loyalty in this marketplace.

In the *lean* supply chain, forecasts are made at the generic product category level rather than at the individual stock-keeping unit (SKU) level, and everything that can possibly be done to smooth the flow of product through supply chains is embraced. Hence the emergence of EDLP. Wal-Mart and Procter & Gamble joined forces so that they could smooth the flow of product and take out costs incurred in demand surges associated with promotional activity.[7] There was some collaboration in this arrangement as well, that is if you can collabourate with a gorilla. EDLP has since been implemented in various forms by many retailers, especially supermarkets, to increase their market share. Often the promotion of EDLP is to 'roll back the price' and pass the savings on to the consumer.

Unfortunately, the price reduction is often due to an imbalance in the supply chain that allows powerful retailers to 'shop around' and select cheaper suppliers, or through coercive tactics that force suppliers to reduce their sale price or lose the contract.

While logically the low-cost/reliability-driven consumers should be responding well to the lower prices offered by EDLP, it seems they are a little confused. Many still view the EDLP's reduction in prices (which is often identified with a yellow ticket) as a 'special' rather than an on-going approach that delivers lower prices for each and every visit to the supermarket. Their confusion is perhaps unsurprising because supermarkets continue to offer specials in parallel with EDLP pricing. It will take a while before shoppers understand EDLP. In the United States and elsewhere, EDLP has apparently worked for Wal-Mart. However, employees can find it difficult to manage the inherent conflict between promotional activities and EDLP. Businesses in the *lean* supply chain need to explain EDLP better to consumers – an educational campaign, for instance, could be useful. EDLP works best when the offer is aligned with buyer behaviour. It can have a significant impact when the customers are 'trained' to expect more for less.

But the Wal-Mart experience raises a number of *lean* issues that are retail specific, e.g., leverage on suppliers; standard products versus 'own brand'; wide SKU range reduces dependency on a supplier; local and national market dominance impact on rivals' competitive strategies; vulnerability to monopoly legislation; vulnerability to suppliers' cartels for protection, or as a way of balancing the power equation. And finally, the EDLP strategy simply doesn't work with monopoly suppliers.

The manufacturing equivalent of Wal-Mart is of course Ford, whose demand for yearly supplier price reductions has a similar effect. However, the underlying difference is that Ford will 'help' its suppliers to achieve these price reductions, whereas Wal-Mart pushes the responsibility on to the suppliers entirely. Wal-Mart's recent foray into RFID is a good example of its unilateral approach, telling suppliers what standards have to be met, and then leaving suppliers to foot the bill for development of its own systems. This strategy has led to several state, rather than federal, law suits.

A revolution is on the way[8]

Is your company prepared for the coming revolution? The revolution is coming in the form of *business process innovation and management* and it could potentially envelop all four generic types of supply chain and their variants. Unfortunately, business process improvement – a vital area of management – has largely been underestimated in the past, as evidenced by the numbers in Figure 6.3. But we believe it is *fundamental to sustained alignment* and, by implication, *future competitiveness*. Business processes must endure for the life of the enterprise, and evolve as the enterprise transforms to stay in *dynamic alignment* with its customers and operating environment.

Unfortunately, we have not yet seen enough of this more enlightened approach. Indeed, conventional wisdom has been to create a radical once-and-for-all process improvement. Put the ERP system in and then … what? It has been a bit like the old 'set it and forget it' approach to production. But making radical changes implies accurate knowledge of emergent conditions in the future, and there is also the lag in implementing new processes and systems that has to be taken into account. So-called 'best practices' are really only best practices under specific market conditions. Today's ERP systems can only handle a limited menu of 'best practice' processes anyway. All this has connotations of a cat chasing its tail. The fundamental issue is that current ERP systems embody

Benefit category	'System replacement' No fundamental business changes (%)	'Re-engineered' Key processes re-engineered (%)	'Transformed' Processes and organization aligned with strategy (%)
Revenue uplift	0	1–3	5–10
COGS reduction	0–1	1–2	3–8
Overhead reduction	0–1	1–2	3–5
Inventory reduction	(30)–5	5–20	25–50

FIGURE 6.3 ◆ **Benefits flowing from different degrees of process re-engineering**

Source Adapted from Table 1.1.3 in Gattorna (2003), p. 8

business processes in software applications and are by definition limited in their flexibility. A new way must be found to meet the flexibility requirements of increasingly turbulent markets. The solution lies in accepting the principle of 'multiple alignment' outlined earlier in Chapter 2.

In this environment, we move away from trying to hit a moving target with constant and costly exceptions, and instead hard-wire into the enterprise up to four unique combinations of standard processes, each supported by the appropriate systems applications and underpinning organization structures and subcultures. Then, as operating conditions in the marketplace change and cause customers to move to alternative 'dominant buying behaviours', we are likely to have these covered already. The pre-canned responses will already be embedded in the enterprise. 'Flexibility' takes on a new meaning under these circumstances, and most importantly, it becomes feasible at a lower cost.

A sure way to *leanness*

Can you imagine the complexity involved in managing supply chain networks spreading out from national to regional and – in many cases – to global markets? Such scale is difficult, but not impossible, to manage. The example of the newsprint company outlined in Chapter 2 gave us an insight into how radically to alter the business to compete internationally. But we need to revisit this important issue from a *lean* supply chain perspective – how to minimize the total costs of running large networks and keep them sustainable. This leads us to the topic of Network Optimization Models as foreshadowed earlier. In a complex supply chain network, strategic and tactical decisions about network design and the optimal use of the network go beyond the scope of experience-based or spreadsheet-assisted decisions. In these situations, where there are a myriad of trade-offs and interdependencies to be considered, sophisticated decision support is essential. For this task the Network Optimization Model has become the accepted tool.

Building a Network Optimization Model (NOM) involves capturing all relevant costs, capacities, volumes and constraints in a particular supply chain network. The result is a very large data set. The data set is used to populate a model 'shell' containing literally thousands of equations. This algorithm is then 'solved' to satisfy an objective function, usually either to minimize the cost of operating the network or (if revenue has been included in the model) to maximize profitability. Although the backbone of the model is usually off-the-shelf software with a mathematical 'optimizer', the characteristics of each supply chain need to be carefully configured and entered into the model's data sets to ensure it accurately reflects what is happening in the enterprise. A base 'validation' model is built to match a period of sales and operations – typically using a period of a year. Next, a set of scenarios are identified by the organization and the impact of these different strategies on the performance of the network can be assessed by running the data in the NOM.

The model is a strategic view of the supply chain. In order to produce results which make sense at the strategic level, aggregations of the key elements are usually required. Thus products, suppliers and customers are typically aggregated into logistically meaningful groups. For product 'groups', the *key driver* is typically handling characteristics. For customers and suppliers, location is, of course, a *key driver* as it determines transport time and cost. This alone, however, is rarely sufficient to capture different service requirements, and therefore determine the cost of servicing different types of customers. It is in this aspect of designing a supply chain model that alignment principles have been used to significantly enhance the power and efficacy of the results. This is amply demonstrated in the following example.[9]

Building products manufacturer/supplier

A building products supplier had a broad customer base which ranged from distributors and large commercial building contracts to large and small end-user installers. These customers were buying the same or very similar products, but their service expectations, buying patterns and underlying needs were very different.

When an optimization model was developed for this business a critical aspect was to capture the key buying differences in the customer groupings and to factor in the format of the order and 'service package' that was purchased. The customer groups for this NOM were developed using behavioural segmentation based on the customer's purchase preference (project or non-project) and the level of direct support required from the supplier. On one end of the spectrum were distributors

▶

(including all formats of resellers) who ordered regularly for stock and whose priority was for reliable and consistent service. 'Commercial project' and 'residential project' were segments of customers identified as having long-term relationships with the supplier and ordered for one-off projects with specific requirements. Their priority was responsiveness and flexibility. At the other end of the spectrum the 'commercial' and 'residential support' customers were generally (but not always) smaller end-users who required delivery to site, but also often needed easy access for last minute requirements. These customers valued technical support and day-to-day relationships with their supplier who they saw as the 'hub' of their trade network.

The service and product packages these customers purchased were defined for modelling as: bulk (larger, stock orders picked up or delivered); crane-ups (deliveries, with narrow delivery windows to meet crane schedules); house lots (larger mixed orders picked up or delivered); standard orders (smaller mixed orders picked up or delivered); and immediate orders (pick ups with no advance notice). Many of these packages were purchased by more than one type of customer.

Product groups were determined by the product's weight, handling characteristics and manufacturing characteristics (as manufacturing was also considered in the model). The network developed using these parameters, and evolved by trying various management scenarios and model runs, is illustrated in Figure 6.4.

The resultant Metropolitan Distribution Network (MDN) features three major pathways to the customer. The *bulk* pathway is in effect the same as our *lean* supply chain, and is designed for high-volume, regular activity and includes supply to facilities in the other two pathways. The *pick* pathway, or *agile* supply chain, is more responsive, capable of shorter lead-times and geared for a less predictable workload. There would be one or two of these facilities to support each metropolitan area. The *trade centre* pathway, or *continuous replenishment* supply chain, is a multi-facility network located close to the end-user's home or site location, providing not only small-volume and top-up products but also technical support and the relationship aspect of the tradesman's service needs.

The strength of combining the decision support capability of the Network Optimization Model with the concept of *dynamic alignment* is the ability to minimize cost within the context of a focused and appropriate

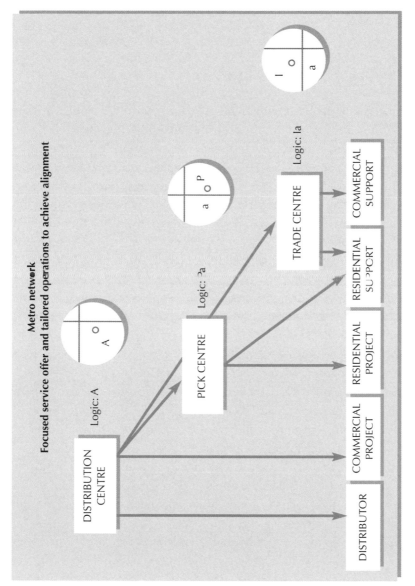

FIGURE 6.4 ◆ Resultant Metropolitan Distribution Network (MDN)

Source Carpenter Ellis (consultants), with permission

service network. By bringing together the physical aspects of the business and its products, and the dominant buying behaviour of customers, the natural 'pathways' through the complexity of a supply chain network begin to emerge.

Mixed supply chain logics

As we saw in Chapter 5, many companies have various combinations of the main four supply chains. In real life, business does not fall neatly within the defined boundaries of categories, no matter how much we might try! A company such as Tesco, for instance, once carried out inventory and order-picking in its own distribution centres. These activities are now performed by manufacturers/suppliers at an earlier stage in the supply chain, which has allowed Tesco to reduce inventory by one-third, and cut supply chain costs by 20 per cent per case. It is an example of *continuous replenishment* and *lean* supply chains combining. Benetton is another example of a company that has re-engineered its processes. *Lean* is the dominant logic during production of components, while *agile* is the dominant logic when finalizing the garments, such as dying the garment the latest 'in' colour.

As *lean* initiatives are essentially designed to strip out waste from supply chains, including inventory and excess capacity, one outcome is to make the system less stable. Indeed, as with 'fly-by-wire' technology in aeronautics, the issue is stability. How close can you get to zero inventory and full utilization of resources without the system failing? In this case the failure is in meeting customers' expectations. On the other hand, if we try to increase stability by building in inventory, time and capacity buffers, agility is likely to be reduced. So the solution is to combine the two in some way rather than adopt one or other approach alone. We will talk more about this in Chapter 7.

A good example of a company that is endeavouring to become leaner yet more responsive to its markets is BlueScope Steel (BSS), a global leader in adding value to commodity flat steel products to produce branded products used in the building sector. BSS has revenues of US$4.3 billion and a network of steel manufacturing and processing facilities in 16 countries. BlueScope's progress on the project is described below.[10]

BlueScope Steel

In phase 1, BlueScope re-segmented its customers and aligned its key value propositions to match the new segments. It aimed to reduce order lead-times using Vendor Managed Inventory (VMI) and other methods. On the manufacturing side, BSS focused on identifying and managing the controllables and sought to standardize processes wherever possible.

In phase 2, the company emphasized aligning key supply chain processes in manufacturing, distribution, planning and scheduling, and performance measurement. It introduced a 'supply chain velocity' pro-gramme across the organization with the aim of developing and implementing lean manufacturing.

Phase 3 involved focusing on reducing and managing variation, as it became obvious that the key to achieving more responsiveness in the delivery to customers was to have the ability to 'flex' capacity to follow more closely forecast demand and supply variations.

Overall, improvement in delivery performance as measured by DIFOT has so far proved elusive, despite all the initiatives. However, external customer surveys have revealed a steady increase in customer satisfaction. The project remains 'unfinished business'.

Lean works

So, approached in the right way, *lean,* low-cost, reliable supply chains can be designed and operated to provide the efficiencies, predictability and low costs desired by customers. But, as the examples highlight, it's not simply about reducing freight rates, or squeezing the providers of third-party services; it is much more creative than that. It is about smoothing product flow, reducing errors and producing goods to forecast right across the supply chain. And, just as importantly, a *lean,* low-cost supply chain will only deliver value when aligned with the appropriate buyer behaviour. Indeed, *lean* protocols will be quite dysfunctional in an operating environment where customers demand high levels of responsiveness in unpredictable conditions. This is your great challenge: 'go *lean*' where it is appropriate, but recognize that other pathways to customers with different requirements must also be working in parallel, or in series, and above all, in synch. That is what it's all about: *dynamic alignment* with all segments of your supply chain. In summary, perhaps the most critical element of *lean* is the ability to collaborate with suppliers on the supply-side in order to smooth out inventory holding and associated costs as you grapple with customers on the sales-side who sometimes treat you and your product like a common commodity.

Living lessons

1   Original *lean* concepts developed for the manufacturing environment do not easily translate across to the more unpredictable supply chain operating environments of today.

2   Hence there is some confusion between *lean* ideas extrapolated from manufacturing, which seem to assume the presence of collaborative relationships between **all** members of supply chains. As we have seen, this is not necessarily so. At best we can shoot for collaboration on the supply-side.

3   The lower cost-to-serve is achieved primarily by ensuring that customers are not over-serviced. Our term is *dynamic alignment*. It is critical to focus on customers to ensure your standard offerings remain relevant. You can invoke *lean* principles as much as you like, but not at the expense of giving the customers what they want!

CHAPTER 7

Agile supply chains

Where quick response is paramount

I t is the third millennium. We all want to be better, cheaper and faster. Let's make that faster, faster and faster. Stop the planet, I want to get off! The new breed of enterprises such as Zara, Dell, Cisco and Li & Fung are certainly demonstrating what is possible when it comes to responding to customers in a fast-moving environment, where life cycles are short and variety reigns. The winners in this environment are those that can respond urgently and effectively. Think of the ultimate example set by the crew during a pit stop in a Formula One car race. The highly skilled individuals in the crew work in perfectly executed concert, racing against the clock and doing so in a confined space. This is a world where milliseconds count, where we worry about speed of execution first and the spare capacity required and the cost involved a long way second. Races have been won and lost during pit stops. But good planning is also involved to underpin the quick response. Many pit stops are scheduled and therefore predictable – planned to the lap. It's the unplanned pit stops where you see the real hash-ups.

The world for businesses in the *agile* supply chain is similar; the only thing is we have neither the budget nor the capacity of an F1 team standing on alert 24/7, 365 days a year. Yes, speed is paramount in this twenty-first-century world. But in keeping the roving, foraging customer firmly in our sights, we need to deliver in a cost-effective way; otherwise we will find ourselves careering off the track in a high-cost, high-speed wreck. Possibly, we are getting a little carried away. But the point is: is such an extreme response necessary for all our customers? As with the *continuous replenishment* and *lean* supply chains, there is a time and place for everything. The focus in *agile* supply chains is on being fast and also on being smart in how you align with demanding customers. Often high responsiveness requires an ability to forecast capacity accurately, rather than predicting the next hit product, and being prepared to switch into high-priority production when the time comes. The challenge for companies is to know how to satisfy their customers as they migrate from the predictable to unpredictable operating environments. And here is another reason why we must know our customers so well.

Watch out, they are hostile

We thought the customers were relentless in *lean* supply chains. Now they are virtually hostile, or at least the operating environment is. You might have a customer who is absolutely chaotic, but still expects lightning service, at a discount. Or else you are dealing with a business whose customer is just plain disorganized. Sometimes it's justified – their behaviour could be driven by uncertainties caused by world oil prices, terrorism-related demand changes or new regulations. The unpredictability is not so much the result of one customer causing chaos; it's the combined effect of an uncertain world rippling up and down the supply chain. Often the longer the supply chains, the more complexity and increased potential for the bull-whip effect. We are now under increasing pressure to respond to the demands of all categories of customers, from consumers and end-users through to the most sophisticated corporate enterprises. You know when fast response is important when a company such as IBM uses a television campaign to promote its 'on-demand' supply chain capabilities.[1] In industries such as fashion and consumer technology, the plethora of products seems to increase exponentially while at the same time life cycles are forever contracting.

Remember, though, that sometimes the urgency is needed, sometimes it's not. We need to work out when the demand is genuine and therefore absolutely necessary, and if so, respond in quick time. And we need to know when the customer does not absolutely need the product immediately, or if they do, there is a price premium involved. Perhaps the best solution is the fast (and regular) rhythms used by Spanish retailer Zara to replenish its global network of retail stores, which it does at least twice a week. This is a 'best of both worlds' strategy: predictable yet fast, very fast. This is exactly what fashion-loving customers demand, and get. Other enterprises with similarly perishable products going to a known network of customers would do well to replicate the example of Zara. However, you also have to do all the other things that make this a great strategy; more about this later.

It will come as no surprise to you that the dominant buying behaviour of customers in an *agile* supply chain is *demanding/quick response*. These customers seek a rapid response to unpredictable supply and demand conditions, but all too often this is a response designed to compensate for a lack of prior planning rather than an essential requirement. However, where market conditions are genuinely unpredictable, high priority is placed on getting an urgent response from suppliers, and there is little time for relationship development. The exception is if a relationship between buyer and seller has been in place for some time, or the parties agree to collaborate to achieve a fast response, as is the case with Ericsson and some of its telecom customers.

There is usually an opportunistic edge to the *demanding/quick response* buying behaviour. Suppliers may be treated as an ad hoc source of supply and loyalty is relatively low, overshadowed by an almost obsessive quest for a particular outcome. In some ways, this is simply the commercial real world: one tinged with pragmatism and driven by a focus on results, but not to the point that lowest price is essential. People who live and work in this world understand that trade-offs sometimes have to be made between high-performance responsiveness and the corresponding cost.

Can you predict what the inherent problem will be with these customers? It's not so much the 'need for speed', but in a similar way to the *cost/efficiency-driven* customers discussed in Chapter 5, it's the impact on the rest of your customer base. The *demanding/quick response* buying behaviour of these customers requires an *agile* response and they can derail your efforts to deliver consistent and reliable service to the rest of your customers. This is particularly the case for loyal customers, simply because your organization could be swamped by surprise demands from other powerful customers. The resulting disruption as the enterprise attempts to satisfy *all demands from all customer types* is one of the fundamental reasons why the resolution of complexity in supply chains has fallen short of early expectations. Indeed, it is not too far-fetched to suggest that if *demanding/quick response* customers are given free rein, they would create chaos across the business. This is not to say they are not valued, but rather to suggest that they must be managed carefully and with a plan in mind, rather than on an ad hoc or reactive basis. The use of Decision Support System (DSS) applications can help immeasurably in these tight situations, and an overall awareness of the particular customer's contribution to the business is mandatory for quality decision-making.[2]

In some situations it may be prudent to embargo parts of production, or even an entire factory, to reduce the negative impacts caused by customers placing random demands on your enterprise. As indicated in Chapter 5, global dairy producer Fonterra recognized the negative impact of demanding customers on its loyal customers in 2000, and took steps to protect the latter.[3]

Being quick *and* cost-effective

How can we respond to the growing band of *demanding/quick response* customers without being overwhelmed by them? Quite aptly, the *agile* supply chain is also described as a surge flow supply chain because demand surges during unpredictable, high-variety market conditions. We need to focus on embedding responsiveness in the extended enterprise to match uncertain business conditions into the future. I think it's safe to say these markets are not going to go away. If we get it right, we can capture significant new business. Surges through supply chains are also the result of commercial practices, e.g., pricing policy, payment terms, so to some extent the solution is in our own hands.

Make-to-Order or Assemble-to-Order capabilities are critical for quick response to customer demands. Hewlett-Packard has long adopted the practice of postponing final assembly of its printers until the exact country market and configuration is known; manuals are added, with the power plugs and leads, at the last moment. Likewise, Vision Express meets delivery deadlines for prescription spectacles measured in hours by assembling frames and custom lenses at the last moment. And Dell Computer is a past master at assembling-to-order and delivering a customer order within days – but they get paid even quicker! However, responsiveness comes at a price unless you are very well organized.

Typically, high responsiveness cannot be achieved for minimal cost. Customers (and suppliers) have to make a choice. Otherwise they become unmanageable and unprofitable. There is always an incremental cost associated with servicing demanding customers, but those who genuinely need urgent service will pay a premium, albeit grudgingly at times. They have already done their sums, made their own internal trade-offs and decided it is worth it. Of course, in practice we often see a mix of Make-to-Forecast and Build-to-Order processes. Companies will Make-to-Forecast for high-volume products that are subject to predictable demand; they will also build low volumes of unpredictable product configurations to specific customer orders.

The unique value proposition of *agile* supply chains is that they can and do respond rapidly and with high priority in unpredictable supply and demand conditions. To do this sometimes means holding spare or redundant capacity aside to cope with unpredictable surges in the pipeline, but that is part of the cost you pay. Anyone who knows about fluid mechanics is familiar with the essential role of surge tanks in absorbing rapid changes in flow volumes through pipelines; the same is true for supply chains. For instance, Zara has two very large distribution centres at La Coruña and Zaragoza in Spain which at times may only be 50 per cent utilized. This is a conscious strategy rather than an oversight. Zara management understands the cost of redundancy, but they also know the benefit and indeed the necessity of having transient capacity available to support their rapid-fire replenishment business model. So this is yet another example where the previous one-dimensional emphasis on incessant cost reduction for its own sake is flawed. Going back to the F1 pit-stop analogy, the team's success is partly due to in-built redundant capacity being kept on high alert for the duration of the race, ready for action at a moment's notice, at speed. Maintaining this capacity pays off.

A vivid example of agility occurred in the immediate aftermath of Hurricane Katrina, which swept through the US state of Louisiana in September 2005. One of the most affected companies was a major oil company, which lost all of its computing equipment in its service centres. The company contacted Hewlett-Packard, its regular hardware supplier, with a priority request to replace 1,000 specially configured PCs as quickly as possible. HP got back a few days later with a commitment to deliver the replacements by Christmas – Christmas 2005! This was not the answer the oil company wanted to hear, so it called Dell, which had not previously been a preferred supplier and asked the same question. Back came the answer almost immediately: 'Is Monday okay?' Dell got the business and won a new customer as well. Obviously the story improves with the telling, but the essentials remain: one supplier could meet an urgent request and the other could not.

How could Dell deliver in such a short time? Probably a combination of lots of spare capacity built into their network; power over their suppliers; and good scenario planning? Clearly, Dell demonstrated the more responsive culture on this occasion. And all that accompanies this, including an *agile* supply chain for new product. Dell's embedded agility enabled it to respond inside HP's cycle time. But this is not necessarily the case across Dell's entire business; my own experience in trying to obtain a replacement battery for my Dell Latitude D800 laptop is a case in point. Two months and still counting! So here is an organization that is agile in Make-to-Order new products, but quite the opposite when it comes to spares and after-sales support. What this says is that even the best enterprises still have work to do. Few if any have got it all right.

Others have found ways around the after-sales service problem. Michelin has been highly innovative in its approach, introducing e-tyres for its customers. The e-tyre is a device like a RFID (radio frequency identification) chip, inserted at the time of manufacture; it monitors air pressure in the tyre when in use. With the right air pressure, tyres perform optimally and last longer; correctly inflated tyres also reduce fuel consumption, which is a significant cost in the transportation business. In this case 'service' has been added to the product itself, and becomes a source of differentiation for Michelin compared to its competitors. And this agility does not necessarily mean higher cost.

Companies such as Haier, the giant Chinese domestic appliance company, combine low production costs with rapid innovation to devastating effect. An example of this 'quick-cycle' mindset came after the company discovered the reason for an unusually high incidence of service calls to repair failures in some of its washing machines – customers in rural China were washing their vegetables in the machines! Haier rapidly re-designed the valving in the affected models to accommodate this unusual application and the level of service calls reduced significantly.[4]

It seems that in the harsh environment of the emerging markets of Brazil, Russia, India and China, the so-called BRIC countries, companies learn survival techniques fast. These markets are characterized by high volatility in demand, low disposable incomes and high consumer expectations. According to Donald Sull,[5] there are perhaps 10 to 20 companies in the emerging markets today that are potentially category killers, and in a decade there will be ten times this number. Maybe such threatening news will at last prod Western enterprises into accelerating their own transformations. The alternative is to be swamped by companies with access to relatively low-cost labour, and the ability to adapt and innovate faster than their Western counterparts. A frightening thought.

Superior agility doesn't just happen by accident. It is the result of combining specific processes and techniques with a responsive mindset. Techniques such as strategic sourcing and postponement play a central role in this. Everything must align if a quick and cost-effective result is to be achieved without plunging the enterprise into uncontrolled and costly chaos. Agile success is also dependent on the ability to 'compartmentalize' lean activities into modules, and have the in-built flexibility to recompile (or reconfigure) the modules in ways that provide the desired responses. This requires quick decision-making cycles, and absolute clarity regarding the roles, responsibilities and level of 'empowerment' that is available to the personnel involved, i.e., what staff are able to commit to the customer. This becomes part of having the appropriate subculture in place to underpin the strategy.

Getting the subculture right

It is beginning to sound as if we are going to need employees with roller-blades on! It would be very handy indeed to have all the cross-directional momentum made possible by roller-blades in order to serve some of our unpredictable customers. The subculture embedded in *agile* supply chains is the *rational* subculture: it's action-oriented, competitive and, above all, driven to perform. It is a culture that values achievement and promotes a sense of urgency. High levels of activity can sometimes disguise less than optimal effectiveness, but brute energy makes up for this. Maybe we should trade the roller-blades for hockey sticks and ice-skates! In this subculture the focus is predominantly on the external operating environment. The policies and rules so evident in the internal-oriented *hierarchical* subculture are replaced by softer guidelines, where individual employees are expected to behave proactively, guided by the principle that you do what is best for the customer. We will now look at what conditions are necessary for a *rational* subculture to develop in the first place. Having said that, look at what is happening with many leading US-based companies, e.g., Dow and ExxonMobil, who are reducing headcount in their global organizations and bringing key decision-making back to the centre. Where is the flex in that? Decision-making speed, an action orientation and solution-based logical thinking are all key elements of this vital subculture.

1. Organization design

Who needs structure anyway? This is the point where we diverge from conventional organization structures, because they are simply incapable of consistently supporting the rapid response inherent in *agile* supply chains. What is needed is a 'modular' design, as depicted in Figure 7.1.

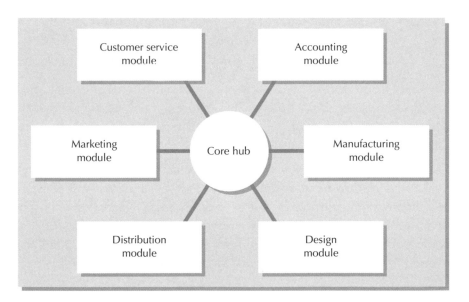

FIGURE 7.1 ◆ 'Modular' organization design

Indeed, both the *agile* and *fully flexible* supply chains can be supported by designs that are combinations of departmental modules and individuals. In any event, what you need is a 'cluster'. Such a cluster (or network) of multidisciplinary personnel, working together in a loosely bound collaborative group, make quick decisions and act fast, which is key. Both are forms of project team that come together for an express purpose, and disband when the particular task they were designed for no longer exists. Very often these teams operate virtually, but the essential ingredients are collaboration and individualism, or *collaborative individualism*.

Companies such as Zara, Li & Fung and Sears Canada have managed to breed this type of responsive culture into their organizations, as has Virgin Atlantic and South West Airlines. In all these cases their success to date, and continuing success, depends on the responsiveness they are able to produce from **inside** their organizations, mirroring their customers' desires. Dow Chemical, especially in Europe, had evolved from a narrow but successful product flow function in the early 1980s, to materials management in the late 1980s, to a strong integrated supply chain management function by the mid-1990s. These were all functional organizations, with loose business alignment, until 1998 when the pendulum swung back in favour of individual business units and perhaps went too far. Dow's full-blooded business alignment resulted in a loss of leverage, lots of duplication, and did not deliver the uplift in earnings before interest and tax (EBIT) that was expected. So the story continues to unfold today with perhaps some misgivings. The company still cannot find the right formula, and this is one of the world's best chemical companies. What hope is there for the rest?

In real life, however, pure examples of particular business models seldom exist. We live in a hybrid world, which brings with it dangers for the unsuspecting. Charles Fine, the notable MIT professor and management writer, highlights just what can happen when two business models come together, as was the case with the acquisition of Chrysler by Daimler-Benz in 1998 to form DaimlerChrysler AG.[6] A 'modular' supply chain in Fine's terms is roughly equivalent to *agile* in my terms, displaying 'relatively flexible and interchangeable relationships among suppliers, customers, and partners'.[7] This was Chrysler pre-takeover. Daimler-Benz had a much more integral product and organization architecture, equivalent in my terms to a cross between *collaborative* and *lean* supply chains, underpinned by a functional organizational structure. In this case, the two architectures were like oil and water, one reason why the merged entity has struggled to perform ever since.

Fine highlights the imperative to 'align' supply chain and product architectures because 'they have a powerful impact on each other'.[8] He uses three companies to exemplify this point – Toyota cars, Dell and Nokia:

> *Toyota cars, known for their reliability and flawless performance, have an integral supply chain and product design. Dell's renowned modular designs match its standardized multi-vendor supply chain. Nokia employs a deliberately designed hybrid approach, with a modular semiconductor and software core, highly integrated components for the rest, and a complementary supply chain design.*[9]

Zara's business model uses cross-functional teams known as 'commercials' to manage the design and production of clothing lines in specific fashion ranges, for women, men or children. These teams work closely with the store product managers and travel extensively to observe purchases and communicate with the local store managers. Employees are given a high level of autonomy to make decisions within their business. However, a note of caution is also appropriate here, because there is increasingly too much rhetoric on company websites and in company reports about how they are shaping a more 'responsive culture', and in the same breath they claim to be cutting costs and working on becoming lean. The two can coexist – but such precision, call it 'partnership' if you like, is still relatively rare. In effect, what has to happen is that individuals are empowered to pull together the appropriate modular components to make things happen the way the customer wants them to happen, fast.

Some years ago, McKinsey & Co. tried out the notion of 'atoms' at British Petroleum, and subsequently proposed the same structure to Fletcher Challenge Energy, but it was never implemented. The idea was to break the organization up into the smallest viable decision-making units to achieve increased accountability at lower levels of the organization structure. The 'atoms' could vary in size from as low as 50 people to several multiples of this number. Not a bad idea but it also brings with it innate problems, especially for supply chains. Why? Because the more you break the entire organization up into relatively small groups or 'atoms', the more fragmented the organization becomes, which paradoxically makes it harder to coordinate – unless you have almost real-time information systems in place, outside and inside the business, as Zara does. So with this organizational format, you lose as much as you gain. Upon reflection it is easy to see now why a pure atomic structure will not work, but the right solution might be a mix of different organization formats, of which the 'atom' structure is one. This is effectively what I am proposing.

2. Processes

The further we move to the right along the continuum of supply chain types, the less we need formal *processes*. But you still need good processes, and plenty of them, to cover the more predictable side of your business. This is not 'either/or', but 'and'. In the *agile* supply chain, processes are still necessary, but they are fewer by definition. Any process that slows down response time is dispensed with via creative process re-engineering. Short-cuts are invoked and the risks increase, but not to the point where safety is compromised. Ways are found to by pass regulations, and there is generally an opportunistic flair embedded in the remaining processes. However, we are not talking about creating a myriad of costly exceptions. Quite the contrary, the processes that drive and support *agile* supply chains are mostly *unique combinations of standard or modular processes*. This is the key to containing costs while delivering rapid bursts of obsessive service over short periods of time.

3. Systems/IT

Agile supply chains are best underpinned by an ERP system similar to those used in other supply chain types, but that is where the similarity ends. We need to invest in an array of additional systems applications designed to optimize capacity and reduce the risk of interfering with the more standard regimes in the *continuous replenishment* and *lean* supply chains. You will have less need to invest large lumps of capital in systems technology, but capital must nevertheless be invested in applications that support scenario development and analysis, e.g., the broad category of supply chain management systems which include supply chain planning; advanced planning and scheduling; supply chain event management;

supplemented by postponement methods. Because of rapid obsolescence, and the changing nature of the marketplace, one wonders if many of the tools being offered by the ERP providers are just too cumbersome. Let's see what MySAP and Netweaver are going to offer in terms of modularity, flexibility and, most importantly, **value**. The uncertain nature of demand on the *agile* supply chain type means there is significantly more management involvement. Experienced, multiskilled staff members are preferred because the complexity that has to be resolved is greater than in the *continuous replenishment* and *lean* supply chains. Above all, you should remember it is fruitless to seek forecast accuracy in unpredictable demand situations when forecasting is not really possible at any level. The guiding principle here is to *plan for capacity... and execute to demand.*

Companies such as Zara follow this principle to perfection, sourcing raw materials and components from distant markets in the Far East, pre-booking manufacturing capacity in advance in locations closer to consuming markets and using postponement techniques and *agile* organizational formats to rapidly produce up-to-the-minute fashion for swift delivery to regional markets. The formula has not been successfully replicated to any significant degree by competitors to date, and Zara has the capacity to enter other apparel markets at will and work well inside the delivery cycle times of more traditional retailers such as Marks & Spencer. If Zara chooses to follow this route it will be bad news indeed for their new direct competitors. Benetton is probably in a position to do likewise.

A strong component of systems in this type of supply chain is the decision-support and analytics capability, which helps you understand the cost of doing business with various customer accounts. Indeed, Customer Account Profitability (CAP) analyses should be undertaken for all major customer accounts that fall into the *demanding/quick response* category of buying behaviour.

Zara's ability to achieve responsiveness in the fashion industry has been due to its determination to monitor constantly *both* what is popular in the marketplace and what sells well in its stores, in close to real-time. There are formalized (and well proven) communication links between the store network and its designer 'commercials', which provide daily updates of sales information, including customer comments. This gives Zara accurate information not only for product re-orders but also of 'what the customer wants', so it can produce designs within very short lead-times.

Of course, the ultimate example of postponement that provides almost infinite agility is the mixing of paint colours at the point of purchase. In the automotive industry it is at the point of application.

The other sizable global enterprise that follows the same principle is Li & Fung. Typical is the case when Li & Fung heard that Levi Strauss was planning to order 1 million garments – style and colour unknown.[10] Since the specifications would only be revealed four weeks before delivery, Li & Fung went ahead on trust with both customer and suppliers to reserve undyed yarn while coincidentally locking-up production capacity at mills and the downstream manufacturer of the finished garment. Li & Fung orchestrated the lot and achieved the relatively short delivery cycle required by Levi's.

Finally, for this type of supply chain it is almost mandatory to develop and maintain a Network Optimization Model (NOM), because this has the capability to materially improve the quality of decision making at the executive level when key issues need to be resolved, e.g., should we close a particular distribution centre? Will we continue to use a particular third-party logistics provider (3PL)? What part of the product range should we produce in particular plants throughout our production network, including outsourcing? With a NOM facility available to undertake intense analytical work, the chances of achieving optimal alignment between the enterprise and its various customer segments, including the *demanding/quick response* segment, are significantly enhanced. Point-of-sale and RFID systems also help drive the required responsiveness.

4. Key Performance Indicators

In the *rational* subculture, the key performance metrics are absolute speed of response to customer enquiries and firm orders, and the ability to be first into the marketplace. Measurements such as elapsed time from concept to launch of new products, including delivery lead-time to customers, are a fundamental indicator of good or bad performance. Another good indicator is optimization of capacity at different points along the supply chain, and overall optimization of the entire supply chain in terms of the service/cost equation. Frankly, this area is one of the biggest challenges facing the supply chain community. You have to get it right.

5. Incentives

The most appropriate incentives are those that encourage results-oriented behaviour, such as achieving budgets and stretch targets. Rewards come in the form of cash bonuses, increased salaries and fringe benefits. The achievement-oriented *rational* subculture is motivated by tangible rewards and recognized performance. But here again, be careful to choose the right incentives for your company. Many would argue that these types of cash incentives can have the opposite effect, and destroy agility – because the business becomes self-centred rather than customer centric. Maybe this is one reason why Dow has not performed up to early expectations?

6. Job design

Job designs that help shape the *rational* subculture focus on clear output requirements. Authority and autonomy is established by clear structural limits, and control is centralized by setting clear guidelines and principles for action.

7. Internal communications

Competing in an *agile* supply chain, you will do best to adopt internal communications that are relatively formal, regular and very action-oriented. The underlying theme to all communications is that 'we respond'. Communications are open and preferably face-to-face, although email, short message service (SMS) and mobile telephones are used for convenience and time efficiency. With the emphasis on results, the tone is impersonal and business-like. The risk you need to watch out for is that staff will withhold information; if this happens silos will start to form within the business. In a cost-saving exercise Dow had eliminated most of the cell phones in the company, only then to face some significant communication problems after Katrina. So much for false economies!

8. Training and development

Your training and development programmes should emphasize resource management. Staff should study *rational* models and execute challenging assignments on problem solving. The aim is to develop competencies in areas such as time optimization, communications and influencing skills. Staff will not just be participating in the process – the backbone of this culture is results, results, results.

9. Recruitment

Your business should be eagerly seeking personnel with a 'driven' personality and a desire to achieve results. Decisive, analytical, energetic and objective are words to describe the people who are most appropriate and indeed essential to shaping a *rational* subculture. The ideal recruits will have a pragmatic mix of operational and strategic mindsets, be very customer-focused and be prepared to take measured risks.

10. Leadership style

The members of your top management team should exhibit the leadership styles that mirror the subcultures you need to drive your company strategies into the marketplace. A *Company Baron* leadership style is the most appropriate to shape a *rational* subculture and realize value in an *agile* supply chain. *Company Barons* lead by objectives; they embrace change, go for growth and focus only on what is important. They are challenging individuals, practical, analytical and seek fact-based commercial solutions. Above all they get their way through force of personality; they are a typical ESTP (extrovert-sensor-thinker-perceiver) in the Myers-Briggs Type Indicator®.

Mixed supply chain logics

If only the world was linear! Then we could more easily manage supply chains to match our customer segments. But there are inherent subtleties in different types of supply chains. As you have probably been thinking, there are unlikely combinations of supply chains out there. Take for example the Hunter Valley Coal Chain in Australia. The case study below describes how its supply chain is a combination of *lean* from its mine pit to port and *agile* at the port. It blends the two supply chains so well we could call it a 'leagile' supply chain.

Previously, the customers' ore carriers would arrive and only then would the specific blend of coal be notified. The 'leagile' solution is unique because it has been achieved through the collaboration of all stake-holders in the operation, comprising mine-owners, rail track owner, train operator and port authority. They are all committed to run the coal chain as though there was just a single shareholder. This solution brings into play three distinctly different behavioural logics which combine to deliver a mutually beneficial outcome for all parties involved. A great result, and one that has been recognized around the world.

Hunter Valley Coal Chain Logistics Team (HVCCLT)

www.hvcclt.com.au

The HVCCLT began as a collaborative project of multiple partners in the supply chain (including market competitors) who are working together to maximize the export capacity of a commodity product: ther-mal coal. The Hunter Valley Coal Chain is the largest (by volume) coal distribution chain in the world, stretching some 200 kilometres to the north-west of Sydney in Australia to Japan, where about 70 per cent of the product is exported, and as far away as Europe and Mexico. The coal chain comprises approximately 30 mines, with more than 23 load points owned by coal producers, two government track owners, two private and competing train operators (one government and one privately owned), an industry-owned shiploading facility and a port authority. In total there are more than 17 organizations involved in the export of each tonne of coal through the chain. The chain ships 80 to 150 brands of coal on to more than 1,000 bulk material vessels every year.

Until recently each operator worked to maximize their own capacity and juggle maintenance schedules. The supply chain partners are now work-ing together to utilize better infrastructure capacity and create economy of scale. They have prepared a coherent plan for long-term capital and maintenance investment in the system, resulting in reduced and coordi-nated 'days out'[11] (which are the days when coal could not be delivered to the port or loaded on to the coal carriers as one or more parts of the infrastructure were undergoing repairs), as well as driving more efficient decision making on investment in new infrastructure required to meet future demand. The project started in 2003 when the port and rail operators agreed to set up a co-located centre. The initiative now includes two competing rail providers (Queensland Rail National and Pacific National), two government track providers (ARTC (Federal) and RailCorp (State)), the coal mining industry-owned shiploading facility (Port Waratah Coal Services) and the port authority (Newcastle Port Corp).

The vision of the members is to:

a) maximize throughput in the distribution chain;

b) create a logistics team with a true end-to-end perspective from the coal site to the customer; and

c) help members to coordinate future expansion so as to improve investment efficiency and drive growth.

The system has moved from a fragmented approach to managing assets in the coal chain, where the individual silos had multiple views and significant variances, to a single-entity, cooperative model. The HVCCLT partners significantly improved asset coordination and turnaround time which led to increased throughput of product, with only minimal capital expenditure. Instead of over 50 vessels waiting up to three to four weeks at the port before being loaded – with demurrage of US$50,000 per vessel per day after an initial 'free' period – there were only 10 to 15 vessels in the operational queue in 2005, with substantially reduced demurrage being incurred by the industry. In two and a half years the initiative increased the amount of coal shipped from 68 million tonnes per annum to more than 81 million tonnes in 2005.

The partners have realized that by cooperating on the distribution of the product they are increasing the size of the market. They all benefit by sharing the increased profits.

This success has been enabled by:

a) recognizing the coal chain as a system rather than a series of component parts;

b) creating a model that provides common success for all; and

c) strong leadership in making the first step to entrust asset planning to a somewhat independent third party.

In 2005 the HVCCLT was formalized as a joint venture comprising the track, train and port operators. Until recently, the coordination of the delivery and loading of coal was determined by a largely manual scheduling system that required a team to determine the daily movements through the system. This has been replaced by a multi-million dollar constraint-based scheduling system. This will not only speed up the planning process, but allows for scenario planning and optimization modelling to be utilized in the day-to-day operational decision-making. With significant growth in thermal coal exports being forecast over the next five to ten years, the next major challenge for HVCCLT is to improve the coordination of capital investment in the infrastructure through collaborative long-term planning by all members.

Another outstanding example of the successful application of mixed supply chain logics is the case of the Korean company Daewoo Shipyards,[12] described below.

Daewoo Shipyards

Daewoo Shipyards completes a new super-tanker or container ship every 36 hours, or more than 200 a year valued at US$75 million to US$100 million. How can that be possible? Several ships are constructed line abreast, and up to 20 sections or blocks for each ship are built off-line, simultaneously. This is the *lean* part of the supply chain. These blocks, weighing several thousand tonnes each, are completed with all the fittings inside – piping, electricals, hydraulics – everything. They are transported from other areas of the site at the last minute and welded together, painted and launched, as fast as possible as the next ship is waiting to be assembled. This is postponement in action on a massive scale. So it is not just a phenomenon that happens with apparel and electronics. This is heavy industry with a capital 'H'. All of this is also achieved with a well-paid labour force – Korea is no longer a low-cost labour country. So, here again, we see an innovative combination of *lean* and *agile* supply chains at work.

Moving from ships to grain, the story is the same, this time in New Zealand. Terry O'Connor, General Manager Corporate Services, ABB Grain, talks about what it is doing for New Zealand customers:

With New Zealand's geographic isolation and its dependence on imported grain for the animal feed and flour industries, efficient supply chain management requires suppliers like ourselves to understand millers' annual requirements and sometimes unexpected demands. Our solution is to locate strategic storage at sites adjacent to the mills. This provides the millers with certainty of supply, and also flexibility in purchasing to meet demand either on a spot or forward basis. The advantage of this is to optimize supply chain efficiencies both in the country of origin, sea freight and on-shore New Zealand storage sites.[13]

A further demonstration of the combination of *lean* and *agile* supply chain principles is provided by the development of the Land Rover Freelander, otherwise know as the CB40 Project.[14] This project has many unique features, but for the purposes of this chapter we will focus on two: the design of a large part of the new vehicle using standard components and processes (*lean*); and the combined in-built 'design redundancy' of other components to shorten the time required at assembly in order to reduce the waiting time for customers (*agile*). To achieve this, the supply base was limited to 146, and fully integrated into the project at the concept phase. Suppliers were also encouraged to participate in component design and subsequent logistics processes and physical operations. In truth, this was one of the first projects in any industry to invoke a higher-order level of collaboration between multiple parties in the extensive supply chains involved, right through to the dealer network.[15] It set the scene for others to follow.

A final noteworthy example of mixed logics: Fantastic Furniture, Australia's fastest-growing furniture chain, has its own Fantastic Lounge Factory which produced 113,000 sofas in fiscal 2004–05, about one every three minutes! It was clearly using postponement techniques and a *lean/agile* supply chain combination, albeit on a somewhat smaller scale than Daewoo Shipyards, but just as effective. As always, you look behind the scenes and you find an entrepreneur and quality leadership at the top; it never fails. Who said Australia can't match the lower labour-cost countries for productivity, work practices and sheer passion?

At this point we should remember, however, that sometimes enterprises can go too far in a blind pursuit of leanness and cost reduction. This philosophy was a major factor in Marks & Spencer's fall from grace in the late 1990s. According to McKinsey & Co.:[16]

...while many companies benefit from sending work to places where labour is cheap, manufacturers [and retailers] often over-rate the value of wage savings and underestimate the inventory, obsolescence, intellectual-property, and currency risks of offshoring. Some also overlook the benefits of producing goods close to their markets so that customers can get them in days instead of months.

Both points raised by McKinsey are relevant in today's fast-moving global trading environment. McKinsey found that Californian manufacturers that had adopted lean practices would only realize marginal savings if they moved to Asia: 13 per cent for apparel; 6 per cent for plastics; and less than 1 per cent for high technology products.[17] Given the declining importance of direct labour, which according to McKinsey may now only represent 7 to 15 per cent of cost of goods sold,[18] some manufacturers are questioning the logic of going offshore. Consider the case of the Los Angeles-based fashion apparel company, described below.

Fashion apparel company[19]

The company had 1,500 workers making casual wear in a dilapidated multistorey building in Los Angeles. The workers were paid above-award labour rates. However, labour costs only represented 3 per cent of retail price, and on the decline. If production was moved offshore, the additional logistics costs would certainly overshadow any savings in labour. But just as importantly, responsiveness, and therefore sales, would suffer as the lead-time blew out from days to weeks because of the greater distance from consumer markets.

This is exactly why appliance and electronics manufacturer, the Haier Group, is expanding its manufacturing base to the United States, and forsaking the lower production costs in China. In the words of Haier's CEO, Zhang Ruimin, 'our strategy is to satisfy consumers as quickly as possible'.[20] So the world is full of contradictions. While many manufacturers are racing to source their manufactured goods in China, a Chinese company is going in the opposite direction! At least it is doing so for part of its production. Those companies moving their production to China are also changing the nature of their business at the same time. Consider the case of Redan, a Polish textiles and apparel company.[21] It has moved from

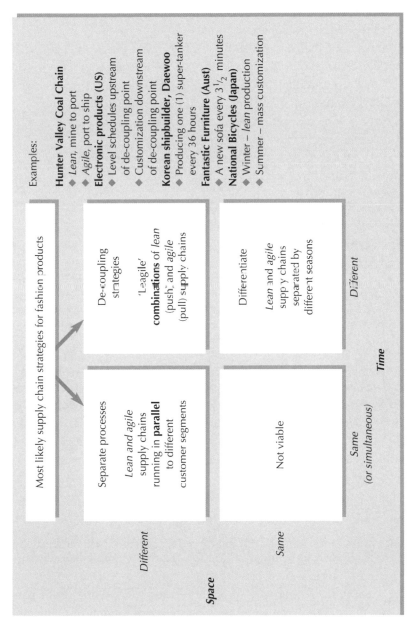

Examples:

Hunter Valley Coal Chain
- ◆ *Lean*, mine to port
- ◆ *Agile*, port to ship

Electronic products (US)
- ◆ Level schedules upstream of de-coupling point
- ◆ Customization downstream of de-coupling point

Korean shipbuilder, Daewoo
- ◆ Producing one (1) super-tanker every 36 hours

Fantastic Furniture (Aust)
- ◆ A new sofa every 3½ minutes

National Bicycles (Japan)
- ◆ Winter – *lean* production
- ◆ Summer – mass customization

Most likely supply chain strategies for fashion products

De-coupling strategies

'Leagile' **combinations** of *lean* (push) and *agile* (pull) supply chains

Differentiate

Lean and *agile* supply chains separated by different seasons

Different

Separate processes

Lean and agile supply chains running in **parallel** to different customer segments

Not viable

Same (or simultaneous)

Time

Different

Same

Space

FIGURE 7.2 ◆ **Different combinations of *lean* and *agile* supply chains in a time/space matrix**

Source Adapted from Figure 2 in Towill and Christopher (2002), p. 303

producing and selling its own goods, to creating its own brands at the retail level and leaving the sewing to others. This is the early phase of Haier's defence against Chinese manufacturers flooding its home markets in Poland with low-priced apparel.

The Ministry of Defence (MoD) in Britain has some challenges with mixed supply chain logics. It has to switch between maintenance mode (peace) and response mode (war). If it tries to manage both supply chains with the same management system, it will be very difficult to optimize either effectively – as a result, MoD carries huge inventories of stock and has incompatible performance management systems.

It is clear that the most common combination of supply chains is *lean–agile*, which itself has several variants; the matrix in Figure 7.2 neatly summarizes this situation.

Shades of things to come

Are you inspired by finding examples of what the future may look like? Igus, a Cologne-based company that makes 28,000 different industrial (mostly customized) products, is a hive of constant innovation. The plant layout is flexible and can be rapidly changed as demand shifts across the product range. And the workforce has a culture that embraces change, every working day. This is the ultimate *agile factory* where everything is designed for speed and responsiveness.[22] They are being smart and fast in how they deliver to their customers. A bit like a Formula One team, only better! The competitive edge used to be about superior product, now it's about the quality product together with the capacity to customize and deliver. All we need now is to re-create the same formula in the rest of our supply chains.

Living lessons

1 Forget about forecasting at the product/SKU level – just forecast the capacity you will need at different points along your supply chains.

2 Accept that you will almost always need to add 'redundant capacity' in the form of inventory/labour/factory space.

3 You can only participate successfully in a fast unpredictable market if you have developed a 'responsive' subculture in your business. If this is not possible, forget it – you won't succeed.

CHAPTER 8

Fully flexible supply chains

Where nothing is impossible

W ith new-breed companies leading the pack in winning difficult customers in fast-moving environments, we all thought the ultimate had been achieved. Agility to match the unpredictability! But there's always a new Himalaya to conquer when we are tackling the supply chain, and today it's the emerging phenomenon of 'emergency supply chains'. Increasingly, organizations are finding themselves at the centre of unforeseen, unplannable events – emergencies, breakdowns and other critical events that threaten their global supply chains. We thought we had it all figured out when we mastered the logistics systems, making it lean and mean and delivered straight to the customer. But such systems are not good at coping with unplannable crises, on any scale. The post-9/11 era has focused attention on the need to develop new capabilities that can be rapidly deployed when necessary.

Can you see times when your business might need a fast, flexible response to unexpected conditions? The *fully flexible* supply chain is pursuing the ultimate quest for a **creative solution** to an unusual supply chain issue. Often this supply chain occurs when non-government and government organizations are coping with a disaster on a massive scale. But there are also times when businesses like yours might need the capability to manage an unexpected event, to avoid disruption and damage to your competitiveness. You can incorporate some of the strategies you use during a crisis into your supply chain in the long term, or adopt the strategies you learn from other agencies as they find solutions in incredibly complex circumstances. *Fully flexible* supply chains – wherever their location – are designed to find a solution to the problem, and find it **very fast**. If this requires creative thinking, innovative behaviour and a high cost, then so be it. The final result is paramount.

In general, this is a costly supply chain to configure for just routine supply, but you will need the capability anyhow to mitigate risk and ensure business continuity. This capability could be regarded as a required competence and positioned within the business development function. The *entrepreneurial* subculture that underpins this type of supply chain is ideal for start-ups and incubation of fledgling businesses. Indeed, it is essential for any activity that is at the edge of the core business, or is subject to imminent market discontinuities through competitive, regulatory or other external forces – with unpredictable outcomes.

Two types of dynamic flexibility

In our *dynamic alignment* model, *fully flexible* supply chains share common features, but they also fall into two distinct categories: the 'business event' and 'emergency response/humanitarian' supply chains.[1] Important features such as the purpose of the supply chain, its life cycle and where and how funds are sourced can vary; this means the organizations managing them need to approach these two types of *fully flexible* supply chain in different ways.

'Business event' *fully flexible* supply chain

Have you ever had to contend with a situation that demanded full-frontal flexibility in your supply chain? Did you have the money to do it? The 'business event' supply chain is normally found in the business sector, as its name suggests, but unlike most business projects the supply chain is not overly cost-sensitive. Managers in this supply chain already have adequate supply chain options for everyday business. But when an unexpected problem arises, and an innovative solution is needed, they will be given substantial – almost unlimited – funds. The attitude is often 'just do it', with the implication, 'to heck with the cost'. Funds are normally provided by the customer, who has a clearly defined focus and pre-determined timeline. An example comes from the oil company mentioned in Chapter 7, which sought to have 1,000 PCs replaced urgently in the aftermath of Hurricane Katrina. The 'business event' supply chain is necessary to solve a transient rather than on-going business problem. So we are looking at a solution to a one-off 'event' that is supported by substantial funds.

'Emergency response/humanitarian' *fully flexible* supply chain

Unfortunately we all recognize the large-scale emergencies that prompt the need for an 'emergency response/humanitarian' supply chain. The 9/11 terrorist strikes in 2001 and the Bali bombings of 2003 called for an immediate, crisis response on a large scale, as did the natural disasters of the Asian tsunami of 2004 and the Pakistan–Afghanistan earthquake of 2005. The 'emergency response/humanitarian' supply chain differs from the 'business event' supply chain largely because of the source of its funding and its sensitivity to cost. Funds are limited because they are often provided by donations from a wide mixture of third parties: national governments, the United Nations, individual donors and non-government organizations (NGOs) such as charities, community and aid organizations. The groups who build this type of supply chain also have an extra factor to consider – governance. They need to be highly accountable for all the funds they collect and apply to disaster operations. This supply chain is not only price sensitive, but is accountability sensitive too.

In many emergencies, the normal supply chains that underpin business and community activities are completely disrupted or destroyed. Urgent help is required to save lives or, in environmental cases, to protect the natural environment. After the initial critical response period, the 'emergency response/humanitarian' supply chain usually develops into longer-term humanitarian aid and/or environmental 'restoration'. Examples include on-going aid in war-torn areas (e.g., UN aid in Afghanistan 2001–02; Niger in mid-2005) or rebuilding communities after a natural disaster, such as the Iranian earthquake of 2002, the south-east Asian tsunami in 2004 and Katrina in the United States in 2005. In each of these situations there is an initial event (or series of events) that dictates the requirement for a *fully flexible* supply chain, although the characteristics of the supply chain can evolve dramatically as the situation develops from the critical response phase into the on-going rebuilding phase.

It's urgent, and we mean it

I can hear you asking, 'So who is the customer?' *Fully flexible* supply chains are unlike most supply chain types because 'the customer' varies from normal market environments and market behaviours. The customers in the 'business event' supply chain are the everyday customers of the enterprise who start behaving in a new way. They seek *innovative solutions* to rare and seemingly intractable problems; they are trying to avoid the problem taking on crisis proportions – unless it's a crisis already! Customers in the 'emergency response/humanitarian' supply chain are not only the end-consumer – the survivor or victim of a tragedy or natural dis- aster – they are also the many organizations within the supply chain demanding emergency services and assistance for the affected population. They could be local authorities, domestic national governments, commu- nity groups, emergency service organizations and local arms of non-government organizations.

'Business event' *fully flexible* supply chain

The customer in this supply chain will normally display one or more of the other three buying behaviours: collaborative; low-cost; or demanding. But they will move into an *innovative solution* behaviour for short periods when a crisis occurs. They are likely to return to their preferred or natural buying behaviour when the crisis subsides – see Figure 8.1.

In September 1992 the international airline Qantas, then owned by the Australian government, acquired the domestic airline Australian Airlines. To ensure the merger of the two airlines was successful, Qantas urgently needed to integrate the Australian Airlines' legacy IT systems with its own within 90 days. Up until that point Qantas had been very price sensitive in its dealings with suppliers. But its system integrators, from an external enterprise, found the airline quickly shifted to a 'fix at any cost' mindset because the task was so vital. Suddenly it demanded a *fully flexible* response to its problem. Once the task was completed, Qantas returned to its former *lean* buying behaviour for subsequent transactions involving sys- tems technology.

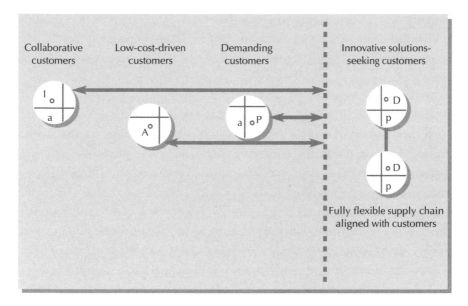

FIGURE 8.1 ◆ 'Business event' fully flexible supply chain and its innovation solutions-seeking customers

Occasionally, due to extreme external pressures this *innovative solution* becomes a new supply chain incorporated into on-going operations of the company. The government bus authority in Israel, Egged, operates about 70 per cent of public bus services. This company continues to operate under incredibly difficult conditions – as a target of terrorism. Company chairman Arik Feldman sums up the resilient attitude of this organizational culture: 'Drivers and managers have learned to adapt to the realities of the situation ... if a bus blows up, it doesn't stop us from running public transportation ... it gives us more courage to continue ...'[2] Such an on-going flexible type of supply chain as that developed by Egged is extremely rare. How often do you hear of a company continuing to offer its customers service under such extreme conditions? They are still operating the bus service today.

DHL has made an art form of handling extreme challenges on an almost daily basis. Request for replacement equipment following a breakdown at a remote mine site, or moving important exhibitions for galleries and museums, or even dangerous goods, all fall within the company's capabilities, albeit requiring the intensive focus of those creative personnel skilled in finding innovative solutions for customers, ultra-fast.

'Emergency response/humanitarian' fully flexible supply chain

Emergency or humanitarian situations usually involve both customers/buyers of services on the ground and consumers/survivors who are caught up in a disaster; natural or man-made. The immediate aim is to quickly provide life-saving essentials to the survivors, who often have no choice of buyer behaviour. Instead, the buying behaviour in the initial phase following a crisis is a response to 'whatever is provided'; required initially by individuals who rapidly move into community clusters as people try to re-establish what was familiar. In the next stage, when basic living requirements are restored, and later as the community is rebuilt, survivors will exhibit a greater range of buyer behaviours as the situation permits – see Figure 8.2.

This situation occurs when an entire complex of supply chains need to be created from scratch because of a major disruption to normal living and business due to situations such as war, terrorist attacks, famine and natural disasters like earthquakes or tsunamis. The third parties providing the funding – and normally there are multiple parties involved – often have conflicting objectives. These groups may become temporary partners at best, or competing enemies at worst, all working in a situation where there are no straightforward answers to the short- and longer-term issues involved. Sarah Murray outlined some of the difficulties faced by humanitarian agencies in her article in the *Financial Times*, including the many lessons learned on the ground from having to bring essential supplies to people in the worst-hit regions of the world.[3]

The singular focus in the 'emergency response/humanitarian' segment is on finding a solution to the problem, and very often the customer has no idea what that solution might look like. Indeed, it is one of those rare occasions where customers look to their suppliers for a supplier-led solution involving lots of innovation and creativity. There is a corresponding risk involved, but customers are usually quite prepared to take risks (in the case of the 'business event' supply chain) to get to a solution, or have no

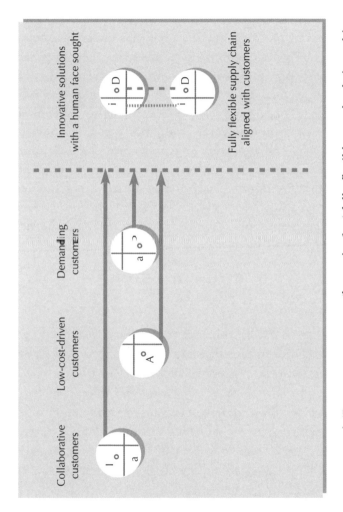

FIGURE 8.2 ◆ 'Emergency response/humanitarian' fully flexible supply chain and its innovative solutions-seeking customers (with a human face)

choice but to take whatever is offered (in the case survivors at the end of 'emergency response/humanitarian' supply chains).

So, the demand characteristics in this market are very unpredictable, much more so than in the *demanding/quick response* customer segment. There is relatively higher risk involved for all parties and a desire for an innovative, flexible response by customers/consumers. A genuine 'solutions' mindset is prevalent for the time that the crisis exists, and price sensitivity is nowhere in sight. As such, this type of buying behaviour represents a real opportunity for suppliers with the capacity to respond appropriately. Sometimes a solution in this situation can be the breakthrough to a new longer-term relationship with the customer involved.

The London bombings in July 2005 were a good example of what can be achieved in terms of providing fast response to the victims and maintaining and restoring service during a crisis. Interestingly, the British government and its agencies have already started a thorough review of the old plans to see what lessons can be learned for the future. Scenario planning is an important tool for anticipating what skill sets might be needed in all sorts of possible disasters.

Response strategies

Now this is where the situation gets really difficult. How do you possibly respond in such extreme, changeable circumstances? *Fully flexible* (or cavitation flow in Chapter 2) supply chains are configured around hedge and deploy principles that are able to provide maximum responsiveness on a selective basis, for short periods. The value proposition is aimed at meeting unplanned and *unplannable* demand with fast, effective, customer-centric solutions that are usually unavailable under normal circumstances. The *emergency* supply chains are a good example, and are activated to meet sudden humanitarian crises anywhere around the globe. In the same way, the 'business event' supply chain is activated quickly and demands urgent attention from suppliers to unforeseen or unexpected events. DHL was requested to transport a replacement mast from Sydney to Newport, Rhode Island, during one of the America's Cup races in the 1980s. The Australian team had broken a main mast on its lead boat.

DHL took on the challenge and managed to load the 100-foot mast by removing the front cockpit window and threading it down through the plane and then replacing the window. The reverse process was performed at the destination end. This is a living example of a 'business event' *fully flexible* supply chain!

Emergency supply chains, whether in response to a natural disaster or the outcome of war, are extreme examples where the *fully flexible* supply chain configuration comes into its own. It has to be created quickly, often from a zero base, and under extremely difficult conditions to service thousands, sometimes millions, of people, who are subsisting under extremely poor conditions. Whether for reasons of distribution of food and clothing, medical aid and treatment, or security and safety, these supply chains are generally highly complex.

Coincidentally, they face huge impediments such as substandard or zero infrastructure, limited capital, multiple partners, language difficulties and usually the involvement of more that one political group. Beyond this initial mission there are always added demands for assistance that can cut across the original task of distributing food, aid and evacuation services. And, of course, political complexities are involved in dealing with the host and donor nations alike, who often place divergent demands on the supply chain network and so stretch human and financial resources to the limit. The people who work in extreme situations are often highly motivated; some will volunteer their services, work for lower salaries than normal, or work for extended periods without recompense. It takes special people to work in these conditions.

Getting the subculture right

The subculture needed to underpin the *fully flexible* supply chain is seldom found in commercial enterprises. It is an *entrepreneurial* subculture: entrepreneurial in the sense that it is a place for unpredictability, opportunity and risk. Entrepreneurial individuals who are attracted to working in *fully flexible* supply chains are highly creative and innovative; they embrace risk and change like no other group in the quest for satisfactory solutions, delivered at speed. *Entrepreneurial* leaders have a proactive leadership style. If you have a 'business event' supply chain, you will need to encourage the *entrepreneurial* subculture while also protecting it against other subcultures in your enterprise. You need to protect the subculture so that it will be available should the need arise. In the initial stage of setting up an 'emergency response/humanitarian' supply chain the entrepreneurial subculture is often the only one present, and the issue is not so much protecting this subculture, but being able to phase in other types of subcultures as the situation stabilizes and more stable processes evolve.

There are, however, some important cultural differences between the two types of *fully flexible* supply chains. The 'business event' supply chain tends to foster individualism and autonomy. In contrast, the success of the 'emergency response/humanitarian' supply chain relies on cohesion of the team, and the ability of the individuals within the team to work with widely divergent groups – who often have very different or conflicting ideologies – for the purpose of the greater good.

1. Organization design

The classic organization for the *entrepreneurial* subculture is a loose structure that involves small 'clusters' or project teams. As depicted in Figure 8.3, the cluster can be either temporary or semi-permanent. There are few, if any, hierarchical elements to the 'cluster' structure, with most emphasis placed on innovation and self-reliance. People will work in a highly cooperative manner either as individuals or in teams.

The Special Air Services (SAS) in the armed forces of several Western nations is the ultimate example of a 'cluster' organization involving individuals. The team comes together for a specific mission, and is composed of individuals who each have specialist skills and competences. Despite this accent on individual skills and flair, the team functions as a unit and under pressure has the capability to adapt to changing conditions with the individuals concerned taking on other roles as required.

It is no accident that modern armies have adopted an array of different organization structures to fight under varying battlefield conditions. The large-scale, slow-moving standing army takes time to position and build up for the main attack. For example, it took the coalition forces six

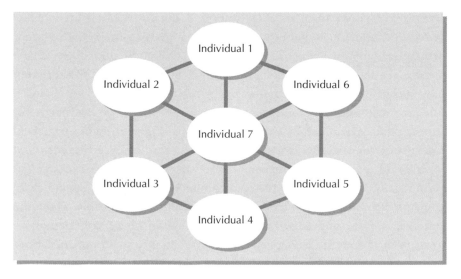

FIGURE 8.3 ◆ 'Cluster' organization design

months to prepare for the first Gulf war. The smaller 'quick reaction' force adopted by the European Union moves faster and can be rapidly deployed to regional trouble spots at relatively short notice. This is a semi-agile type of response. The SAS (Britain and Australia) or the Green Berets (United States) can deploy in small groups within 24 hours to undertake key missions practically anywhere in the world; these were used extensively up to and during the second Gulf war. This is the *fully flexible* supply chain organization par excellence.

We are likely to see more of this organizational configuration in the commercial world as operating environments become even more turbulent and unpredictable. The downside is that they are, by definition, costly to develop and maintain. This is a primary example where extreme flexibility comes at a cost. As you've heard before, 'You get what you pay for.' The classic hedge and deploy strategy, where capabilities and especially capacity is held in reserve for unforeseeable situations, is only worthwhile if the stakes are high enough to warrant the cost. In the commercial world this means having customers who will pay for a high-powered response. And they do exist. Indeed, the major international courier companies such as DHL, UPS and FedEx all have customers who demand this type of 'express' response from time to time, and each of these providers has developed internal capabilities to meet their customers' exceptional demands. Other businesses that foster innovation and high responsiveness using a cluster-type of organization are 3M and Google – often offering solutions before the customer knows they need them.

The most commonly recognized enterprises that have these types of supply chain organization structure are usually government-supported emergency services, such as the ambulance service, fire brigades and search and rescue teams. Another group comprises the voluntary (yet highly trained and organized) organizations such as surf lifesaving clubs and bushfire brigade services in Australia. They raise funds through a combination of donations, government grants and industry partners to support their operations. A third group is the global cluster organizations such as the United Nations Joint Logistics Centre (JLC) that is a consortium of the World Food Programme (WFP), UNICEF and the World Health Organization (WHO).

2. Processes

Processes? How can these be planned for? Perhaps not surprisingly, there are practically no *standard* processes in the *entrepreneurial* subculture. But there are some processes – the most basic and the most complex. The point to remember is that you are in uncharted waters and you step in where others have feared to tread. There are no road maps, you are 'making it up as you go along'. The trail-blazing, however, may reap huge benefits and could uncover new approaches to business problems in the future. Or, it could be a one-off solution. Organizations will embrace the processes that work best locally in the midst of an emergency. The teams can operate either virtually or in physical proximity to each other. Autonomy is paramount and the ability to operate as separate unconnected 'cells' for extended periods is mandatory. Australia's SAS uses 'scenario dreaming' to achieve high flexibility and reduce reaction time to events that *may* happen in the future. Unfortunately, due to the constraints placed on resources in businesses today, there is little opportunity to invest time, money or labour into scenario development. The potential here is huge, though the benefits are unpredictable.

Despite the challenges, process design is not impossible in this type of supply chain. I am indebted to Chris Morgan of Cranfield University for providing the following insights into process design:[4]

◆ Establish clear overarching goals (and update in real-time consistent with emerging situation).

◆ Break goals into manageable subgoals (and update in real-time).

◆ Establish a communications framework (robust technology for remote communications; internal and external structures).

◆ Establish key milestones and collective review (international vectors and review in line with goal variations).

◆ Recruit people who can cope with evolutionary project iteration and risk evaluation.

3. Systems/IT

The requirement for high-cost transactional systems/IT in the *fully flexible* environment is relatively low, and consequently there is an equivalent lower requirement for capital investment. However, contrary to practices in *collaborative* and *lean* supply chains, there is a heavy emphasis on intervention by management, coupled with the presence of highly skilled and experienced permanent staff. Web technology is embraced as required, and some form of enterprise profit optimization (EPO) system is used to gauge the profitability of any innovative solutions that are applied to customer problem situations. Investment in high-technology applications may be necessary from time to time.

Overall, the main systems used in *fully flexible* supply chains can, and do, vary across the full spectrum, from those required for financially and time-limited humanitarian supply chains, to those needed to deliver high-cost creative solutions. The key is to apply the **appropriate** degree of systems sophistication and avoid unnecessary over-engineering. Indeed, it is not unusual for manual systems such as Gantt charts to be used at one extreme, and online rules-based ordering systems of the type developed by Cisco Systems at the other end of the spectrum. Originally, Cisco, which produces complex modular products and components to meet its high-tech customers' specifications, found it was reworking many of its products because it failed to meet customers' demanding specifications. Now customers order for themselves through an online ordering system that provides parameters around what they are likely to want. So Cisco, working with its partners on this novel solution, has become a world leader in this particular technological space. Scenario analyses, using say Monte Carlo methodologies, are also likely to be a required business modelling capability.

4. Key Performance Indicators

KPIs in this area of the business emphasize finding creative solutions in the very short lead-times demanded, and in the case of 'business event' supply chains, measure customer satisfaction with the solutions. The 'emergency/humanitarian response' supply chains can be more complex because of the number of parties involved – normal business style measures may not suffice when issues such as governance and political expectations, not to mention saving lives, can all be part of the mix of 'performance' in this critical supply chain. Best to say that little is important in the heat of this operating environment save for getting results. Risk-taking is encouraged and mistakes are not punished, unless of course they become the norm. Basically the KPIs for an aid organization are to 'get there fast and save lives' with an eye kept on the expenditure of funds due to increased accountability in this sphere.

5. Incentives

Rewards for individuals who lead or contribute to the development of creative solutions and new ideas that meet the required KPIs can be tailored to the particular individuals/teams involved; whatever they prefer is what they are given. Usually, the rewards are 'in kind' rather than monetary, e.g., research grants, industrial sabbaticals, further education and overseas travel to investigate advanced practices or the satisfaction of achieving more altruistic goals. In the 'business event' supply chain, personal development and personal challenge is uppermost in the minds of the individuals involved, and this is one of their main motivators. In the 'emergency response/humanitarian' supply chain, self-development and challenge can be overtaken by the personal and emotional benefits of supporting a humanitarian cause and helping people, animals or the environment.

6. Job design

Do you like job descriptions? That's going to be difficult. To foster an *entrepreneurial* subculture you need to have loosely defined roles rather than tight job descriptions. Your focus should be squarely on encouraging flexibility and rapid response – nothing should be allowed to get in the way of achieving your objective. The vision of the organization, to which everyone agrees, provides the broad boundaries for individual and team action. You can empower people to perform various roles within those boundaries. Control is achieved through adherence to this vision and an agreed set of values. This is a very self-regulating subculture, but it is important to have boundaries in place. Empowerment without boundaries is a recipe for chaos at worst – and inaction at best.

7. Internal communications

The style of internal communications is spontaneous and ad hoc. If you are not around, you will not hear what is going on inside the organization. The underlying message is that 'we participate in the search for creative solutions'. The method of communications is mostly face-to-face, and is usually very open and informal. This is not a place for hidden agendae. However, there are downsides; including the haphazard nature of internal communications leading to confusion and a lack of information reaching the right people. This is the 'business event' situation. In the 'emergency' situation, where armed forces or emergency response teams are involved, the level of communications is necessarily much better because of the life and death situations usually involved.

8. Training and development

You can expand and reinforce the skills of individuals who work in the entrepreneurial subculture by providing training in lateral thinking and problem solving, and by enabling them to gain cross-industry experience. This is a very cerebral if not conceptual world, where techniques such as brainstorming are used to extract ideas. Individuals have their communication skills developed through training and are taught how to build rapport in team environments. The reason for risk-taking is explained and risk-management skills are further developed and refined.

9. Recruitment

People with special qualities are required to work in *fully flexible* supply chains. You should be looking for recruits who are comfortable with taking risks and are highly intuitive and flexible in their working style. This category of employee needs to have an almost contradictory combination of independent thought with a team-orientation. They also need to be self-confident, passionate, have good listening skills, be good net-workers and resilient in order to maintain their ability to function in extreme 'business' environments that would challenge most other human beings. Your recruits should be the type to challenge the status quo, be strategic in their orientation, resourceful and original. These are rare and talented individuals indeed.

Generating and retaining an *entrepreneurial* subculture in the appropriate locations in an enterprise is not easy. Some enterprises have found it impossible to do so as they seem inevitably to become dominated by an 'operational' mindset. They are not alone. The mindset pervades too many businesses today. However, an operational focus will only take the enterprise as far as operational excellence – the **first** level in the performance and capability continuum. Going to higher levels of performance requires entirely different capabilities and competencies, some of which include the more risk-taking *entrepreneurial* subculture. But for this to occur, a necessary condition is to already have in place leaders in the executive who are naturally *visionary*.

10. Leadership style

Visionary leaders lead their enterprises by inspiration. They tend to be informal yet decisive, and they genuinely care about ideas generated by others as well as themselves. They are not people who feel threatened by subordinates, and they certainly don't curtail talent that has the potential eventually to challenge their position. Such leaders are inherently strategic, and they ooze innovation and creativity: leaders such as Richard Branson (Virgin) and perhaps even Carly Fiorina (ex Hewlett-Packard). Their Myers-Briggs Type Indicator style is usually INTP (introvert-intuition-thinker-perceiver) to ENFJ (extrovert-intuition-feeler-judger), or thereabouts. Branson, in particular, stands out. He has a very unconventional leadership style nurtured since he was very young; he invariably challenges conventional wisdom. For instance, Branson believes strongly that employees matter most, and if you create an exciting workplace environment for staff, this will motivate them to serve their customers. As a result, shareholders also do well. I can vouch for this approach having flown Virgin Atlantic on the Shanghai–London sector in June 2005; it was a much more enjoyable experience than flights I have previously taken on many other airlines. So Branson is a living example of alignment. He has been quick to see opportunities and understand exactly what customers want in all sorts of diverse markets. But that is not the end of the story. He has been able to develop matching value propositions and find ways to breed appropriate subcultures in these businesses to drive his strategies into the marketplace. The results are there for all to see, as the Virgin group, established only 20 years ago, is now one of the world's biggest brands; the group now boasts more than 270 branded companies, all doing well in their respective markets. Branson exemplifies what can be achieved when the natural energy **inside** the enterprise is harnessed to service customers.

The combination of autonomous independence and the ability to work in cohesive teams is rare; these are usually individuals with a strong team commitment. They can either be individuals with the ability to move from one extreme to the other on the I–P axis of the P-A-D-I framework, as outlined in Chapter 3, **or** they are in balance and are able to select 'appropriate' ways to respond along the axis given the requirements of any particular situation. The preferred mode of behaviour would be Dp (or Developer–producer) for individuals working with 'business event' supply chains and more towards Di (Developer–integrator) for the 'emergency response/humanitarian' supply chain. If a Myers-Briggs assessment was to be completed on individuals working in *fully flexible* supply chains this group would probably yield widely divergent personalities. However, we could expect a high degree of similar characteristics in the individuals who are leading both variants of this supply chain.

Mixed supply chain logics

For example, in an emergency response supply chain, the first thought is a rapid response to save lives and help stabilize the situation (Phase One – *fully flexible*). This can evolve over time into a more scheduled re-building

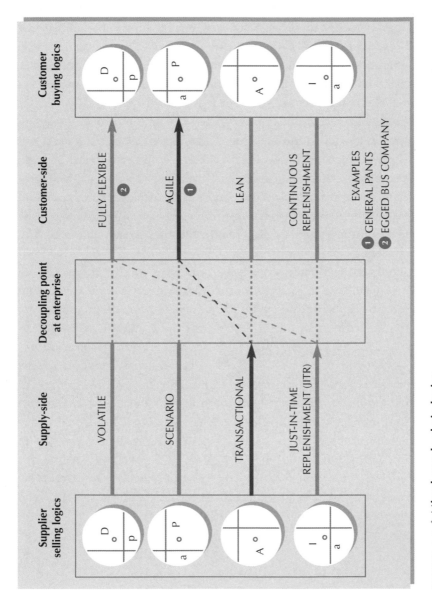

FIGURE 8.4 ◆ Mixed supply chain logics

programme as routine is restored (Phase Two). And underneath this, you are receiving cooperation from NGOs and the government(s) involved – the collaborative culture. As normality is restored, this should be replaced by an array of supply chains that reflect natural buying behaviours in the affected community.

So, practically any combination of supply-side and demand-side supply chains are possible, as depicted in Figure 8.4. A few final examples are embedded in the graphic itself.

So where are these supply chains going? If anything we can expect to see increasing focus and resources being poured into the development of this vital capability, both at the business and public levels, which is very consistent with the uncertain age we live in. The good news, if there is any in this area of extreme crises and extreme solutions, is that techniques and practices developed under pressure in these types of operating environments will eventually be refined and flow through to the mainstream of the enterprise as everyday best practice.

Living lessons

1 Don't be afraid to 'walk on the grass'. Anything goes.

2 The key to success is speed, innovation and passion.

3 Everything in the *fully flexible* supply chain is assessed at the instant it happens, and the 'most appropriate' responses are framed and launched as expeditiously as possible – this is decision-making on the **run**, without apologies. Only decisive thinkers need apply!

CHAPTER 9

New business models for new supply chains

The miracle of 'embedded alignment'

A 'business model' is simply the way an enterprise organizes itself to make money. It's the core logic for how your business creates value in a sustainable way. *New* business models are just that – new and often innovative ways of organizing the enterprise to make money. Can you think of a genuinely **new** business model? Today they come in both formal and informal arrangements. Perhaps the best known are the models nurtured in industry clusters identified by Michael Porter.[1] Examples include information technology in Silicon Valley and biotechnology at nine locations across the United States. Other examples include banking in Switzerland and movie production in Hollywood and India's own Bollywood. These clusters act as 'incubators' for new ideas and set the direction for industry. Rubbing shoulders with each other helps to share knowledge, excite passions and encourage more than a bit of intense competition, as well as intensifying the development of associated industries. This simply doesn't happen in other environments, at least not in such an intense, industry-focused way. Industry clusters in Europe have generated world-class industries, from ceramics in Italy, fashion in Paris/Milan and London and more recently New York and Tokyo, to the original watch/clock industry, and cut flowers in the Netherlands, as our example overleaf describes.

Have you seen the seeds of new ideas appearing in your industry? Fortunately, new business models are emerging in a multitude of different formats in different industries around the world. In particular, new business solutions in publishing,[2] tobacco,[3] and aviation fuel[4] exist today. The airline industry has its alliances and brokers, call centres; SMART cars (with their Daimler-Chrysler and SWATCH association, as well as their environmentally friendly design); eco-tourism and many other examples are at different stages of development. All of these new-breed business models are based on the principle that it is better to bring together the required combinations of *capabilities*, fast, in a new organization rather than trying to develop them organically. The resulting hybrid business brings to life the idea of 'embedded alignment'. The desired alignment with customers is created and embedded almost instantaneously in a new organization. There's an end to the hard work of trying to change your internal culture to achieve alignment; the alignment is embedded from the very start. Sound easy? We will get to the hard part later.

Dutch cut flower market

The Dutch cut flower market is an example where a highly perishable luxury product has been transformed into a global product through an innovative business model. The market origins are from the late 1800s when vegetable growers started auctions to sell their own produce instead of selling through wholesalers. The wholesalers tended to foster intense competition between the growers – driving down prices. This developed into the flower auctions known today, that are owned by the growers in a cooperative that helps set market prices and provides an exchange of information on future market trends. Basically an antecedent of the 'open auctions' that were all the buzz when first 'discovered' in the 1990s.

This innovative solution to unbalanced power in the supply chain (where the wholesalers dominated) fostered a cluster of industries with strong links to the cut flower market. Not all of these industries are directly involved in the 'Dutch auctions', yet have formed as a service or supplier to the industry. For example, the Netherlands, which has limited land mass, has cut flowers as one of its exports – which initially is counter-intuitive. However, due to the early development and adoption of glasshouses in this country the cut flower market was facilitated by a state-of-the-art glass production industry. Glasshouses provided the means for intensive cultivation of land, resulting in both high yields and more standardized product.

Other well-developed industries closely associated with cut flowers in the Netherlands are the strong agricultural businesses (dairy, agronomy), horticulture products (fertilizers and pesticides), horticultural education and training, along with the innovative logistics developed

▶

since the mid-1990s that allow the transportation of perishable products around the globe. The cluster comprises a range of products and services – from horticultural advice and innovative packaging for the global transport of flowers, to state-of-the-art logistics systems, fertilizers and pesticides, and glass products for green houses.

You might ask: 'Why do we need new organizational formats in the first place? My business is travelling along very well, thank you.' One very good reason, particularly if you are a small to medium-sized business, is **scale**. Scale is critical simply because it gives other businesses greater operating efficiencies and competitiveness. That means, they'll be better than you, maybe not yet … but watch them enter your market soon! Let's face it, in many smaller economies the size of entire industries is less than a single organization in some parts of the world, particularly in the northern hemisphere. If you are in a smaller economy and you want to compete, you need to find new ways to achieve scale – even if only artificially. In this vein, a recent report by Booz Allen Hamilton proposed the concept of 'virtual scale', which allows smaller companies to 'compete with industry giants by pooling resources with carefully chosen partners'.[5] This is not an unreasonable concept, but it relies heavily on the companies' ability to form strong and lasting alliances. The new scaled-up organization will only survive if there is an 'equity' structure to hold it together when the going gets tough, as it surely will, as we shall see.

There is also the *diminishing returns* effect of just doing more of the same, as depicted in the first two levels of Figure 9.1. Re-inventing the organization, even using sophisticated alignment principles described in earlier chapters, has its limitations, mostly to do with the time to execute to plan. Therefore, we have to seek out more radical forms of organization formats.

Why are radical formats necessary? Surely, they are too risky? I don't think they are – I believe they are essential. For too long enterprises have segmented their customer base using institutional, geographical or internal parameters. This immediately 'disconnects' the non-customer-facing logistics operations from the most important people: *customers*. No wonder they fail to have a clear view of what the customers want! The idea of weaving multiple supply chains into the fabric of a business is still a foreign concept. In addition, the underlying mechanisms that cause cultural

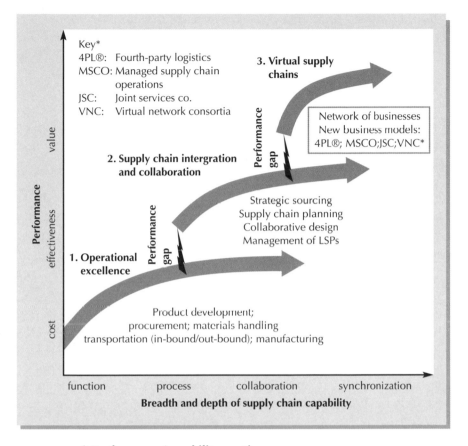

FIGURE 9.1 ◆ Performance/capability continuum

Source Adapted from Figure I.1 in Gattorna (2003), p. xi

resistance to change are still largely a mystery to executives brought up in a functional world, where specializations are preferred and rewarded. Cross-functional interaction seems almost too difficult to contemplate. We can see why the old models of doing business have prevailed!

I am an optimist though. Businesses will inevitably overcome the factors that have retarded new business models from emerging and shaping future supply chains. But they need to watch out for the two things that can stand in the way: a lack of **management will** to embrace the changes inherent in new models; and a lack of understanding of what is involved, both good and the bad. We will pursue this theme in more depth in the following pages. Ultimately, you have to move to Level 3 in Figure 9.1. This will involve pulling the existing organization apart and re-configuring it in some way, but doing so in conjunction with partners who have capabilities to complement your own. I call this the *Humpty Dumpty effect*.

The imperative of new operating models for next generation supply chains

You should take decisive action when it's clear that you need radically to re-align the needs of your market with your current internal capabilities. Similarly, a fundamentally new approach is called for when an enterprise cannot break through the *capability wall* to deliver its own strategies.

But embracing new operating models is not an easy task for today's C-level executives. Many are innately conservative, and this is only reinforced by the increasingly stringent scrutiny being applied by analysts and investors alike. The investment community today is looking more critically at top management's plans and strategies for growth, profitability and projected returns on investment. Senior executives must convince investors they have the ability to 'execute to plan'. And if they are proposing a new operating model, they have to show that it will indeed be a more efficient way of deploying shareholder capital. The bar just keeps getting higher!

And we can't expect that to change in the future. If anything, the scrutiny is set to increase. With supply chains accounting for up to 80 per cent of the enterprise's invested capital and 50 per cent of working capital,[6] they are already coming under almost daily scrutiny by financial analysts around the world. It is therefore imperative that management find new supply chain operating models that are more capital efficient[7] and less demanding on up-front investment requirements. One of the most exciting recent developments has been the wider adoption of the Cash Flow Return on Investment (CFROI)[8] metric developed by Boston Consulting to measure the health and relative wealth of an enterprise. CSFB Holt's ValueSearch database of cash flow and valuations of tens of thousands of companies across the globe has detected a significant trend relationship between future share price performance (expressed as market capitalization) and CFROI as described by Joel Litman and Mark Frigo in

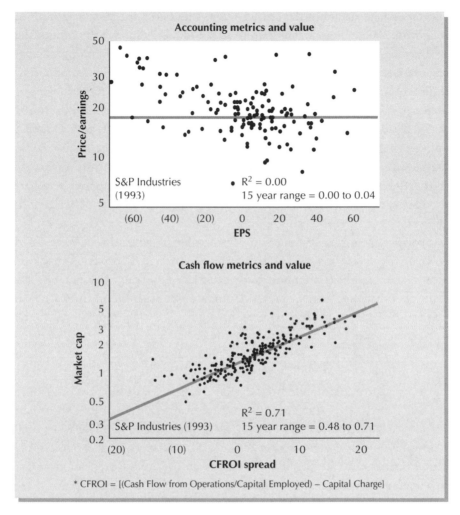

FIGURE 9.2 ◆ CFROI and traditional accounting metrics

Source CSFB Holt

their recent paper.[9] On this basis it seems that this financial metric is superior to other more traditional accounting approaches, as depicted in Figure 9.2; CFROI gets under the covers and exposes what is really going on inside a company's operations.

Indeed, if we look at some leading companies of the last decade, their market performance is matched by their CFROI. Nokia – one of the biggest change stories of the last 25 years – has had a spectacular growth in its CFROI. While transforming itself from a timber company into one of the world's leading high-tech companies, Nokia has ensured that ample funds are available to sustain high investment levels in competitive-building assets. This in turn has helped the company out-perform the market in terms of share price. Li & Fung is another enterprise that has successfully transformed from a small trading company[10] to a global high-performance, full-line supply chain service provider. In fact HSBC is reported in the *Wall Street Journal* as saying Li & Fung's current profit measure, EBIT/Revenue (3.4 per cent in 2004), understates the company's real performance, which when measured by EBIT/Gross Profit is 36.9 per cent in the same year.[11] At the other extreme is Enron, whose demise was probably predictable given 18 consecutive years during which its CFROI failed to beat the cost of capital. This could be attributed in part to the way Enron's leadership responded to the quarterly reporting pressures for ongoing performance improvement. Compare this with the more European style of Nokia's leadership, where the emphasis has been on satisfying all key stakeholders to achieve a sustainable business.

The CFROI metric gives us a mechanism to help predict the future performance of publicly listed companies. It's no surprise that the best performing companies on world share markets exhibit relatively high CFROIs over a five-year period – and have superior alignment with their respective marketplaces. Take a look at BMW, Gillette and Wal-Mart – all examples of this phenomenon.[12] They also have cost-effective supply chain operations, supported by strong asset investment programmes. But other equally well-known companies, many of them global brands, are struggling to achieve acceptable levels of performance, and probably do not have the luxury of time to take a long-term view about performance improvement. It is this latter group that must look for new business models that will improve their performance, fast, just to survive.

However, because CFROI is a complicated equation, some analysts prefer to use Return on Invested Capital (ROIC), Economic Profit (EP) and Total Return to Shareholders (TRS). The combination of these three metrics provides very powerful insights into the operating performance of a business – and its ability to return value to its shareholders – as depicted in Figure 9.3.

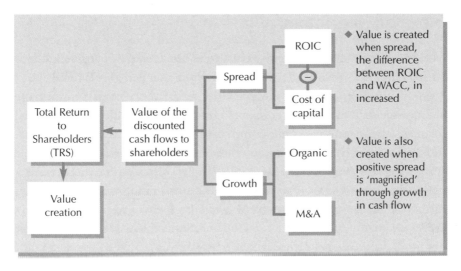

FIGURE 9.3 ◆ Value creation road map

Source The Accenture Value Creation Road Map, copyright 2005

ROIC is calculated as NOPLAT (or EBITA*1-tax)/Invested Capital, and in simple terms this is a measure of how well a business performs in terms of generating operating profit from the capital it has invested in the business. When we subtract the costs associated with investing this capital – otherwise known as the weighted average cost of capital (WACC) – we come to an economic profit figure, representing the true value that a business has generated from its operations. Economic Profit is currently regarded as the most important metric when analyzing the value creation ability of a business. Furthermore, there have been several studies into the correlation of EP and TRS over the years: showing a strong R^2, i.e., providing evidence that to improve shareholder returns, managers should focus on optimizing their Economic Profit. However, it is important to note that EP only calculates the historical cash-flow generation of a business, and so is not appropriate for calculating current share price, or indeed, future share prices.[13]

Why am I giving you all this detail? If you believe as I do that supply chains **are** the business, as highlighted in Chapter 1, then it's logical to look at overall business performance to see how well your enterprise supply chains are performing.

It has all been painfully slow!

New business models in supply chains were first seriously considered circa 1996 when Accenture[14] invented and trade-marked the Fourth Party Logistics concept, better known simply as 4PL®. Accenture originally defined the 4PL® model 'as a supply chain integrator that assembles and manages the resources, capabilities and technology of its own organization, with those of complementary service providers, to deliver a comprehensive supply chain solution'.[15] The motivation for this organizational innovation grew out of the very real frustration that shippers around the world were experiencing with their third-party logistics providers (3PLs), sometimes referred to as Logistics Service Providers (LSPs). This category of third-party provider first emerged in the mid-1970s as an outgrowth of single-mode transportation and warehouse service companies. Unfortunately, few of these companies have been able to successfully make the transition to the satisfaction of their shipper customers, as evidenced by the 1994 survey carried out in Britain among 250 companies across several industries.[16] Only a third of the sample felt that their expectations were being met on a consistent basis; and two-thirds were unhappy. Hardly a resounding endorsement!

Can you remember the thinking that drove the emergence of 3PLs? About 20 years earlier, some businesses – predominantly fast-moving consumer goods (FMCG) companies – took the first tentative steps towards outsourcing elements of their distribution function. Often it was for the wrong reasons, such as to excise industrial relations issues. However, a genuine rationale existed for outsourcing at the time, and it is worth recalling this:

1 **Strategic:** it was thought that senior management would be freed up to focus on core competences. However, it was found that substantial senior management time was still required after the move to outsourcing, to coordinate and review 3PL performance.

2 **Financial:** a reduction in total costs and associated working capital requirements was thought to be a natural outcome of outsourcing, but in those early days the experience was that a continuous reduction in operating costs was minimal after the initial 'honeymoon period' of 6 to 12 months.

3 **Operational:** a simpler industrial relations climate was expected, but in fact the industrial action was simply transferred to the new 3PL organization, and this factor continued to affect the client's business for a few decades.

One of the biggest factors to undermine the success of outsourcing – and perhaps the most unexpected – was on-going internal resistance. People inside the client organization strongly opposed the outsourcing arrangement and this inevitably made life difficult for both parties. In other words, the biggest competitors that the early 3PLs faced were in fact internal competitors, and this situation continues today.

But perhaps the biggest issue for the fledgling 3PL organizations between 1970 and 2000 was their inability to develop the 'creative solutions' so much sought by their shipper clients. Clearly these new logistics service organizations lacked the essential *innovation gene* needed for success. This failing was due to their lack of scale in talent and strategic thinking, which in turn was a throwback to their operational roots. Currently DHL is putting significant resources into addressing this very issue. Over the succeeding three decades, much has changed in the global, regional and local 3PL marketplace; fewer, larger, more sophisticated organizations now fill this space and there has been a discernible closing of the original *capability gap* between shippers' expectations and their perceptions of 3PL capabilities to meet these expectations.[17]

The 4PL® business model, which brings together a select combination of principal parties with a number of minor equity parties with special capabilities, was born as a direct result of the doubt that accompanied the early development of 3PLs. But it too has suffered, albeit in a different way; the original design concept and operational philosophy behind the 1996 version, depicted in Figure 9.4, has largely been lost or has become confused over the past decade.[18] Indeed, several factors combined to force compromises: relatively long lead-time in the negotiation phase; the pure scale of the proposed new business model; and the apparent rigidity of the 4PL® design. Many current versions of 4PL®s look nothing like the originally intended design.

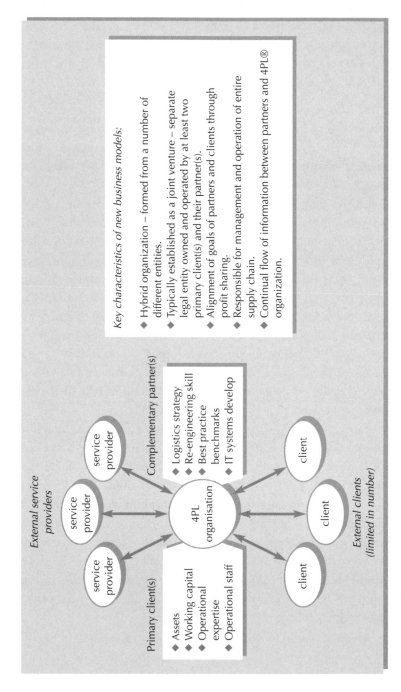

External service providers

service provider

service provider

service provider

Complementary partner(s)

- Logistics strategy
- Re-engineering skill
- Best practice benchmarks
- IT systems develop

4PL organisation

Primary client(s)

- Assets
- Working capital
- Operational expertise
- Operational staff

External clients (limited in number)

client

client

client

Key characteristics of new business models:

- Hybrid organization – formed from a number of different entities.
- Typically established as a joint venture – separate legal entity owned and operated by at least two primary client(s) and their partner(s).
- Alignment of goals of partners and clients through profit sharing.
- Responsible for management and operation of entire supply chain.
- Continual flow of information between partners and 4PL® organization.

FIGURE 9.4 ◆ Classic 4PL® new business model

Source Adapted from Figure 27.4 in Gattorna (1998), p. 43

Nevertheless, some 20 genuine 4PL®s have been designed and built across multiple industries around the world, and Figure 9.5 shows a sample. These 4PL® prototypes taught us many valuable lessons about what does and does not work in the design and implementation of new supply chain business models. These lessons, which are discussed in more detail below, should be heeded as we move to the next generation of business model.

Early adopters of the original 4PL® business models have enjoyed significant financial and operational improvements:

1   **Thames Water Utilities (UK):** 10 per cent reduction in supply chain costs; 40 per cent reduction in inventory; 70 per cent reduction in backorders; and achievement of 97 per cent service levels.

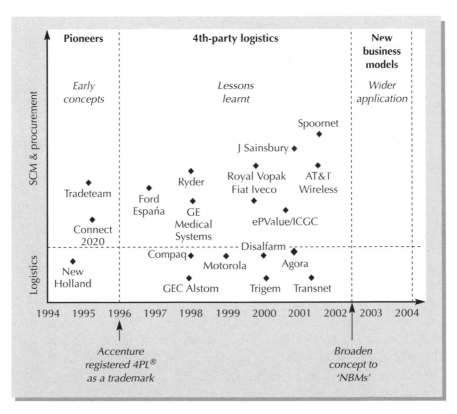

FIGURE 9.5 ◆ **Historical evolution of 4PL® style new business models**

2   **New Holland Logistics (Italy):** US$67 million. Savings in the first seven years of operation; this venture has now been bought back by

New Holland. These savings were achieved through a 20 per cent reduction in inventory; 15 per cent saving in freight; and more than 90 per cent order fulfillment accuracy.

3   **Ford Clasa (Spain):** an on-going annual supply chain operating cost reduction of US$6.7 million, together with increased flexibility in the assembly mix; and reduced in-plant stock.

These examples are consistent with my own experience in building business cases for a range of 4PL®s. In virtually all cases, annual operating costs were reduced by up to 40 per cent, on top of one-off savings in capital investments. And just as importantly, the degree of difficulty in implementing this type of transformation was less than the experience of changing an existing or legacy organization from the inside out. Unfortunately, this is not intuitively obvious.

The original 4PL® design was specifically structured to overcome most if not all the issues encountered by early 3PLs:

1   **Strategic:** a single point of contact for all supply chain requirements designed to reduce the time demands on senior management.

2   **Financial:** continuous improvement and on-going re-negotiation of Service Level Agreements (SLAs) as a central feature of the new 4PL® organization.

3   **Operational:** the simple act of establishing an entirely new entity meant that staff and management could be carefully selected, thereby reducing possible union and internal cultural resistance.

However, despite the subsequent hard-won successes of the 4PL® business model, it has been difficult to maintain the integrity of the design. In fact, it is not unusual these days to hear that companies are requesting 'tenders' for a 4PL® provider, just as you would do in the days when 3PLs were invited to respond to a request for quotation (RFQ) for specific contracts.[19] In the process, some of the essential elements that differentiate 3PL and 4PL® business models have been lost. One thing is for certain: you cannot simply issue a tender for a 4PL®!

Perhaps the only independent research[20] published on the comparative value created by a true 4PL® business model revealed that the EV/EBITDA[21] earned by a genuine 4PL® was a factor of three to five times greater than that generated by standard 3PLs and single-mode transportation providers. See Figure 9.6 for more detail.

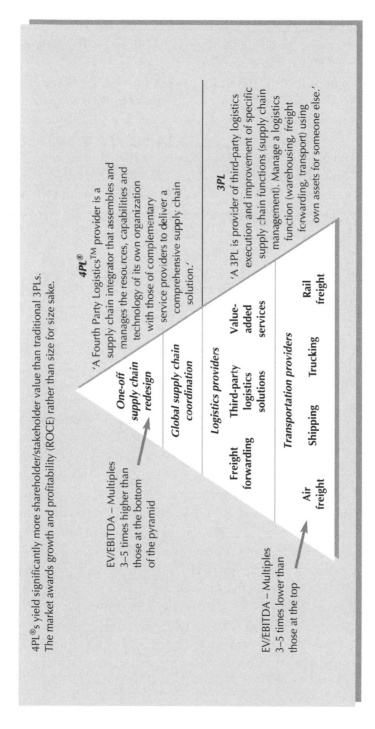

FIGURE 9.6 ◆ Relative profitability of different logistics service provider (LSP) models

Source Adapted from Dr Jochen Vogel, Lehman Bros Report, March 2001

Some single-mode companies developed variations of the 4PL® business model to operate in parallel with their core business. For example, Spoornet, the freight division of South African Railways, has been working on several collaborative industry-level models for the last three years. These models involve developing customized e-marketplaces for suppliers and buyers in several major industries, and attaching a 4PL® style *virtual management company* to coordinate the fulfillment task that is physically carried out by other 3PLs and single-mode transportation companies. The success of this venture is still being assessed, but this configuration could well be the forerunner of future *supply chain industry solution* models (see Figure 9.7). Another example is found in New Zealand with the commodity company M-co, which operates internationally in markets for gas and electricity commodities and telecommunications.[22]

The key lesson that has emerged from the experiment with 4PL® business models in their various forms over the past ten years is that it takes a tremendous leap of faith by management to embrace an organization design that is so radically different from previous experience. But then that is what leadership is about. However, C-level executives simply do not feel comfortable engaging in such new styles of organization that have had relatively little testing under all types of operating conditions; especially given increased market scrutiny and pressure for accountability over the past decade. Typically, the easy way out has been to embrace the 'norm' and undertake large-scale transformations of **existing** organization structures. What if the same mindset had been adopted in the area of product development? Answer: little or no progress, and probably extinction by now. That's why it is so hard to reconcile the slow progress made by many global companies such as Philips, Samsung and Sony in their supply chain business models, compared to the rapid rate of innovation in the product side of their business. Perhaps we should shift some product development executives into logistics and supply chain functions and see what they can achieve in a short time!

The difficulties in delivering on 4PL® designs has led me to search for new and more flexible designs over the last five years. Interestingly, during the same period, significant progress has been made in adapting 4PL® concepts and principles to the service sector, as described in the case study (see pp. 214–18) on British health care logistics provider NHS Logistics.[23]

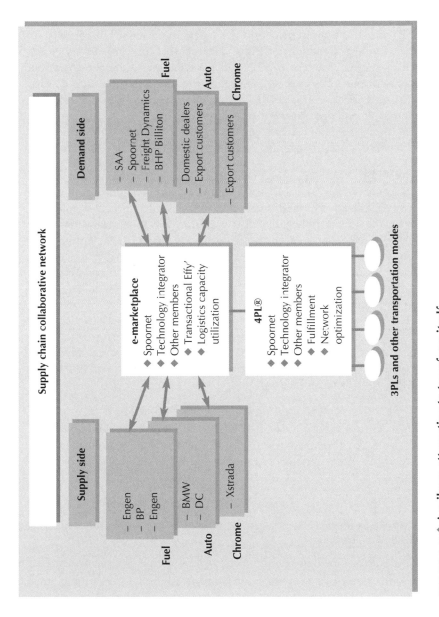

FIGURE 9.7 ◆ A railway attempting to transform itself

NHS Logistics

This case study describes how an in-house public sector not-for-profit (NFP) logistics operation within the English National Health System (NHS) has transformed itself into a successful internal supply chain service provider. The result? NHS has achieved international recognition across multiple industry sectors in both Britain and Europe. At the heart of this transformation are 4PL® principles adapted from the original Andersen Consulting (now Accenture) model, but the final outcome is a hybrid organizational format, which is considered more appropriate to the complex supplier/customer environment in the UK health sector.

Background

NHS Logistics has its roots in the Wholesaling Division of a previous supply organization tasked with providing purchasing and supply services to the English NHS. NHS is a confederation of more than 600 health organizations, each operating as a separate legal entity with autonomy in purchasing and supply matters. NHS Logistics was established in its current form in 2000 as the in-house supply *channel manager* for the NHS on the basis of a NFP, self-funding business within a totally competitive health environment.

The challenge was to turn a traditional wholesaling organization into a successful supply chain service provider. The journey started in 2001 with the appointment of a new Chief Executive who came from the utility sector and had previous experience collaborating with Accenture on 4PL® models in utilities.

Strategy

The Accenture definition of a 4PL®[24] was adopted as the underlying framework for transformation. The initial assessment identified that many of the characteristics required for a 4PL® already existed in the organization in some form or other; see comparative table below.

4PL® principles	Match	Comments
1 Defined ecosystem	✓	Healthcare
2 Multiple customer model	✓	But scope for expansion
3 Multi-year transformation programme	?	Needed, but yet to accelerate
4 Partnering with customers	✓	Good foundation but opportunity to improve
5 Partnering with 3PLs	✓	Yes, but needed to be extended
6 Capital funding	✗	Limited availability but not a constraining factor
7 Gain sharing on outcomes	✓	Yes, with the customers, suppliers and partners

Starting point 2001:

The 4PL® model identifies four core capabilities – architect/integrator; control room; supply chain infomediary; and resource provider. A development programme was instigated to strengthen these areas.

Architect/integrator:

A supply chain consultancy arm was established with a small in-house team of seven highly skilled individuals from diverse industry sector backgrounds supported by 35 external consultancy partners, ranging from specialist sole traders to international consultancies. This group provides a full supply chain review, solution and project management/ implementation service across the total supply chain.

◆ Established NHS Supply Chain Knowledge Centre (www.supply-chain.nhs.uk) to capture best practice from all sectors, promote adoption and provide tools, techniques and supply.

◆ Established NHS supply chain forum to lead the supply chain development agenda across the NHS, with support from academics and leaders from other sectors.

◆ Established UK's only logistics benchmarking club (www.logmark.org) to establish cross-industry comparative metrics and to promote introduction of best practice.

Control room:

◆ Fully e-enabled the total supply chain to provide complete visibility for all concerned.

◆ In particular, focused on arrangements with suppliers to integrate processes and share key data, especially in areas of performance, inventory and demand forecasting via web supplier trading portal.

◆ Positioned the organization as clearly neutral with true partnership working with all parties and benefit sharing.

Supply chain 'infomediary':

◆ Fully e-enabled supply chain providing world-class management information for all parties across the supply chain.

◆ Information used to drive continuous improvement agenda for all parties.

◆ Real-time data for operational excellence.

◆ Data/management information covers all customer demand regardless of supplier.

Resource provider:

◆ Flexible operational resources via third parties but operating under a single brand.

◆ Multiple supply channels established to meet wide range of service requirements.

◆ Resources available on shared basis where this can be used to leverage better deals.

Results

Following are just a selection of the key indicators which point to a transformational change in the organization over the four years to 2005.

Customers/service offer:

	2001/02	2005/06
Customer segmentation	NHS only	NHS
		Private sector service providers
		Military health
		Prisons health
Product range	10,000	43,000
Professional services	Minimal	Consultancy
		Contract management
		Managed services
		E-commerce solutions
		Training
		Emergency support services

Service excellence:

	2001/02	2005/06
Deliveries on time	97.4%	99.4%
Overall product availability	97.7%	98.5%
Customer satisfaction	73%	88%*
Staff satisfaction	51%	63%*

(*2004/05 latest data)

Continuous improvement in internal efficiency:

	2001/02	2005/06
Service charge	11.7%	9.7%
Stock management (Turns per annum)	11.5	16.5
Cost per £100 sales	£7.68	£7.11

Growth in activity levels:

	2001/02	2005/06	Change
Sales value (£M)	559	780	+39%
Order lines (millions)	26.5	33.2	+25%

The above shows direct sales value, but overall NHS Logistics is now responsible, via its procurement arm, for £1.2 billion in spending on health care products.

Recognition across industry sectors

During 2004–05, NHS Logistics has won eight national and international awards, including UK and European Supply Chain of the Year.

Conclusion

The transformed NHS Logistics business is delivering cumulative savings to its internal customers of £110 million per annum plus additional benefits at the rate of circa £10 million per annum. As a not-for-profit business these savings all go back to the front-line health providers via lower product and service charges, and special cash returns when exceptional efficiency savings are achieved.

Suppliers also benefit from the neutral and totally transparent intermediary role played by NHS Logistics. Processes, data and knowledge are shared collaboratively with suppliers to improve the overall effectiveness and efficiency of the total supply chain. The partnership approach with suppliers, as with customers, ensures that benefits are shared.

The commonly held belief that the 4PL® model is best suited within a profit-driven commercial environment has been reversed with this experience in the health sector, as 4PL® principles appear to work equally well in a not-for-profit service environment. The experience in NHS Logistics is that another organizational format is possible which follows 4PL® principles and commercial best practice but where all the benefits are shared with stakeholders rather than shareholders. This is an important distinction.

This hybrid organization model particularly lends itself to the public sector where it is in the best interests of both tax payers and the public to ensure that the maximum benefits flow directly to front-line service provision. In addition, it is a model which works well when the intermediary is working in a complex supply chain with thousands of suppliers and tens of thousands of customers but has no mandated power base. In this scenario an intermediary relies entirely on trust, openness, transparency and benefits being shared right across the supply chain. The profit-driven shareholder model, with power vested in the 4PL® joint venture, can potentially create tension to partnerships working in this type of environment due to the power dynamics and concerns over opposing objectives. A *not-for-profit stakeholder* 4PL® model as described here addresses these concerns through the inclusive involvement of all parties, supports partnership working and provides the potential to maximize benefits right across the supply chain in this particular type of environment. Truly a unique result in this era of zero-sum games!

Outsourcing in the twenty-first century – getting it right

'Outsourcing' is not a term that I use with any relish, because it has too many different meanings, and in any event has largely been devalued by association with high-profile failures in the past. The experience of Marks & Spencer in 1998, when it turned its back on local UK suppliers and opted to outsource all its apparel requirements to distant markets in the Far East is a good example of what can happen when the blind pursuit of cost savings can lead to quite the opposite outcome. We will consider 'outsourcing' further in Chapter 10.

At this stage I prefer to describe the nine principles that should be followed in developing and operating the next generation of supply chain business models:

1 Ensure the new service company is co-owned and co-managed; this holds the disparate members of the consortium together and motivates them to achieve shared goals. This is a criterion that has been largely overlooked in many new business models tried during and after the

e-commerce era when we saw many one-sided marketplace models emerge only to fail.[25] My own preference is to go all the way and develop industry supply chain solutions that involve the equity participation of both sides of a particular industry. The arguments against such an open approach will be discussed later in this chapter.

2   Facilitate rapid realization of benefits (cost savings, profitability and revenue generation); investors and analysts will no longer tolerate back-loaded benefits. Those days are gone for ever.

3   De-risk the implementation of new systems technology and other operational processes; this will help gain the confidence of the investment community.

4   Take advantage of any state-of-the-art assets that are readily available from other specialist players; there is simply not enough time to grow assets, competences and capabilities organically in major competitive markets.

5   Reduce up-front implementation costs through financial engineering practices and careful choice of consortium partners. This lowers investment requirements and enhances asset efficiency.

6   Infuse a subculture of innovation and continuous improvement through some conscious corporate genetic engineering. This is essential for success of the venture and quite feasible if you understand the internal behavioural forces in play.

7   Embed pre-determined KPIs and corresponding incentives (for all parties) in the new organizational design. Every party involved must make a fair return if the consortium is to succeed. See Figure 9.8 for typical commercial arrangements.

8   Recognize all the risks involved in this new style of business model, and confront them head-on.

9   'Out-cycle' your competitors' supply chains, in speed of decision-making as well as action.

The result is a completely new type of execution model that will deliver scale at speed and, paradoxically, at lower risk than traditional change initiatives. Why? As has been argued throughout this book, it's the *people factor* that will ultimately decide the success or failure of a major transformation, and everything else fades into insignificance. I think this approach

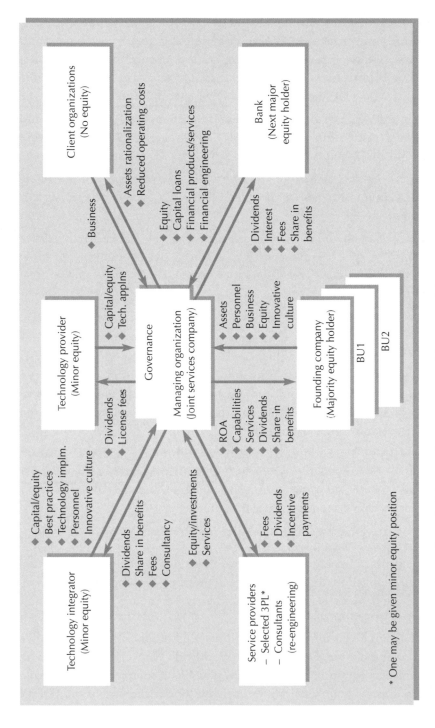

FIGURE 9.8 ◆ How each member of a joint services company (JSC) earns a ROI

of bringing together the *best-of-the-best* resources and capabilities in a consortium-style structure will also overcome the negative aspects of performance observed in numerous mergers and acquisitions (M&A) over the last decade – and they too were in search of scale! An Accenture White Paper[26] documents some of the value-destruction which has occurred during the pursuit of scale via M&A activities, and concludes that: 'the scale-driven perspective is not without merit; it is simply incomplete'.[27] I agree with this point of view, and suggest that we have found the missing piece of the puzzle – the joint services company (JSC).

The next generation of business models

What does the next generation of supply chains look like? The Level 3, *virtual supply chains*, depicted in the performance/capability continuum (see Figure 9.1, p. 201), paints a future involving new business models configured in different ways. We have updated versions of the original 4PL®; and newer business models such as managed supply chain operations (MSCO), joint services companies (JSC) and virtual network consortia (VNC), otherwise known as 'Networked Supply Chains'. The speed with which these models are adopted is largely in the hands of the shipper principals who own the business being transacted. They must take the lead and drive selection of the various equity and capability partners required to make such entities a success for all the parties involved. It takes an entrepreneurial (or deal-making) culture in the set-up stage to do this, but the potential rewards are enormous. For example, I was involved in one business case in the oil industry where the principal partners saved 36 per cent off their baseline operating costs, mainly through rationalizing terminals and transportation capacity. The partners were previously competitors. Such is the quantum of benefits possible from these new models – the potential cannot be ignored for long, irrespective of previous concerns and biases.

The good news is that there is emerging evidence that global and regional LSPs have significantly closed the *capability gap* that was both real and perceived among their shipper customers over the past five years.[28] For example, Deutsche Post Worldwide Network (DPWN), with its recent acquisition of Exel Logistics, now has a complete array of logistics and supply chain capabilities available under the one brand, DHL.

It is therefore an opportune time for a new generation of business models to emerge on to the scene, ones that are far more flexible than previous versions. These would have the following five characteristics in addition to the nine already articulated:

1   **Built-in 'sunset clauses'** that provide consortium members with more flexibility to enter and exit the joint venture as required.

2   The major shareholding principals would have the **option of either rolling-over or folding the entity after a fixed period** (say seven to ten years), and buying the capabilities back on the basis of a pre-agreed formula.

3   More attention should be given to including **both sides of an industry** (buyers and sellers) in the proposed joint services company (JSC); this is an essential ingredient for success in the future. One-sided arrangements simply won't fly in the future – they never have.

4   **Banks and other financial institutions would be encouraged to join the JSC as minority equity partners.** For them there is also the added sweetener of capturing all the other financial services required by consortium members.

5   More attention should be paid to the requirements of government regulatory bodies such as the Mergers & Monopolies Commission (UK); the Australian Competition and Consumer Commission (Australia); and the Commerce Commission (NZ). These statutory bodies should ideally be included in discussions at an early (design) stage. This will assist the approval process because these authorities will see, at close quarters, the cost-based rationale for these new organization structures. It is unlikely that straight out mergers and acquisitions will receive the same sympathetic treatment.

The best chance of introducing these new generation models will be in Europe and Asia Pacific as competitive pressures build, but this is truly a global issue. Pressure for change will ultimately determine the rate and location of adoption.

The only difference between the proposed joint service companies business model and the more advanced virtual network consortia is that the latter version will make it even easier for equity holders to enter and exit the virtual management company on a 'plug-and-play' basis. These differences are summarized in Figure 9.9.

Option 1	Option 2
Joint services company (JSC)	**Virtual network consortium (VNC)**
◆ Co-owned, co-managed service company	◆ Rather than strict equity arrangements, stakeholders in the loose alliance can join and leave the consortium as appropriate (more of a 'plug-and-play' arrangement)
◆ Pre-determined incentives and rewards based on performance	
◆ Infusion of innovation 'culture' in organization design	◆ In most other respects, similar to a JSC
◆ Financial engineering to fund set up and operations	◆ Both models focus on acquiring the capabilities needed at a particular point in time

FIGURE 9.9 ◆ **Execution models that deliver change at speed and scale**

Doctoral research work is currently underway on this category of 'networked' models to determine if operational effectiveness can be further increased through a more informal configuration than even that proposed by the virtual network consortia.[29]

What's so different about the joint services company model?

I have shied away from using the term 'outsourcing' for most of this chapter because it normally conjures up failed contractual arrangements, where one party has given an external party business to carry out on its behalf, usually under tightly worded legal-style conditions. Too often the 'performance' measures become self-fulfilling prophecies of failure! Within two or three years the business is again back in-house and the 3PL is discarded. We have witnessed this scenario many times during the past few decades, as neither the principal (owner of the business being transacted) nor the 3PL provider has been able to find the right balance between capability, price, innovation and service.

The joint service companies model is a far different proposition. The structure of the organization, its motivation/reward systems and funding arrangements are all designed to bring together parties that have the necessary array of capabilities for a particular task. These ingredients are critical for success. The one-to-one contracts used with 3PLs have failed in all but the most common operational situations. As customers become more demanding, particularly in the fast-moving consumer goods, automotive and electronic high-technology industries, suppliers must look for solutions outside their own resources and those of their immediate 3PL contractors. These solutions will require the unique combination of a particular array of capabilities for a specific task that are only available from across multiple organizations. Selecting and bringing such parties together, and keeping them motivated and rewarded for a significant period (say seven to ten years), is the challenge facing many global multinational companies today. While there are three main options (and variations around each), the one most likely to achieve a quantum improvement in performance is the JSC business model, as shown in Figure 9.10.

Based on the parameters in Figure 9.9, it seems almost foolhardy to either a) embark on major change programmes and take all the up-front risk while waiting for the promised benefits to accrue (traditional consulting) or b) lose control of particular business functions in pursuit of short-term cost reductions (traditional outsourcing), when a third option exists. This is the development of a co-owned, co-managed delivery model where capability is built and executed very fast in order to provide shareholders with almost immediate results. This is what global financial centres want to see, and this is how to give it to them. The paradox is that this approach is technically easier and less risky to engineer in change management terms. It will deliver much improved results, faster and better than taking what appears to be the safer, slower, internal change management pathway to improved performance. In the end, it is the internal cultural *forces of darkness* that will undo the best laid transformational plans, and have done many times in the past. But there are risks in the suggested approach as well, which we will now consider more closely.

The structure, motivation and funding options that define strategic transformation programmes place clear daylight between the value of this approach compared to either traditional contract-style outsourcing or 1990s-style consulting services

Feature	Client-hosted solution	Outsourcing solution	Strategic transformation and joint services company
Ownership and risk	Born 100 per cent in-house	Contracted out	Jointly owned
People	Bought-in resources	Transferred	Enhanced career path
Objective	Process improvement	Cost reduction	Share price growth
Motivation	Policy and compliance	Cost reduction	Mutual shared goals
Incentives	Milestones	Cost-based service rewards	Fusion of all partners' share prices
Funding	100 per cent in-house	Outsourcing provider	Own, other third parties
Focus	Template roll-out	Cost reduction	Capability at speed
Control	Programme management	By contract only	Improved and flexible
Future option	Sustain non-core activity	Return difficult	ROI easier to get
Strategy	Better IT	Cost reduction	Market leadership

Why should a company embark on such a pivotal change programme and either (a) take all the risk and the upfront costs while waiting for the benefits (traditional consulting) or (b) lose control of business functions in pursuit of short-term cost reductions (traditional outsourcing) when there is a co-owned execution model able to build capability to drive shareholder value with immediate results?

FIGURE 9.10 ◆ **Comparing the three outsourcing options**

Risks associated with forming a JSC

Clearly, forming any new business model carries its share of risks. But for 4PLs®, many if not most of these risks were flushed out during the prototype era of 1994 to 2004. The way to reduce the risks is to study them in detail and consider the remedies.

1. Founding partners

The first and perhaps most difficult task is to find at least two founding partners of like minds for the JSC. The principal partners can be drawn from the same industry, or a related industry. The key is to find two enterprises, preferably at the big end of their industry, that have products with the same or similar *handling* characteristics and/or going to the same or similar delivery destinations. If two such parties cannot be found, or if they can be found but are not willing to pool their businesses to significantly increase scale, then it's simply not possible to launch this class of business model. In other words, don't try it!

But you could try looking in the large process industries, where companies have downsized for several years and cannot find any new avenues for reducing costs. They offer a good potential source for partner enterprises. Another source could be fragmented industries where only a few majors exist, beyond which there is a long tail of small to medium-sized enterprises; an example is the pharmaceutical industry. In both cases, a JSC configuration will bring major benefits to both major and minor (complementary) parties that join the original venture.

By the way, the idea often gets stifled at this point by senior executives who use the 'we are not prepared to give up our competitive advantage in logistics' argument, or, 'we really believe this is the way to go but we don't want to be the first'. Interestingly, every time I hear these comments opposing the formation of a JSC, it invariably comes from executives in enterprises whose logistics and supply chain performance is nothing near 'competitive' in the first place; they are quite simply in denial.

2. Ownership structure

Once the two (or three, maximum) principal partners have been identified and agree to spin-off a new management company to manage their joint logistics operations, it is time to agree the all-important equity structure. The principal partners will usually take the majority of the equity between them. The next task is to decide on what specialist capabilities are needed to service the combined business, and from where these are likely to be sourced. It is all about *capabilities*, and these should be sourced from 'best practice' enterprises which then become complementary or minor equity partners in the new venture. **Equity** is essential for all active members of the consortium, because it provides the basic motivation to stay together and help each other in a non-contractual environment. The other part of this motivation is provided by setting appropriate performance milestones and corresponding incentives/rewards, which all parties share according to their equity position. These elements of the organization design will make a big difference if and when the going gets tough. No such fall-back is in place for the so-called 4PL® provider that is formed through the tender process. Yet, several enterprises have tried to go this route.[30]

3. Perceived independence

A board and executive team should be installed to run the new entity so that the newly formed JSC is perceived to be independent from its major shareholders. Independence could become a vital issue if you later decide to publicly list the new company and launch it as a supply chain provider in its own right. Such a scenario would have been thought impossible some years ago, but it's likely to be played out in a number of countries as pressure on margins builds to intolerable levels.

4. Secondment of best talent

You should look to second or permanently transfer the best talent from the founding enterprises to the new (virtual) management company. This is an essential ingredient for success. Transferring staff can help you to sidestep the usual internal resistance to change and put in place only those personnel who passionately want to be involved in the new venture. It is important to minimize the cultural differences between staff in the JSC, and indeed to shape a new culture quickly. The design of the organization structure will be an important factor in success, and should be approached using the principles outlined in Chapters 5–8.

5. Organization life cycle

The principal shareholders should reach initial agreement on the life of the organization, minimum seven years, but preferably ten years, in the first phase. To lessen the concern in the formation stage it is recommended that a 'pre-nuptial' clause be agreed between all parties to the effect that at the end of the initially agreed life of the entity, the principals have the option to buy back their respective business and capabilities according to a pre-agreed formula. On the other hand, if the principals agree, the arrangement can be extended for another term, at which time a similar review and decision is contemplated. This clause provides the flexibility that did not exist in early versions of the original 4PL® business model and its absence may have contributed to the slow acceptance of that model.

6. Scope of operations

At a very early stage in the development of the JSC, you should define and agree on the exact scope of operations among all partners, and the partners' specific roles within that scope. The principle is that no party should be part of the JSC unless they bring one or more of the unique assets or capabilities required to execute the business of the venture.

7. Financial engineering

One of the most vital roles is the financial engineering of the new venture. The financials have to make the JSC immediately viable, and it is here that major financial service institutions (FSIs) have an opportunity to lead. Sadly, too many of our modern FSIs are not prepared to do so, and are missing out on huge opportunities to capture future revenue streams; but they must take some risk at the outset to reap later rewards. I strongly believe there is **less** risk for banks and other financial institutions in getting involved in this type of business model. As a principal partner, they would invariably have a seat at the board table, and would be able to influence the management of the new entity, rather than simply stand aside as an external observer and/or mortgage broker.

Some limited activity is already starting to happen in this area of financial engineering, with GE Commercial Finance (GECF) and Barclays

Bank taking the lead. GECF has combined with DHL to roll out a new inventory ownership product called Trade Distribution Services. This product is directly designed to address concerns of manufacturers with their cash-to-cash cycles and the consequent impact on working capital. Under the proposed arrangement, GE Commercial Finance takes ownership of the finished goods inventory from the seller's point of shipment until the buyer's just-in-time point of purchase. GE owns the inventory and DHL manages it while in transit between seller and buyer. There are benefits in this arrangement for all the parties involved, so we are likely to see more of the same as other enterprises recognize the benefits potentially available, at relatively low risk. Meanwhile Barclays have formed a dedicated group under the name Barclays Logistics, and they are pursuing the development of new financing products and limited involvement in JVs. They are treating this development as very much 'experimental' in the early stages.

8. Ability to meet performance milestones

Clearly, if targeted savings/benefits are not achieved on time the whole venture is at risk, as the equity players will not realize the forecasted ROI. But if the partners can meet the conditions described above it is unlikely that they will fail to achieve their targeted savings. At the outset, JSC managers should lay out the proposed milestones for the life of the venture; transparency in the initial stages is important for the cohesiveness of the new organization structure. This approach was followed by the former Andersen Consulting and North Sea oil exploration consortium in 1994, and proved to be a winning initiative.

But how will we achieve the *embedded alignment* referred to at the start of this chapter? The new 'service company' will ideally own little or no infrastructure, other than technology, and will in effect coordinate and manage an array of hand-picked 3PLs to achieve the desired outcomes. One of these outcomes will be to fulfil all the Service Level Agreements (SLAs) entered into with the owner-principals and other external organizations. This will by definition require the JSC to deliver different levels of service to achieve the multiple supply chain alignment already discussed in Chapter 2. However, it is more than likely that the new entity will be capable of delivering the required responses, in parallel, and cost-effectively; because it will be specifically designed to do this from the outset. This is in effect *embedded alignment*.

Going beyond the business that the founding partners bring to the JSC, there is a risk that future expansion will be limited if other companies in the industry, especially direct competitors, are unwilling to add their business to the growing pool. They may not have a choice if the model is designed well from the start, but if the cost economies of the JSC are not clearly evident, other companies may choose not to join the burgeoning industry supply chain solution. This is now less of a risk than a decade ago, but it becomes real if the JSC is launched without at least two major industry players.[31]

9. Availability of best 3PLs

Another early risk in forming a JSC is that the best 3PLs in the logistics industry, and relatively few exist across the globe, may not be immediately available because of long-term contractual commitments that cannot easily be set aside in the short term. It may be necessary to negotiate exits from existing contracts in crucial cases.

10. Excessive disruption

There is always the risk of excessive disruption to the existing business during the establishment phase of the JSC. The best strategy is to plan for this and then execute as fast as possible. Given that an entirely new organization is being set up, the risk of 'cultural resistance' will be minimal, and if the new staff members are selected carefully, most will welcome the rapid pace of change. Going slow in implementing change these days is a recipe for failure, because a slow pace allows competitors and internal forces alike to mount more strident defences. In any case it's unlikely that the disruption will be any worse than that encountered in an internal transformation project. At least in the case of the JSC, most if not all the action takes place 'off-line', thereby minimizing disruption to the mainstream business.

11. Culture

The cultural challenge for JSCs is to encourage *entrepreneurial* behaviour and embed an *innovation* subculture early in the life of the new organization, while encouraging a focus on continuous improvement. The current crop of 3PLs generally lack these cultural capabilities and will probably never have the resources and mindset to fully develop and sustain them. And yet these are the very attributes that client organizations desire most, because they know that it will reduce costs on a progressive and sustainable basis over time. The 'rate game' cannot be sustained indefinitely; something has to give.

12. The risk of doing nothing

The biggest risk of all of course is doing nothing, or just as bad, continuing to embrace traditional change management practices because they appear to be safe and risk free. Indeed, nothing could be further from the truth, as we have already demonstrated in Chapter 3. Transforming organizations is a risky business at the best of times, and attempting to carry out major change coincidentally with operating the company is akin to *DIY brain surgery* – which is seldom successful. Therefore, other less conventional ways must be sought to achieve the quantum improvements in operational and financial performance that await the brave.

Going forward

Increasingly in the future we can expect to see enterprises of all types experimenting with different combinations and permutations of business models in search of performance improvement. Although the risks associated with introducing new organization formats were once considered unacceptably high, the situation now is quite the reverse; the risk of **not** embracing new business models is even higher, and from what we now know about the difficulties of transforming organizations from the inside out, it is easy to see why this is so. However, as always, everything comes back to the quality of executive leadership, and their individual and joint resolve to innovate to succeed in the difficult times that surely lie ahead.

Living lessons

1   Incredible opportunities exist for those prepared to step up to the plate and go well beyond simple 'operational excellence'. We must wake up to the fact that it is 'supply chain versus supply chain' from now on!

2   Go all-out for cultural compatibility and alignment of objectives with your key partners and other consortium members, from the very start.

3   For any new model to be successful, it has to be equity-based; I regard this as one of my most important insights over the last few years. This type of arrangement helps to keep the consortium together and focused when the going gets tough, as it surely will at times.

CHAPTER 10

Delivering living supply chains

A bridge to the future

T his is not the end; rather, it is the beginning of the new era of *living supply chains*. We now know much more about the sometimes mysterious mechanisms that shape and drive today's complex supply chains. We know that viewing supply chains as a linear set of inanimate structures and systems both misunderstands the modern supply chain and underestimates its potential for being a source of competitive advantage. The real driver in the supply chain today is people: we are dealing with living systems propelled by the personality and behaviour of people both inside and outside of enterprises. Our *dynamic alignment model* showed us how to treat the supply chain as a set of dynamic mechanisms. This is no more linear than the complex, changing world in which we operate! For the first time, this model gives us a clearer view of our customer segments and helps us to show how to align the culture and leadership styles of the business to the dominant buying behaviour of each customer group. The *dynamic alignment* framework then helps us to work through the different types of supply chains likely to affect our business: how to understand, manage and synchronize to our advantage.

What do you think are the top strategic issues facing your supply chains? I believe that understanding the dynamism of the supply chain will help us to face the major challenges expected to appear over the horizon during the next ten years. There are certainly many – from the need to be socially responsible and sustainable, to managing fluctuating oil prices and their impact on supply and demand throughout the supply chain, through to gaining top talent in our supply chains and managing partnerships in new forms of outsourcing arrangements. Each new issue is likely to have a different impact on your business depending on your preparedness – whether you analyze and prioritize the issues as they emerge or whether you fail to consider the future and simply react to crisis after crisis, engulfing your business in uncertainty. In this final chapter we will explore how *dynamic alignment* in our supply chains can help us to weather the storm and make life more beneficial for customers, employees and shareholders alike.

Here come the Exocets

As we begin to understand more about the world in which supply chains operate, it is a case of the more we find out, the more we realize we don't know. We have come a fair way in the past 40 years, but there is a lot more we need to learn in the next decade. There is always some warning of future events, however subtle, and Kenneth McGee of Gartner, Inc., quotes examples such as Three Mile Island and the Space Shuttle *Challenger*, to demonstrate this point.[1]

After scanning the horizon, I have come up with 13 issues, or Exocets, that I think will affect the way enterprise supply chains perform during the next ten years. To help us prioritize this list, I will use an issues analysis technique that I developed in the 1980s.[2] It is simple to use, but very effective. Indeed, I still find executives using this technique 15 years after I first introduced them to it. First, however, let me define an 'issue'. An 'issue' is anything that is either impacting now or will impact at some time in the future on the performance of the organizational unit under review; in this case, enterprise supply chains. An 'issue' defined in this way can come from anywhere in the organization's operating environment, which is why I refer to them as Exocets. But unlike a real Exocet, they may have either a positive or negative influence on their target. My approach involves listing and briefly describing each issue in no particular order, then assessing the priority of each to the business and plotting each issue on the impact/urgency matrix; see Figure 10.1. The guidelines for this approach are described in each box of the 3 × 3 matrix. This is, in effect, a prioritization technique designed to help you to assess the issues and then guide decisions about where to allocate resources in order to alleviate or enhance their impact.

		Impact		
		Low	Significant	Major
Urgency	Low	New entry	Periodic review	Monitor continuously
	Significant	Periodic review	Closely monitor	Planned/ delayed response
	Pressing	Monitor	Planned/ quick response	Crisis – response immediately

FIGURE 10.1 ◆ **Critical strategic issues impact/urgency matrix framework**

How do issues emerge in your business? Do they suddenly occur in a crash, as a crisis? Or do they linger on the horizon for some time before unleashing their full force? You will see in Figure 10.1 that issues normally enter the matrix at the top left-hand box, where they very often go unnoticed. Over the succeeding years they can drift around in the matrix, and may not be noticed until they reach crisis proportions and appear in the bottom right-hand box. Then it's time for 'crisis management'. Many executives spend their lives doing nothing more than reacting to the issues that become crises. The idea of the impact/urgency matrix is to push back the boundaries, study the issues as they occur, so that you can get out of crisis mode. Interestingly, issues are like radio waves – they are in the air that surrounds us, but we can only do something about them early if we tune in to the right wavelength. So, once we have clearly identified an issue and understood the likely implications of its presence, we can either continue to monitor its progress or take immediate or more measured action. If the matrix is re-visited on a regular (say quarterly or six-monthly) basis, the movement of issues can be monitored and action taken in a proactive way. The aim of course is to avoid further crises.

I remember working with John Rickard, Group Chief Executive of Hooper Baillie Industries, an Australian mini conglomerate, during the mid-1980s. His problem was that the board was acquiring diverse companies often without involving him; e.g., tanneries, vineyards and office interiors. John was always in a 'crisis'. One day about a year after we had been systematically plotting and managing the issues that arose across his various businesses, he remarked to me, 'I feel there's something wrong – I don't seem to have any crises these days,' or words to this effect! What had happened was that the issues management technique had helped him get ahead of the crisis and anticipate events so that he had more time to do what he was paid for as Chief Executive: lead the conglomerate, provide direction and work more systematically on shaping his portfolio of businesses to achieve the desired performance.

Global critical strategic issues facing supply chains of the future

The 13 strategic issues likely to have an impact on the performance of your supply chains over the next ten years are listed below. I have listed them in no particular order – and kept them that way – because it is important to keep our minds open and avoid jumping to conclusions too early. Instead, we want to appraise honestly the priority of each. The issues are briefly summarized below – I will give a more detailed analysis shortly:

1 **Sustainability** in supply chains in the light of pressures for ecological, social and corporate responsibility.

2 The **impact of oil prices** on the cost-to-serve.

3 The future practice of **outsourcing**, in all its forms.

4 The adoption of supply chain 'principles' by **service organizations**.

5 **Vulnerability** of supply chains; designs with embedded **resilience**.

6 The rise of **genuine collaboration** in supply chains.

7 Tapping the **talent** inside and outside enterprises.

8 Learning to design and manage **multiple organization formats**.

9 Coping with the national, regional and global **spread of supply chain networks**.

10 Adoption of the **whole-of-enterprise mindset** in managing supply chain operations.

11 **Collaborating with the enemy.**

12 **Innovation, product design and product life cycles.**

13 Learning to manage **inherent complexity** in supply chains.

Is that a priority? Assessing where to put the effort

Your enterprise could be operating in quite a unique environment and therefore have different strategic issues to those listed above. But I have judged these issues using my experience across a broad range of sectors and assigned each a specific level of priority, as shown in Figure 10.2.

I will discuss each of the top-priority issues and comment briefly on how the application of *dynamic alignment* principles may assist in resolving each. I will start with 1 and 5; then 2 and 12; and finally 3, 8, 6 and 13 in that order. This is the suggested order of priority for your business, until resources run out.

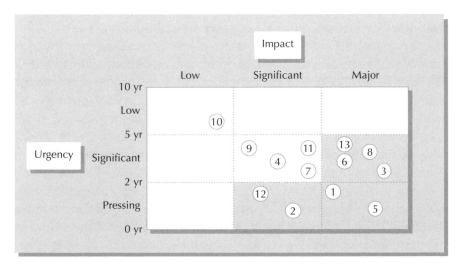

FIGURE 10.2 ◆ **Assessment of critical strategic issues facing enterprise supply chains**

Sustainability in supply chains

Sustainability is a big issue, looming large in the minds of all types of enterprises, public and private. Rising community pressure over human rights and globalization brought sustainability to prominence in the 1990s. Businesses were forced to 'take a closer look at sustainable development, particularly its social dimension', writes Charles Holliday in his book *Walking the Talk*:

> *Companies such as Shell, Nike, and BP were unprepared for consumers' ability to get their concerns into the boardrooms. In a globalised and transparent world, managing a company's reputation becomes a central element in managing a corporation.*[3]

Sustainability is therefore a relatively new concept, albeit a complex one. When supply chains, also underdeveloped as a concept, are added to the mix, complexity increases. 'Nevertheless, this is where business, value creation and sustainability meet reality, in difficult-to-manage and increasingly globalised and commoditized supply chains,' a report on sustainability in the supply chain points out. 'Sustainability in the supply chain is fundamentally about identifying problematic social, environmental and H&S [Health & Safety] issues throughout the supply chain, assessing their impacts and risks, and then trying to improve them.'[4]

Investors and fund managers are not only increasingly scrutinizing companies for their supply chain performance, as discussed in Chapter 9, but they are also looking at the enterprise's performance on sustainability issues, including the environment, human rights, occupational health and safety, ethics and social responsibility. Australian funds manager AMP Capital Investors is one such firm. Senior research analyst Dr Ian Woods reviews company performance against sustainability criteria in order to decide whether to recommend investment in such firms. The reason for doing so is clear, says Woods: 'sustainable companies in the end will outperform other enterprises'.[5] AMP and other firms have mounted a Sustainable Future Funds Research effort to understand if there are any risks associated in investing in these companies, beyond the normal financial analyses. A recent article in *Fortune* magazine seems to reinforce this trend to look beyond the bottom line and demand corporate social responsibility from the Fortune Global 100 and others.[6] This subject is getting hot!

Putting in place sustainability policies, and often publicly reporting on the results, is paying off for enterprises such as BP, BT, Intel, Procter & Gamble and Tesco; they have all been acknowledged and admired for their stand on corporate social responsibility.[7] Interestingly, they all have strongly performing supply chains integral to their businesses. While not suggesting there is a causal link here, the same sound thinking that drove them to pursue sustainable growth policies is likely to be the same as their approach to their supply chains. This demonstrates an ability to think and behave in the face of complexity. The pharmaceutical company Novo Nordisk's approach to sustainable supply chain management is firmly rooted in the twin principles of company values and risk management. The company has developed its own self-evaluation programme which it administers to suppliers, and if necessary it requires its suppliers to submit to social and environmental audits. One company that does see things a little differently from many others is IKEA. Goran Carstedt, former Volvo and IKEA Senior Executive, thinks the leadership challenge 'is to stop treating companies like machines that need to be driven', and as his friend Aric de Geus wrote seven years ago in *The Living Company*, 'accept that a company is a community with all the complexity of a living organism'.[8] His attitude to sustainability is summed up as follows: 'it's so sad when people think the purpose of business is shareholder value alone. That's like saying the purpose of life is oxygen. Of course it's needed, but it's the customers, co-workers, and the organization's place in society that create that value, and that's why they have to come first.'[9]

There is a cost to sustainability, a real cost in terms of the financial and human resources required, with no immediate prospects of payback. But it's becoming a requirement of doing business, just as occupational health and safety (OH&S) is now part of every business. The companies that don't move forward with sustainability initiatives will in the end be forced to do so by government policy. If they wait until they are coerced, the danger is they will be well behind their competitors. Leading companies are acting to ensure they are ahead of the regulatory game. Witness environmental policies that are now commonplace – clean air requirements to reduce air pollution, environmental impact assessments for new developments and reporting on greenhouse gas emissions. Interestingly, one notable company which is not high on the corporate social responsibility list is Wal-Mart. However, after being criticized for its operating practices, the company has developed a new set of priorities that signals a substantial shift (for the better) in its stance on environmental and social issues.[10] No firm is too big to ignore the growing demands for more sustainable practices.

Several companies are starting to extend sustainability principles across their supply chain. Nestlé Philippines Inc. (NPI) has launched a Greening of the Supply Chain (GSC) initiative involving 42 of its upstream channel partners.[11] The GSC initiative involves educating business partners on environmental management. The initiative has improved performance and relationships between NPI and its suppliers. Adidas-Salomon, the footwear and apparel company, which outsources most of its production to more than 500 factories around the world, demands that all its suppliers adopt self-governance on the sustainability issue. Adidas-Salomon has implemented a system of scoring and monitoring suppliers' performance on social and environmental matters.[12] Major competitor Nike, the global footwear and sports clothing company, was the first in the industry to disclose its supplier base in its new corporate social responsibility report. Nike believes 'the potential benefits to industry and factory workers outweigh the possible competitive risks'.[13]

The issue is not going away and indeed will loom larger in the next decade, particularly for those companies falling behind in this area. Application of *dynamic alignment* principles will help us to pinpoint and understand the areas of potential mis-alignment between all the stakeholders in particular industry supply chains and more broadly – remember, *dynamic alignment*, first and foremost applies to whole enterprises, not just to the supply chains they are part of. However, it can be used to guide the formulation of strategies to close identified gaps where sustainability is the focus, and the benefits that flow from this action to stakeholders will vary.

Vulnerability of supply chains[14]

Sudden failures in supply chains can be due to a multitude of causes, including the following:[15]

◆ Disruptions: natural disasters, terrorism and war.

◆ Delays: due to inflexibility of supply.

◆ Systems: failure of technology infrastructure.

◆ Forecast: inaccurate forecasts; lack of forecasting.

◆ Capacity: capacity inflexibility ... and the list goes on.

One such failure occurred in March 2000 when lightening hit a power pole in Albuquerque, New Mexico. The strike caused a massive surge in the surrounding electrical grid, which in turn started a fire at a local plant owned by Royal Philips Electronics, NV, damaging millions of microchips. Nokia, a major customer of the plant, almost immediately began switching its chip orders to other Philips plants, as well as to other Japanese and American suppliers. Thanks to its multiple-supplier strategy and responsiveness, Nokia's production suffered little during the crisis. In contrast, L.M. Ericsson, another mobile-phone customer of the Philips plant, employed a single-sourcing policy. As a result, when the Philips plant shut down after the fire, Ericsson had no other source of microchips, which disrupted its production for months. Ultimately, Ericsson lost $400 million in sales.[16]

This was a spectacular example where two different approaches to risk led to very different outcomes; but many more risks abound in the way supply chains are designed and operated. For instance, if *lean* principles are taken too far, and stocks of components and finished goods in the pipeline are reduced to very low levels to cut costs, it will become susceptible to even the smallest disruption in supply or fluctuation in demand. In these situations, it is prudent to hold reserves of inventory along the supply chain in different stages of completion. This in-built redundancy costs money, but this has to be offset against the cost of lost sales and lost customers through non-supply.

Given the rise of terrorism, which has injected even more uncertainty into the operation of global supply chains, the solution is to put much more thought into developing risk mitigation strategies, **before** something happens. Hau Lee and Michael Wolfe suggest six strategies:[17]

1 Comprehensive tracking and monitoring – to detect a security breach at the earliest possible stage.

2 Total supply chain visibility – so that you can respond in a meaningful way once the extent and location of a security breach or other disruption is known.

3   Flexible sourcing strategies – we saw how important this is in the case of the fire at the Philips microchip plant.

4   Balanced inventory management – the importance of reviewing 'safety stocks' has been brought back into focus, after years of cutting and trimming inventories to reduce costs.

5   Product and process re-design – this has taken on new significance, and led directly to the development of postponement techniques. Indeed, one of the strategies used by Nokia to mitigate the problems caused by the fire at the Philips plant was to re-design its microchips so that they could be sourced from alternative suppliers.

6   Demand-based management – which means influencing demand with pricing and other offers to upgrade to the next level of product. Dell does this very well.

The *fully flexible* supply chain configuration, described in detail in Chapter 8, would help to secure supply chains in most eventualities and protect them against vulnerability to sudden shocks. In particular, the cluster organization design and corresponding *entrepreneurial* subculture are essential ingredients for success in such unforgiving circumstances. Indeed, Professor Yossi Sheffi of MIT highlights the role of culture in his book *The Resilient Enterprise*.[18] He too believes that resilience and flexibility in an organization derive largely from having the appropriate culture in place.

In the context of the *dynamic alignment* model, a fast-reacting entrepreneurial subculture will often be the key to aligning your firm successfully, irrespective of the processes and technology. Nokia demonstrated this when the fire occurred at its microchip supplier; Dell epitomizes the fast-moving culture of a high-tech company, as does DHL in its express business. All the necessary traits for developing a resilient organization, underpinned by an *entrepreneurial* subculture, have been discussed in Chapter 8. Yossi Sheffi has also defined similar elements for achieving the necessary dynamic culture for a *fully flexible* supply chain; these are:[19]

◆   continuous communications among informed employees;

◆   distributed power;

◆   passion for work; and

◆   conditioning for disruption.

Changing and shaping the culture so that it can cope with sudden disruptive events in supply chains is the key starting point in preparing for unexpected events. Anything can happen – it's just a matter of where and when. So we shall see much more emphasis on developing both variants of *fully flexible* supply chains in the future.

Impact of oil prices on cost-to-serve

No one knows where the oil price will go over the next five to ten years, but high oil prices will clearly have a negative impact on the global economy, and therefore on the supply chains that link national and regional economies. If, for instance, rising oil prices cause a shift in customer buying behaviours throughout supply chains, it may mean each supply chain party has to change their emphasis. High oil prices of more than US$60 per barrel will significantly affect both the energy input costs for manufacturing and the fuel costs for all types of transport. To stay aligned with any shifts in customer preferences, enterprises will need to watch markets very carefully, and adjust inputs to production, production processes and transportation arrangements. If you do this, you will postpone any rise in cost-to-serve for as long as possible.

Innovation, product design and product life cycles

The variability of supply and demand are the two big killers of smooth supply chain operations. However, you can reduce some of the variability in supply through smart design that allows for ease of manufacture and assembly (postponement). You will need to have quality assessment routines in place, particularly in the early stages of a new product launch. Innovation will also be vital, not just in the product development stage but throughout the supply chain itself. Today many enterprises favour innovation in product and product design rather than innovation in manufacturing and supply chain areas. On the demand side, you can avoid variability by strategically stocking product at various locations along the supply chain, essentially building capacity ahead of demand. This also means ensuring contract manufacturers build manufacturing capacity and trained people capacity, ahead of demand. This may break some *lean* principles, but if a specific product requires unrelenting agility, then building in redundant capacity is the only answer. The cost has to be weighed against the potential for lost revenue by keeping to more conventional cost-based methods in managing the supply chain. Finally, in some product-supply chain combinations, complexity rises exponentially quicker than the growth in product sales, and in this situation significant innovation is usually required at process, technology and people levels. To achieve *dynamic alignment*, continuous improvement and innovation must be pursued in all four types of supply chain, although here again the subcultures that underpin innovation are not naturally present in *continuous replenishment* and *lean* supply chains, and therefore the task is all that much harder.

Future practice of outsourcing, in all its forms

It is becoming clear that outsourcing is not a simple exercise, for either the outsourcer or outsourcee. As was outlined in Chapter 9, enterprises outsource for one main reason: to access required *capabilities* and to do so at a minimum cost. Unfortunately, most companies that have either outsourced the manufacture of key products and components, or outsourced logistics functions, have often not had a happy ending to their adventures.

Management consultancy Booz Allen Hamilton reported in 2001 that high-tech companies such as Cisco, Sony, Palm, Compaq (now Hewlett-Packard), Apple and Philips had found that outsourcing had not met their expectations and had in fact caused some of the difficulties in their operational and financial performance.[20] The report highlighted one of the major flaws in outsourcing: the inevitable and basic conflict of objectives between the original equipment manufacturers (OEMs) and contract equipment manufacturers (CEMs) who actually made the product. In short, OEMs such as Cisco need 'flexibility' to meet sudden changes in demand; and CEMs such as Solectron and Jabil Circuit need 'predictability' rather than flexibility for their production schedules. Never the two shall meet! This remains a big issue today, which is making supply chains rougher rather than smoother to manage.

A more recent study by Deloitte Consulting highlights that some of the world's largest organizations have started to recognize 'the real costs and inherent risks of outsourcing'.[21] The report argues that 'organizations looking for differentiated growth solutions should avoid outsourcing when based solely on cost saving'. Further, 'companies should outsource only commodity functions to guard against a loss of knowledge and should plan for short-term outsourcing to prevent vendor dependency'.[22] Zara does just this; in fact, it keeps the difficult work inside and only outsources the simple tasks.

Do any of the problems and issues highlighted by Deloitte sound familiar to you? I believe the new business model proposed in Chapter 9 will deliver a more successful approach to outsourcing for today's economy and labour market. The model brings together companies that want work done along their supply chains, with other parties that have the particular capabilities to best carry out these tasks. The organizational format can be a partnership or, better still, an equity-based consortium. The parties in a consortium should be able to make good returns, but most importantly of all, the principals (OEMs or retail distributors) which own the business retain control of their business, and are rewarded for creating scale of operations and knowledge. The *dynamic alignment* model is useful in these circumstances because it helps to ensure that rapid alignment is achieved in the new joint venture, highlighting how to make the objectives, culture and leadership of all the parties compatible.

When I worked at the Australian consulting firm Accenture, our consulting assignments certainly revealed some of the best and the worst of outsourcing arrangements operating at the time. Accenture has listed its top five considerations in achieving better outsourcing[23] and it is useful to discuss these here as they reinforce the features of the JSC model we discussed in Chapter 9. Get these features of the outsourcing arrangement right and the benefits will flow.

1. Have a partnering approach to outsourcing

Your selection of the right partner is crucial, and is now regarded as one of the new *competences* that enterprises must be good at. Once the selection is complete, you have to commit to each other in virtually a 'professional marriage', and managing the relationship becomes the key to success. It's important that the partner be both competency and culturally compatible. Key attributes to look for in a partner are:

◆ *demonstrated leadership*, capability and a track record for delivery in outsourced activity;

- *flexibility* in approach, and willingness to shape a contract that works for both parties;

- willingness to take on business risk-reward contract structure – business is of a strategic nature to the supplier as well as the buyer; and

- willingness to be transparent and open in working towards mutual trust as well as risk and reward.

So, *flexibility, team approach, trust, shared objectives and compatible culture* are all vital ingredients of success in outsourcing deals. For these to occur, both companies need to share similar relationship values and business outcomes. The cultures need to mesh so that both parties are in agreement about what end results to focus on. The *dynamic alignment* model will be a useful tool at this point.

2. Use outsourcing to drive strategic change

A significant success factor is to use outsourcing to achieve enterprise-wide strategic impact on the buyer's organization, rather than outsourcing to accomplish lower operational costs or higher process efficiencies. The outsourcing relationship should be used to achieve business objectives that cannot be accomplished by the buyer organization without leveraging the strong points of the service provider's organization.

3. Use risk-reward structures to motivate performance

Incentive-based pricing structures pay significant dividends. As usual it is a case of 'the greater the risk, the greater the reward'. The reward is not paid to the service provider unless they meet the specified desired result of the buyer organization. Incentive-based pricing or risk-reward structures are always evident in successful outsourcing arrangements. These structures provide an effective way to motivate providers to achieve challenging goals that will greatly impact the buyer organization's ability to compete.

Examples of risk-reward structures include the following:

- Gain share on savings achieved on operational costs.

- A reward for improved performance.

- A combination of the above.

◆ A reward for achieving a unique objective, such as target cost-to-serve or percentage movement in share price.

4. Adopt a beneficial deal structure

You should be prepared to spend time up-front on developing joint objectives. Structure the deal using business principles that are beneficial to both parties. Due diligence is also a critical step and should be used to establish the governance structure, joint business objectives and commercial payment structure. You should also clearly articulate the desired business outcomes and key success factors and measures.

Partnership 'operating principles' should also be built into the programme. Agree working principles that ensure a 'win–win' relationship. Share information openly to secure a robust business case. And spend time understanding each other and company philosophies.

5. Avoid outsourcing problems

Poor due diligence or assessment can have a negative impact on the outsourcing arrangement. Some of the problems include the following:

◆ Buyer not prepared at various stages of the process, e.g., value of assets may not be known; lack of resources through transition and implementation phases. **Recommendation:** you need to work with the partner to capture baseline data, and assign dedicated resources to work on the deal to clearly identify business objectives, desired outcomes and potential risks.

◆ Buyer has unrealistic expectations, eg., buyers often do not understand their roles and responsibilities during and post-transition. **Recommendation:** agree business principles and roles and responsibilities early during discussions with outsourcing partner.

◆ Buyer makes poor judgements, e.g., ineffective service level specifications; lack of linkage of contract to business outcomes. **Recommendation:** agree business outcomes and link service level agreements to outcomes.

Learning to design and manage multiple organization formats

Where to then, for your organization design? Clearly, a simple, straightforward format of days past will not provide the appropriate mixture of supply chains needed to respond effectively to the desires of today's customers. Your supply chain performance will depend on your ability to design and manage three or four organizational formats within your one current organization structure. This sounds like a complex task, and it is. But if we accept that the marketplace for most product categories is fragmenting, then we must also accept that this shift will have to be reflected in the way organization structures are configured. This book has stressed that customers exhibit several dominant buying behaviours; now you will need at least four types of organization structure to cover these primary behaviours, as depicted in Figure 10.3.

No doubt maintaining the coexistence of four sometimes opposing organization formats inside a single enterprise is something you have studiously avoided in the past. But it's become obvious that the old singular formats cannot possibly respond to the emerging range of different buying behaviours of customers today. Leading management thinker Peter Drucker has in effect been saying something similar for more than 30 years. In 1974 he wrote that:

> *an organization should be multiaxial, that is, structured around work and task, and results and performance, and relationships, and decisions. It would function as if it were a biological organism, like the human body with its skeleton and muscles, a number of nervous systems, and with circulatory, digestive, immuno-logical, and respiratory systems, all autonomous yet interdependent. But in social structures we are still limited to designs that express only one primary dimension.*
>
> *So, in designing organizations, we have to choose among different structures, each stressing a different dimension and each, therefore, with distinct costs, specific and fairly stringent requirements, and real limitations. There is no risk-free organization structure. And a design that is the best solution for one task may be only one of a number of equally poor alternatives for another task, and just plain wrong for yet a third kind of work.*[24]

How prophetic his words were!

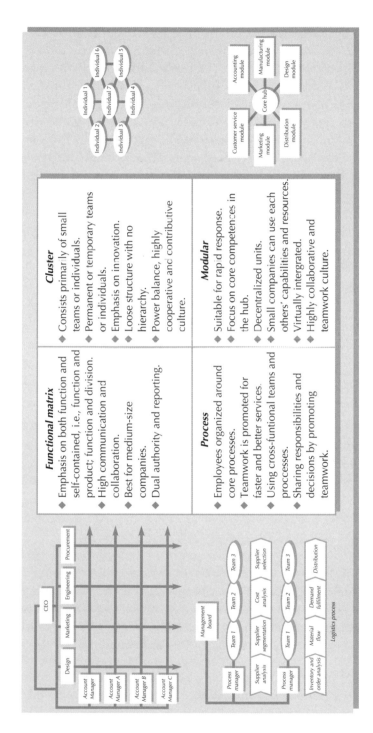

Functional matrix
- Emphasis on both function and self-contained, i.e., function and product; function and division.
- High communication and collaboration.
- Best for medium-size companies.
- Dual authority and reporting.

Cluster
- Consists primarily of small teams or individuals.
- Permanent or temporary teams or individuals.
- Emphasis on innovation.
- Loose structure with no hierarchy.
- Power balance, highly cooperative and contributive culture.

Process
- Employees organized around core processes.
- Teamwork is promoted for faster and better services.
- Using cross-funtional teams and proccesses.
- Sharing responsibilities and decisions by promoting teamwork.

Modular
- Suitable for rapid response.
- Focus on core competences in the hub.
- Decentralized units.
- Small companies can use each others' capabilities and resources.
- Virtually intergrated.
- Highly collaborative and teamwork culture.

FIGURE 10.3 ◆ **Multiple organization formats within an enterprise**

How do you view organizational structures? I see them acting as the 'straitjackets' in which we put people to work; work structures have an inordinately powerful impact on the performance of the enterprise as a whole, and its supply chains in particular. Hierarchies have thrived for too long and largely outlived their usefulness. The functional mindset that dominates so many enterprises needs to be broken down and dispersed into process, modular and cluster organizational formats if maximum value is to be extracted for all stakeholders. Kraft is one of the few organizations that has developed several different formats inside its walls, and linked them in practical ways that work. See Figure 10.4.[25]

Other variants are also urgently required to align the enterprise with its rapidly fragmenting market. The McKinsey 'atom' structure,[26] which disaggregated organizations into smaller decision-making units to force greater accountability at lower levels of the organization, has already been briefly reviewed in Chapter 7. Donald Sull reports that Haier, China's largest home appliance manufacturer, has adopted what he calls a *flexible hierarchy* structure.[27] This is 'an organizational form in which top executives set top–down priorities for the organization, but allow middle managers and employees great latitude in negotiating their specific objectives and autonomy in executing them'.[28] This sounds very much like a mixture of the hierarchical/functional and modular organizational formats depicted in Figure 10.3. Whatever the case, the point is to recognize the importance of organization design in achieving alignment of the enterprise and its supply chains with the marketplace, and focus enough of your thinking and resources to radically improve your current practices. As you've probably gathered by now, this is a crucial area where much work remains to be done in the next decade.

The rise of genuine collaboration in supply chains

Most likely I have said enough about this issue in Chapter 5, but it concerns me that seller enterprises continue to throw resources at buyer enterprises in supply chains, when there is clearly no chance of ever achieving equitable collaboration. You can talk about trust and governance all you like, but if the buyer enterprise doesn't have deeply embedded collaborative values, you can forget about collaboration. The task for management in the future is to read the situation earlier in the cycle of the buyer–seller relationship, and make a call whether or not you are in the *zone of collaboration*. In the meantime, let's cut the rhetoric!

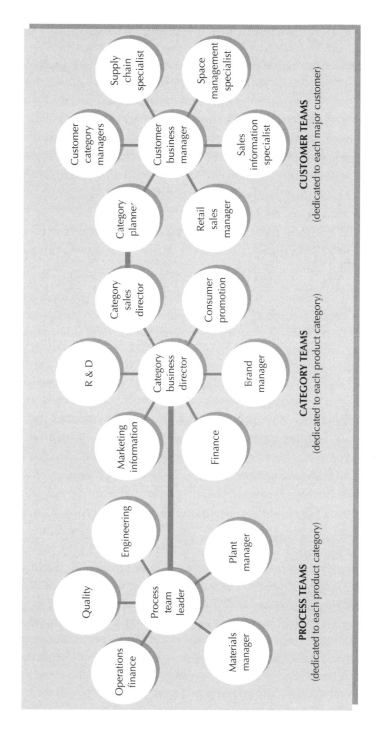

PROCESS TEAMS
(dedicated to each product category)

CATEGORY TEAMS
(dedicated to each product category)

CUSTOMER TEAMS
(dedicated to each major customer)

FIGURE 10.4 ◆ **Managing through different types of teams at Kraft**

Source Adapted from Figure 6.7 in Christopher and Peck (2003), p. 121

Learning to manage inherent complexity in supply chains

I doubt if you or any other senior manager today will argue with my contention that 'complexity' is increasing. Complexity comes in many forms, but to mention a few, there is the proliferation in SKUs; shorter product life cycles; demands by customers for ever quicker service; external factors such as increasing oil prices; an imbalance of power in many industries; and the list goes on. Where can we go for some respite from this multi-headed, accelerating band-wagon which is practically unavoidable in today's world? Our problem is that complexity will define today's and tomorrow's world. There's no hiding from it.

Let's turn to scientific theory for some guidance on how to cope with complexity. *Ashby's Law of Requisite Variety*[29] is one of the laws common to all systems. To paraphrase, it says that as systems become more complex through increased variety, then the corresponding complexity-resolution devices have to become equally sophisticated. In effect, if we want to manage complexity in supply chains – and supply chains are *living systems* – we have to absorb 'variety', otherwise the whole system is likely to become unstable, and worse, it may collapse, in some cases catastrophically. To overcome potential instability, systems have to be designed with in-built redundancy to allow them to suffer unexpected shocks. If we try to eradicate all redundancy, such as in the pursuit of ever lower costs in supply chains, the supply chains are likely to become brittle and fail. We have to embed redundancy into certain types of supply chains, in particular *agile* and *fully flexible* supply chains, if they are to be flexible and resilient enough for some sections of the market. In light of this, perhaps we have brought a lot of complexity upon ourselves by trying to squeeze too much out of our previous supply chain designs. They are simply not equipped to cope with the changing demand patterns. This realization only reinforces the need to recognize and implement the concept of *multiple supply chain alignment*. And this is a dynamic situation – different supply chain configurations will need to operate either in parallel to or in some linear combination. The future world will look like this whether we like it or not.

Monitor the rest

I expect you will find that issues 4, 7, 9, 10 and 11 will fall into the monitoring category. However, like all issues, it's possible that some will move into the (shaded) area of Figure 10.2 and require resources and direct action in the years ahead. In the meantime, a parting word on each.

Adoption of supply chain 'principles' by service organizations

Service enterprises vary in only one respect from product enterprises: their product is an intangible service. They still have networks of nodes, all of which are some form of processing point, or dispensing point for their services. And these nodes where all the activity takes place are usually tied into an information network. Banks, indeed all kinds of financial service institutions, are examples of institutions that have multiple supply chains or pathways running through them. And yet very few of these institutions have systematically adopted supply chain principles to shape their various responses to the marketplace. They are years behind product companies in this respect, and the gap continues to grow. A great opportunity awaits discovery.

Tapping the talent inside and outside enterprises

Growing or acquiring talent is likely to be one of the biggest issues for the most successful (and unsuccessful) businesses over the next decade. For some, especially the large global consultancies, this issue is already at crisis point, and in some cases is holding back the growth of their business. Perhaps an even bigger crisis for enterprises, and supply chain management, is how to develop leadership talent to execute the types of strategies suggested in this book. Unfortunately, 'many executives believe that leadership development is a job for the human resources department. This may be the single biggest misconception they can have.'[30] Going hand-in-hand with talent is the requirement to help these key players in the enterprise with personal knowledge management. These managers will need help to keep track of and manage the information they encounter in their daily working likes.[31] In fact, today's organizational designs are particularly difficult for knowledge workers or professionals because of the difficulties of moving information across functional boundaries.[32] John Mangan and Martin Christopher have provided a comprehensive review of the knowledge areas, competences and skills that tomorrow's supply chain managers will need to have, as a minimum.[33] It reads like a general manager's job description. Surprised? I don't think so.

Coping with the national, regional and global spread of supply chain networks

The globalization of supply chain operations is well established for the leading players in several industries, from electronics high-technology and fashion to automotive and third-party logistics. But for many other companies the wave is just breaking on them. What to do? My advice is to look and learn from the supply chain experiences of enterprises that have gone before you, irrespective of your industry.

Adoption of the whole-of-enterprise mindset in managing supply chain operations

This might seem a long way off, but I hope that one of the outcomes of this book is that more enterprises will realize the value in taking a whole-of-enterprise approach. One day I hope we can sound the death knell for the narrow myopic view of the supply chain that has characterized the development and management of logistics and supply chains over the past two decades. Perhaps no more telling is the realization that supply chain management today is a strategic business issue requiring top management attention. As US supply chain 'guru' Clifford Lynch said recently in a keynote speech delivered in Athens, '…in a globalized business environment, with goods without country, the only true Supply Chain Manager in a corporation is the CEO, because nobody else has full control of the cradle-to-grave process'.[34]

Collaborating with the enemy

Collaborating with competitors is difficult for two reasons. First, most executives cannot cope with the ambiguity of collaborating with a competitor in a joint venture in the supply chain, and at the same time competing in the marketplace. Well, get used to it, as the ambiguity is set to increase in the next decade. In some parts of the world, collaborating with competitors is the only way to achieve the scale to compete on a level footing with major international players that have more natural scale at their disposal.

And second, how do you draw the line between collaboration and collusion? That's tricky, especially when your reputation is at stake over any 'unfair' or restrictive trading practices. In the future you will see that companies have to manage the strict requirements of various government regulatory bodies that have been expressly set up to stop the domination of a few industry players over the majority of smaller players. We mentioned this issue in Chapter 9, but it's a long way from being resolved. Perhaps an education of the regulatory agencies on the modern supply chain is in order! Or at the very least, getting them involved in the design discussions at a very early stage.

Living institutions

Rather than end at the beginning, it seems apt that we should end with evolution. In their book *Presence*, Peter Senge and his colleagues say that 'nowhere is it more important to understand the relation between parts and wholes than in the evolution of global institutions and the larger systems they collectively create'.[35] They point to the observation made by Arie de Geus in his book *The Living Company:* the twentieth century witnessed the emergence of a new species on Earth – large organizations, notably global corporations.[36] 'This is a historic development,' Senge *et al.* commented. 'Prior to the last hundred years, there were few examples of globe-spanning institutions. But today, global institutions are proliferating seemingly without bound, along with global infrastructures for finance, distribution, and supply, and communication they create'.[37] Clearly, these global institutions require the delivery capability, speed, agility and performance made possible by a global network of supply chains.

Even if you are not a global business, no organization can isolate itself from this phenomenon. Trying to segment your business according to single customers and targeting each and every one of them is simply not feasible. Now more than ever we need to understand how people behave and interact as groups within these extended supply chains. The *dynamic alignment* model we have outlined in this book seeks to give you a framework to understand the dominant types of supply chains and the dominant buying behaviours we can expect in these supply chain networks. As the name of Senge's book *Presence* suggests, supply chains are ever present in our lives; they may be unseen, and seemingly operating in a subliminal way, but they underpin the way all businesses deliver goods and services and the way we as customers and consumers demand and receive them. As humans, our behaviour is driving these modern extended supply chains; not the other way around. If events go as predicted, the presence of *living supply chains*, and all that they encompass, will loom large in all our lives in the years ahead.

A final word

e started with an allusion to golf. Let's finish with a more precise description of the art of alignment:

When playing or practicing golf, to strike the ball with power, accuracy and precision the alignment of the left arm, hand, shaft, and clubface relative to the target line at impact is critical! This combination of elements coming together are called the 'impact alignments', and I strongly suggest that no matter what level you play at you should seek to improve and sustain them.

Gary Barter, AAA Member PGA of Australia
Australian PGA Teacher of the Year – 2001
Teaching Professional, The Australian Golf Club, Sydney

Good advice from a master of 'alignment'.

So where are we when it comes to securing our own impact alignment? In this book we have traversed some of the old ways of thinking about the supply chain and found them wanting. Supply chains today are pervasive. And they are so much more than warehouses, transport and technology. Supply chains are by their nature living organisms; they are *living supply chains*.

Understanding supply chains in this way means we can configure and re-configure them, just like any cellular structure. It can make your task of managing the enterprise much simpler and more rewarding in the future. With your supply chain forming part of a much broader business ecosystem, you can survive and thrive by designing and operating supply chain configurations that have an embedded *dynamic* quality that facilitates on-going *dynamic alignment* between the enterprise and its customers and suppliers.

How can you do this? The *dynamic alignment* model and the supply chains described throughout this book show you how to group processes, assets and people into modular structures or 'cells' that can be quickly re-configured and re-aligned to changing customer buying behaviours. As in nature, the secret is to have simple building blocks that are endlessly re-configurable to create sophisticated 'life forms'. This means your enterprise will need several key capabilities available that can be compart-mentalized, and combined and unwound at speed, something akin to 'cellular manufacturing'.

Only unlike cellular manufacturing, alignment is likely to occur in a much less controlled environment, so maintaining all the elements in synch is more difficult over sustained periods. However, if *dynamic align-ment* principles are followed, it is possible. Remember, success is all about understanding customers' buying behaviours, developing matching value propositions and underpinning these with an organization structure that flexes according to your customers' needs. And any and all of this will only happen if the leadership of your enterprise is in harmony with the market-place. Are you in harmony? After understanding customers, leadership is the most important ingredient for success. With the right leadership, the best strategies for identifying and targeting customers in separate supply chains will surely follow – breathing even more life into your *living supply chains*.

Appendix 1A

'Quick' *dynamic alignment* diagnostic

Important note: This diagnostic tool will provide a single overall assessment of the alignment between your enterprise and its marketplace. However, to obtain detailed assessments of alignment against specific customers and customer segments, the 'quick' behavioural segmentation diagnostic outlined in Appendix 2C must first be undertaken.

Part 1 Instructions

1. Marketplace

On the following two pages there are eight questions to answer about your organization's marketplace.

There are two groups of four questions.

The first four questions deal with 'competitive intensity' and the second four with 'uncertainty'. Let's define each of these factors:

Competitive intensity measures the concentration of commercially aggressive behaviour between competing enterprises.

Uncertainty measures the degree of discontinuous change in a marketplace.

When responding to the four questions which describe each of these factors please think about your industry or market in its broadest sense. For example, 'financial services' rather than, say, insurance broking, 'telecommunications' rather than the PABX market, etc. Take your 'first impression' response in each case – it will be right. So don't spend too much time on any one question.

Each question is phrased so that you can rate the strength of your agreement or disagreement with it. Do this by checking the square with the appropriate answer. When you finish each set of questions add up your score in the 'subtotal' box.

I. Competitive intensity

| | Agree | | | Disagree | |
	Strongly	Moderately	Neither	Moderately	Strongly
a) It is very easy for new competitors to establish themselves in our market.	5	4	3	2	1
b) Our market is very attractive even to those companies who have no industry experience.	5	4	3	2	1
c) Our product/service is easy to copy in terms of the benefits it provides to customers.	5	4	3	2	1
d) Our industry is in a late stage of development.	5	4	3	2	1
Subtotal 1					

II. Uncertainty

| | Agree | | | Disagree | |
	Strongly	Moderately	Neither	Moderately	Strongly
a) The environment changes quickly relative to other industries.	5	4	3	2	1
b) Early signs of change in our industry are difficult to identify.	5	4	3	2	1
c) We can't predict how change will impact on our business.	5	4	3	2	1
d) The structure of our market can easily be altered by our buyers/suppliers.	5	4	3	2	1
Subtotal 2					

2. Business strategy

As for the previous the section, this one is also organized in terms of two sets of four questions.

Here we focus on your organization's business strategy and the two factors used to describe it:

Risk and reward measures the trade-off between the risks taken and the potential rewards sought.

Strategic posture measures the intended strategic position of the enterprise.

Do this by checking the square with the appropriate answer. When you finish each set of questions add up your score in the 'subtotal' box.

III. Risk and reward

	Agree			Disagree	
	Strongly	Moderately	Neither	Moderately	Strongly
a) Important decisions are often made on the basis of 'gut-feel'.	5	4	3	2	1
b) When someone has a new idea we take action before everyone has agreed that it has merit.	5	4	3	2	1
c) Our survival depends on our ability to identify and respond to opportunities before our competitors.	5	4	3	2	1
d) Market creation is more important than market share.	5	4	3	2	1
Subtotal 3					

IV. Strategic posture

	Agree			Disagree	
	Strongly	Moderately	Neither	Moderately	Strongly
a) We know more about our business than our customers do.	5	4	3	2	1
b) R&D is a critical success factor in our business.	5	4	3	2	1
c) Our competitive posture could be described as leading the market.	5	4	3	2	1
d) Quality and responsiveness are more important than efficiency and low costs.	5	4	3	2	1
Subtotal 4					

3. Organization culture

The questions about organization culture focus on two factors:

Focus measures the primary focus or the effort the organization exerts to improve its on-going viability and well-being.

Control measures the manner in which the organization achieves the coordination and integration necessary to implement its efforts.

Do this by checking the square with the appropriate answer. When you finish each set of questions add up your score in the 'subtotal' box.

V. Focus

	Agree			Disagree	
	Strongly	**Moderately**	**Neither**	**Moderately**	**Strongly**
a) Management spends most time formulating plans and initiating action.	☐ 5	☐ 4	☐ 3	☐ 2	☐ 1
b) Organization effort is primarily directed at growth and resource acquisition.	☐ 5	☐ 4	☐ 3	☐ 2	☐ 1
c) Profit is more important than people.	☐ 5	☐ 4	☐ 3	☐ 2	☐ 1
d) We are proud of what we have achieved in the marketplace.	☐ 5	☐ 4	☐ 3	☐ 2	☐ 1
Subtotal 5					

VI. Control

	Agree			Disagree	
	Strongly	**Moderately**	**Neither**	**Moderately**	**Strongly**
a) Our structure and decision-making process is de-centralized.	☐ 5	☐ 4	☐ 3	☐ 2	☐ 1
b) Jobs are designed to match an individual's skills and capabilities.	☐ 5	☐ 4	☐ 3	☐ 2	☐ 1
c) The way to succeed in our organization is to behave like an entrepreneur.	☐ 5	☐ 4	☐ 3	☐ 2	☐ 1
d) We all know what the organization is aiming for and how we can contribute.	☐ 5	☐ 4	☐ 3	☐ 2	☐ 1
Subtotal 6					

4. Leadership style

The questions about leadership style focus on two factors:

Orientation measures the extent to which a manager is sensitive to teams or individuals.

Preference measures the extent to which a manager has a preference for thought or action.

Do this by checking the square with the appropriate answer. When you finish each set of questions add up your score in the 'subtotal' box.

VII. Orientation

	Agree			Disagree	
	Strongly	Moderately	Neither	Moderately	Strongly
a) We motivate our people by providing them with challenging but realistic performance targets.	☐ 5	☐ 4	☐ 3	☐ 2	☐ 1
b) Management should get close to their subordinates – familiarity breeds understanding, not contempt.	☐ 5	☐ 4	☐ 3	☐ 2	☐ 1
c) People don't need to feel that they really belong to an organization.	☐ 5	☐ 4	☐ 3	☐ 2	☐ 1
d) We actively encourage innovation and our people respond well to challenge.	☐ 5	☐ 4	☐ 3	☐ 2	☐ 1
Subtotal 7					

VIII. Preference

	Agree			Disagree	
	Strongly	Moderately	Neither	Moderately	Strongly
a) Communication is almost entirely informal in our organization.	☐ 5	☐ 4	☐ 3	☐ 2	☐ 1
b) We believe that generalist skills are more efficient than specialist skills.	☐ 5	☐ 4	☐ 3	☐ 2	☐ 1
c) We focus on developing cohesive and effective work teams.	☐ 5	☐ 4	☐ 3	☐ 2	☐ 1
d) We place a higher value on creativity than on objectivity.	☐ 5	☐ 4	☐ 3	☐ 2	☐ 1
Subtotal 8					

Part 2 Instructions

Each of the four sections in Part 1 of this questionnaire had two sets of questions which determine each organization's position relative to the two axes. We will now outline how you can plot these subtotal scores to build a profile of the organization's alignment.

Step 1: Plot your subtotal scores on each of the graphs on the following pages as per the example below.

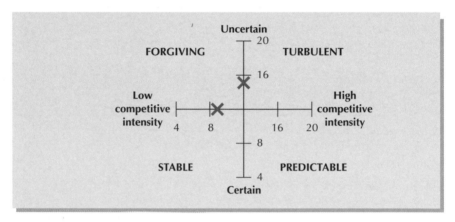

Step 2: Now draw straight lines at right angles to the X and Y axes as shown.

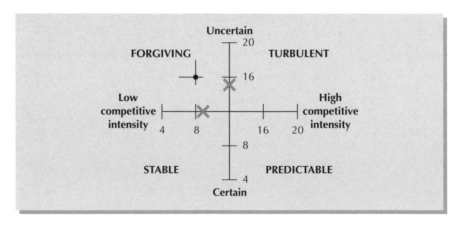

The intersection of the lines through the two ordinates signals the **dominant condition** of the enterprise at that particular level of the 'alignment' framework.

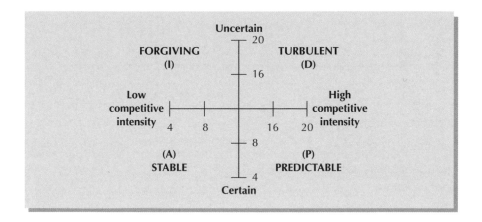

1. Marketplace

Plot the subtotal score from question 1 on the horizontal axis.

2. Uncertainty

Plot the subtotal score from question 2 on the vertical axis.

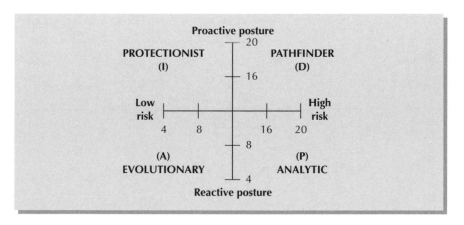

3. Risk

Plot the subtotal score from question 3 on the horizontal axis.

4. Posture

Plot the subtotal score from question 4 on the vertical axis.

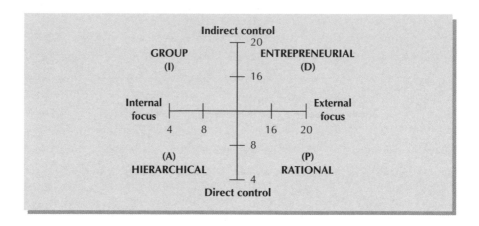

5. Focus

Plot the subtotal score from question 5 on the horizontal axis.

6. Control

Plot the subtotal score from question 6 on the vertical axis.

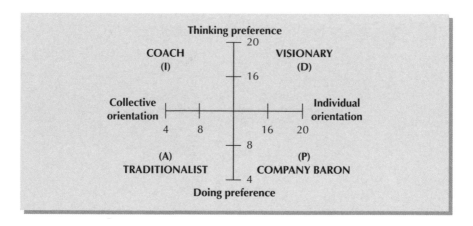

7. Orientation

Plot the subtotal score from question 7 on the horizontal axis.

8. Preference

Plot the subtotal score from question 8 on the vertical axis.

'Quick' *dynamic alignment* diagnostic

MARKETPLACE

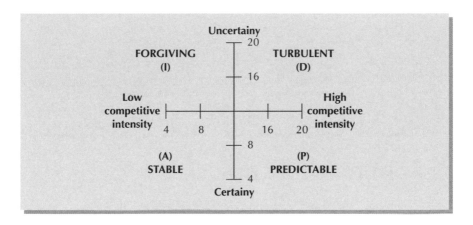

BUSINESS STRATEGY

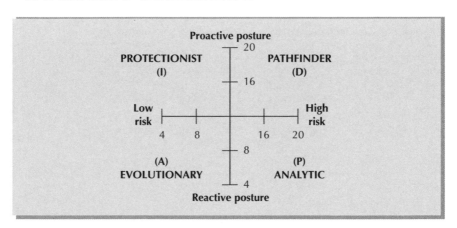

ORGANIZATION CULTURE

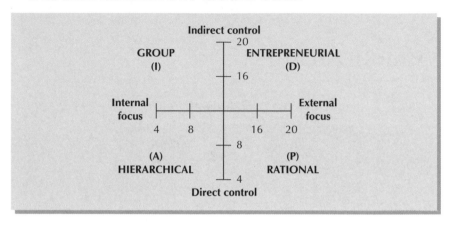

LEADERSHIP STYLE

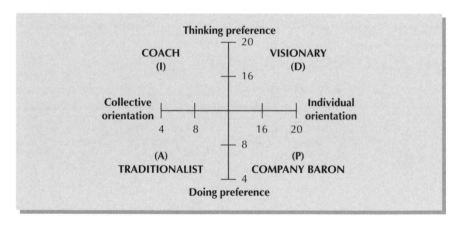

Appendix 2A

Product/service category

Segment members
- Newspapers/mags (same day)
- Legal/financial/ business documents
- Mail/parcels
- Livestock
- Perishables
- Fashion

'Time critical'

Buying priorities
- Time-sensitive
- Not price-sensitive
- Tracking
- JIT
- Safety
- Care

Segment members
- Newspapers/mags (same day)
- Mail/parcels
- Legal/financial/ business documents
- Government
- Advertising agencies

'Reliable'

Buying priorities
- Reliable
- Dependable
- Price-sensitive
- Risk-averse
- Guarantee
- No hassles

Segment members
- Advertising agencies
- Mail/parcels
- Recording
- Dangerous goods
- Mining
- Fashion

'Speciality'

Buying priorities
- Difficult
- Urgency
- Innovation
- Special handling
- Special documentation
- Not price-sensitive

Express small packages

ILLUSTRATIVE

Segment members

- Kodak
- Hewlett-Packard
- LL Bean
- Chrysler
- Bechtel
- Polygram

'Collaborative'

Ia

Buying priorities

- Partnership relationships
- Reliability > price
- Budgets
- Quality and safety
- Stability

Segment members

- Hoechst
- Westinghouse
- 3M
- Nissan Nth America

'Fair Deal'

Ai

Buying priorities

- Reliability – 'on-time'
- Quality and service guarantee
- Customer focus
- Fair negotiations
- Cost effectiveness

Segment members

- AMP
- J&J Medical
- Bank of America
- New Hampton Inc.
- Paul Fredrick Shirt
- Mobile Telesystems Communications Equipment

'Efficiency'

A

Buying priorities

- Reliability > speed
- Cost is the final evaluation criterion
- Access to information
- Timely and accurate information

Segment members

- General Motors
- AT&T
- IQ software
- Motorola Inc.
- Lillian Vernon

'Premium'

aP

Buying priorities

- Reliability > speed
- Product availability
- Flexibility
- Communication
- Competitive pricing

Express logistics

· 274 ·

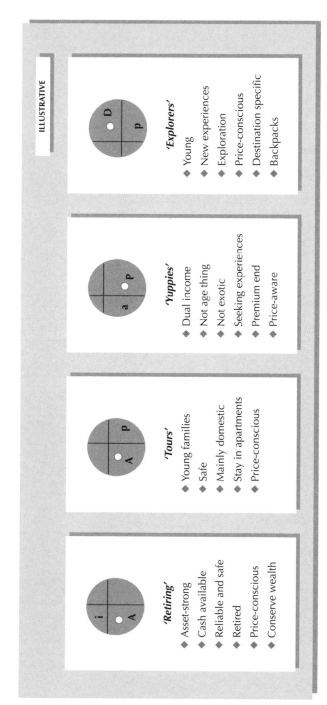

ILLUSTRATIVE

'Retiring'
◆ Asset-strong
◆ Cash available
◆ Reliable and safe
◆ Retired
◆ Price-conscious
◆ Conserve wealth

'Tours'
◆ Young families
◆ Safe
◆ Mainly domestic
◆ Stay in apartments
◆ Price-conscious

'Yuppies'
◆ Dual income
◆ Not age thing
◆ Not exotic
◆ Seeking experiences
◆ Premium end
◆ Price-aware

'Explorers'
◆ Young
◆ New experiences
◆ Exploration
◆ Price-conscious
◆ Destination specific
◆ Backpacks

Leisure travel

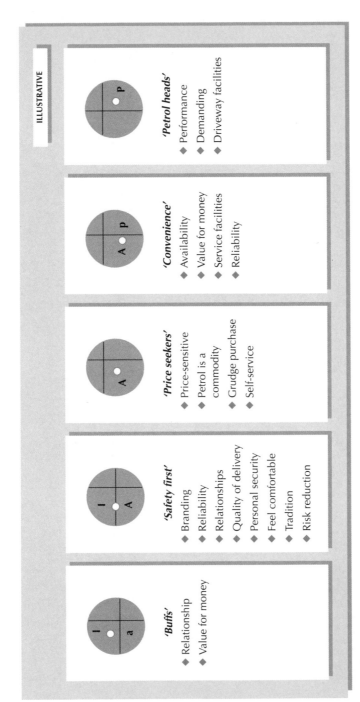

ILLUSTRATIVE

'Bufs'
- Relationship
- Value for money

'Safety first'
- Branding
- Reliability
- Relationships
- Quality of delivery
- Personal security
- Feel comfortable
- Tradition
- Risk reduction

'Price seekers'
- Price-sensitive
- Petrol is a commodity
- Grudge purchase
- Self-service

'Convenience'
- Availability
- Value for money
- Service facilities
- Reliability

'Petrol heads'
- Performance
- Demanding
- Driveway facilities

Gasoline

Multiple supply chains

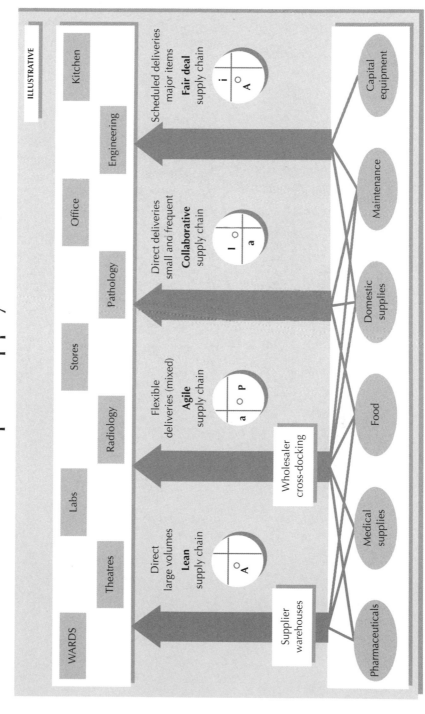

The healthcare industry

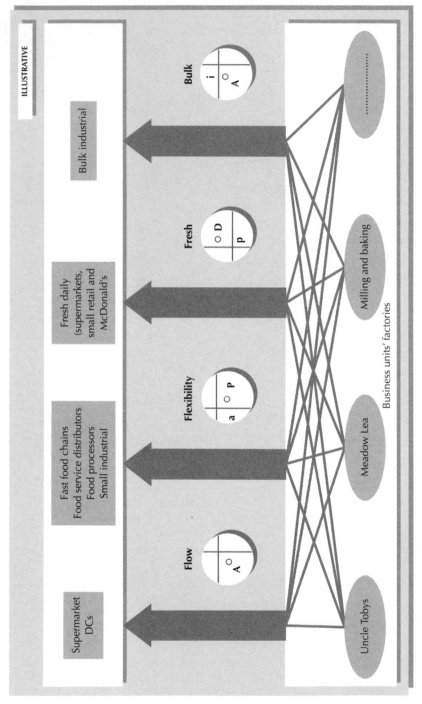

Processed food manufacturer Goodman Fielder

Appendix 2C

'Quick' *behavioural segmentation* DIAGNOSTIC

Exercise to discover the 'buyer behaviours' or 'logics' evident among your customer base.

Instructions

1. List the various customers/clients which buy/use the products/ services of your business.

2. For each customer listed in (1) above, provide four or five *descriptors*, i.e., words or phrases your **customers/clients** might be expected to use in describing their needs/requirements to any provider of the desired product(s)/service(s).

3. Code each descriptor as P, A, D or I (using the following guidelines).

4. Assess the dominant logic(s) for each individual customer/client.

5. Identify any pattern evident in these customer/client logics, and arrive at a 'strawman' segmentation.

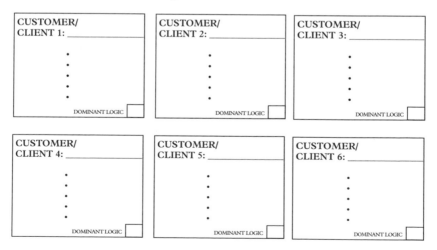

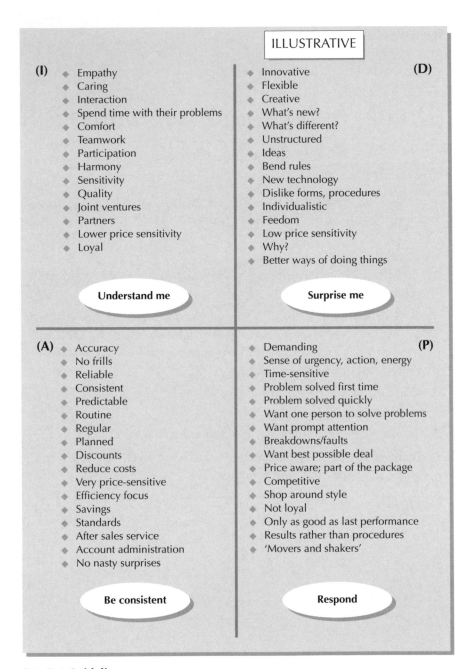

ILLUSTRATIVE

(I)
- Empathy
- Caring
- Interaction
- Spend time with their problems
- Comfort
- Teamwork
- Participation
- Harmony
- Sensitivity
- Quality
- Joint ventures
- Partners
- Lower price sensitivity
- Loyal

Understand me

(D)
- Innovative
- Flexible
- Creative
- What's new?
- What's different?
- Unstructured
- Ideas
- Bend rules
- New technology
- Dislike forms, procedures
- Individualistic
- Feedom
- Low price sensitivity
- Why?
- Better ways of doing things

Surprise me

(A)
- Accuracy
- No frills
- Reliable
- Consistent
- Predictable
- Routine
- Regular
- Planned
- Discounts
- Reduce costs
- Very price-sensitive
- Efficiency focus
- Savings
- Standards
- After sales service
- Account administration
- No nasty surprises

Be consistent

(P)
- Demanding
- Sense of urgency, action, energy
- Time-sensitive
- Problem solved first time
- Problem solved quickly
- Want one person to solve problems
- Want prompt attention
- Breakdowns/faults
- Want best possible deal
- Price aware; part of the package
- Competitive
- Shop around style
- Not loyal
- Only as good as last performance
- Results rather than procedures
- 'Movers and shakers'

Respond

P-A-D-I Guidelines

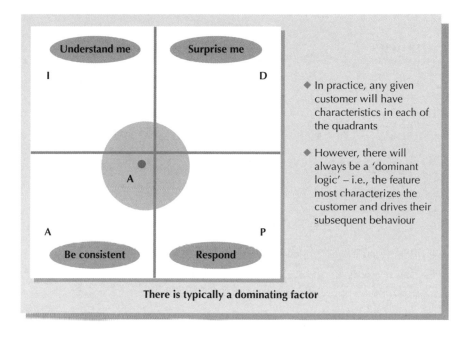

In practice, any given customer will have characteristics in each of the quadrants

However, there will always be a 'dominant logic' – i.e., the feature most characterizes the customer and drives their subsequent behaviour

There is typically a dominating factor

Appendix 2D

'Quick' diagnostic comparing 'current' versus 'ideal' strategies

◆ Firm up your views on the behavioural segments identified earlier.

◆ List the corresponding ideal strategies in terms of the way products/services should be packaged and delivered to each of these client types.

◆ Document the overall thrust of your 'current' strategies.

◆ Look for discrepancies between your 'current' and 'ideal' strategies to identify where there are significant mis-alignments and therefore resource mis-allocations.

◆ Use the framework overleaf to identify and prioritize potential initiatives.

◆ A number of tools and frameworks such as the organizational pyramid below provide a logical route from strategy to operational execution.

◆ Each pyramid element is examined and issues, needs and capability gaps are documented.

◆ Consider each issue and propose corresponding action plans.

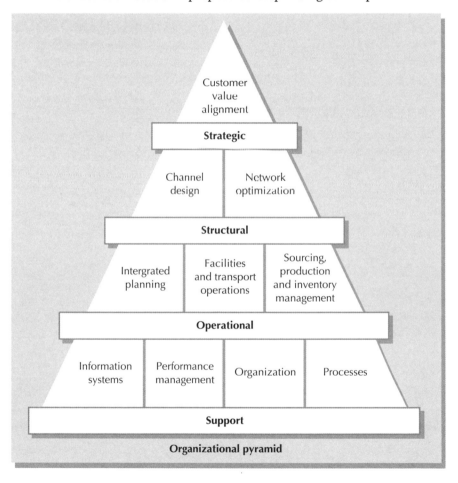

Organizational pyramid

◆ Each initiative is mapped on to the matrix according to the relative business benefit and the relative ease of implementation.

◆ This process is in itself an extremely effective way of promoting valuable interactive and focused discussion among the top management team (TMT).

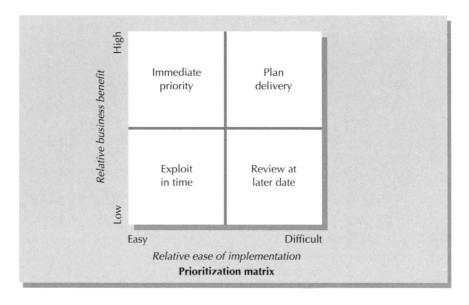

Prioritization matrix

Appendix 3A

Typical culture maps

Total employees
621

Number of
respondents
560

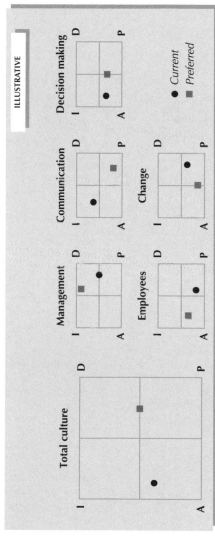

ILLUSTRATIVE

Current culture is 'Ai'
Overall focus is on following rules and procedures, making decisions by consensus, with information being privy to those who belong to cliques or groups.

- Management 'PD' – Managers focus on performance, results and the organization's future direction and opportunities for growth.
- Employees 'Pa' – Employees are given specific goals and objectives to meet and are expected to work efficiently by following established rules and procedures.
- Communication 'Ia' – Closed communication with information available to cliques or members of particular groups and on a 'need to know' basis.
- Change 'Pd' – Change is accepted when people understand the reasons for doing things differently and it becomes the way of life in the organization.
- Decision-making 'Ai' – Individuals need to seek management approval for decisions, provided there is consensus.

Preferred culture is 'DP'
The preferred culture is one where the main focus is on the future direction, opportunities for growth, performance and results.

- Management 'Di' – Prefer managers to focus on the future, opportunities for growth, building teams and supporting them.
- Employees 'Ai' – Employees prefer to work according to rules and procedures where everyone's contribution to the team is valued.
- Communication 'P' – Employees prefer open communication where information is widely shared and easily accessible to all.
- Change 'PA' – Although employees are willing to accept change when the reasons are well understood, they prefer change to be implemented with new systems and procedures.
- Decision-making 'PA' – Employees would like sufficient authority to make decisions to allow them to achieve their objectives and targets.

Source Prepared for John Gattorna by the Ryder Self Group, 2005

Appendix 3B

Culture dimensions

Results

Performance reward
Informal standards

High value is placed on group harmony and human interaction skills	High value is placed on individuals' ability to be flexible and creative
High value is placed on the ability to maintain productivity and efficiency	High value is placed on individuals' ability to meet short-term operational goals

Stability

Formal standards

Change tolerance
Knowledge capability

High willingness

Change implicit in cultural make-up but implementation of specific programmes can be haphazard	
Change is tolerated if the logic for it is fully understood and action is planned in detail	
Change is valued for its own sake, but can only be implemented if there is consensus on how it should be done	
Change is not well tolerated but can be implemented indirectly by altering systems/infrastructre	

Low willingness

System capability

Individual orientation

Internal organizing
Low power distance

People are allowed to work on their own to fulfil their own potential	People are given goals and motivated in order to achieve best results
People are organized into supportive teams to ensure participation and commitment	People are given a clear stucture of rules and procedures to achieve maximum efficiency

Orientation collective

High power distance

Source Developed from Hofstede data

· 286 ·

Communication

Open system

Informal style — Formal style

- Spontaneous, interactive, irregular – information must be discovered by the individual
- Planned, impersonal, regular – information widely shared and easily accessible
- Participative, team-based, continuous – information accessible to group members but inter-group sharing is poor
- Systematized, directive, regular – information shared on a 'need to know' basis only

Closed system

Control

Subjective

Outcomes

- Control is achieved by individuals' commitment to a shared vision of the future
- Control is achieved by individually negotiated and agreed performance standards
- Control is achieved by collective adherence to a set of common values and beliefs
- Control is achieved through conformance to explicit rules and procedures

Objective / Behaviours

External coping

Uncertainty accepting

Expressive — Instrumental

- The organization deals with opportunities in a flexible and creative way
- The organization deals with opportunities by attempting to beat the opposition and overcome obstacles
- The organization deals with opportunities by considering if they are compatible with its own value
- The organization deals with opportunities as threats and attempts to protect itself

Uncertainty avoiding

Source Developed from Hofstede data

Autonomy

Role

	Empowering	Task
	Autonomy is limited only by an individual's creative response to organizational ideals	Autonomy is limited by the need to obtain consensus about the way things should be done
	Autonomy is limited by the need to perform to set objectives and to prove the validity of decisions	Autonomy is minimal, task-specific and limited by the need to make decisions according to a tried and trusted formula

Dependence

Achievement-based

Conflict

Open resolution

	Value alignment	Behaviour alignment
	Conflict arises often as a result of individual expressiveness but usually resolved quickly and easily	Conflict arises when individuals perceive barriers to the achievement of objectives, and is usually resolved by negotiation
	Conflict arises with no consensus on applicable values. Usually resolved through new coalition formation	Conflict arises when there is deviation from processes; it is suppressed and only resolved by enforcement

Closed resolution

Identity

	Subjective	Security-based
	Based on a sense of affiliation with the organization's leadership role	Based on a sense of 'belonging' to a group which shares a common set of values
	Based on a sense of pride in what the organization can and will achieve in the market	Based on a sense of protecting an established history and tradition

Objectives

Source Developed from Hofstede data

Appendix 3C

'Quick' culture mapping diagnostic

Each question has four statements. **Read each question first** and then rank the four statements, allocating a 4, 3, 2 or 1 to each statement to indicate how often that situation occurs at work, where:
4 = Most often and 1 = Least often
*Use 4, 3, 2 or 1 **only once** when ranking the four statements in each question. Rank all statements.*

Management   Current

1. a. Our managers are focused on setting performance
      targets to be achieved, and results   _____ ☐
   b. Our managers are focused on analysis, planning
      and budgets   _____ ☐
   c. Our managers are focused on the company's
      future direction and opportunities for growth   _____ ☐
   d. Our managers are focused on building teams and
      a supportive environment   _____ ☐

Employees

2. a. Each of us is given specific goals and objectives
      to meet   _____ ☐
   b. We have clear rules, guidelines and procedures
      to follow   _____ ☐
   c. As individuals, we are expected to work on
      our own to fulfil our potential   _____ ☐
   d. We value everyone's contribution to
      the team   _____ ☐

Communication

3. a. Information is openly shared and easily accessible   _____ ☐
   b. We get information on a 'need to know only' basis   _____ ☐
   c. We stumble across the information we need   _____ ☐
   d. Those who are part of a clique or group are privy
      to information   _____ ☐

Change   Current

4. a. Change works best when everyone understands the
      reasons for doing things differently   _____ ☐

   b. Change works when new systems, rules and
      procedures are put in place to do things differently _____ ☐

   c. Change is the way of life in our organization   _____ ☐

   d. Change is acceptable when we all agree how
      it should take place   _____ ☐

Decision-making

5. a. We can make decisions that allow us to achieve
      our objectives and targets   _____ ☐

   b. We can only make decisions with management
      approval   _____ ☐

   c. We are free to make any decisions we like   _____ ☐

   d. We can make decisions as long as everyone
      agrees   _____ ☐

Please score your result overleaf

Culture mapping – self scoring

Instructions

1. Transpose your rankings to each question in the culture mapping questionnaire into the following scoring sheet:

	Q1 Management	Q2 Employees	Q3 Communication	Q4 Change	Q5 Decision making	TOTAL
P – Production	1a	2a	3a	4a	5a	
A – Administration	1b	2b	3b	4b	5b	
D – Development	1c	2c	3c	4c	5c	
I – Integration	1d	2d	3d	4d	5d	

2. Add your responses across the table, writing a total score for each row in the total column.

3. Write the total scores into the calculation below to get your Z diagonal and X diagonal plotting scores.

    P total _____ *less* I total _____ = Z plot _____

    A total _____ *less* D total _____ = X plot _____

4. Make a mark on the Z diagonal to represent the Z plot score. If it is a + value, this mark will be somewhere in the P quadrant. If it is a – value, this mark will be somewhere in the I quadrant.

5. Make a mark on the X diagonal to represent the X plot score. If it is a + value, this mark will be somewhere in the A quadrant. If it is a – value, this mark will be somewhere in the D quadrant.

6. Draw a line at right angles to your Z plot and your X plot. Where these lines intersect is the dominant 'subculture'.

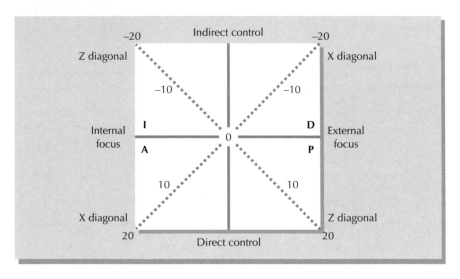

Source Prepared for John Gattorna by the Ryder Self Group, 2005

Appendix 3D

'Evolutionary' change

Option 1: Consolidate current position

◆ Improve cultural coherence

◆ Remove negative climate influences

◆ Measure business unit productivity; reward efficiency

◆ Emphasize past achievements

◆ Define 'how we do things' statement

Option 2: Move towards *Group* culture

◆ Multi-level/functional team-building

◆ Introduce bottom–up planning

◆ Reduce power-distance; TMT role modelling

◆ Joint, peer job design

◆ Personal interaction skills training

Option 3: Move towards *Rational* culture

◆ Individual results – based on job design

◆ Measure performance against objectives

◆ Reward achievement; speed of response

◆ Research and wide communication of prevailing market conditions

◆ Delegate, decentralize decision-making

◆ Install task force issue resolution process

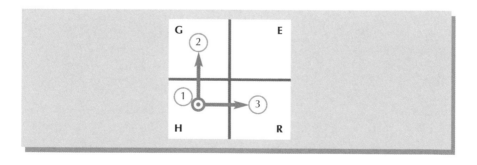

Option 1: Consolidate current position

◆ Improve cultural coherence

◆ Remove negative climate influences

◆ Measure by objectives; reward performance

◆ Emphasize current achievements

◆ Define 'what we are fighting for' statement

Option 2: Move towards *Hierarchical* culture

◆ Direct objectives towards efficiency, productivity, on a collective basis

◆ Centralize 'important' decision-making

◆ Define jobs by method

◆ Develop policy manuals; reward adherence

◆ Control information flows

Option 3: Move towards *Entrepreneurial* culture

◆ Assign open-ended problems; reward creativity of solutions

◆ Emphasize the long-term 'strategic' view of performance

◆ Reward experimentation/ideas

◆ TMT role model – tolerance of risk and error

◆ Remove all systemic barriers to change

◆ Evaluate knowledge capability and spend (lavishly) on individual development

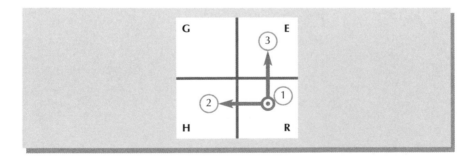

Consolidate current position

- Nurture any signs of the right momentum
- Identify systemic resistance/barriers
- Build change power-base
- Raise status of R&D function

Phase I: Re-direct system focus

- From rules to 'guidelines'
- Set market-related objectives for each job
- De-centralize structure
- Research and communicate pressure for change
- Train all personnel in marketing based skills – internal customer service?
- Streamline administrative/reporting procedures
- Measure market impact; reward individuals
- TMT role modelling – high energy

Phase II: Loosen control mechanisms

- Recruit individuals with 'DP' capability
- Introduce 'what if' scenario building into planning process
- Reduce power-distance; flatten structure
- Make individuals accountable
- Encourage/reward 'good ideas'
- Formulate appropriate human resource management (HRM) strategy

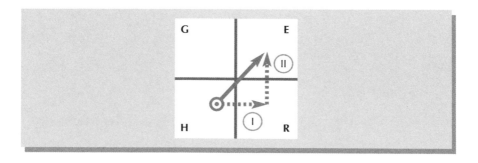

Consolidate current position

◆ Nurture any signs of the right momentum

◆ Identify sources of philosophical resistance

◆ Select and convert change affiliates

◆ Raise status of operations and marketing functions

Phase I: Make values explicit

◆ Define values, and develop policy manuals based on these values

◆ Formalize communication/meeting practices

◆ Define lines of authority, decision-making

◆ Measure and reward productivity, efficiency

◆ Close control loopholes, especially job descriptions

◆ Training in systems, methods and time management

Phase II: Redirect control mechanisms

◆ Recruit individuals with 'AP' capability

◆ Introduce appropriate systems and processes

◆ Market awareness communication campaign

◆ Restructure towards product/market matrix

◆ Introduce individual accountabilities for performance bottom–up planning process

◆ Formulate performance-oriented HRM strategy

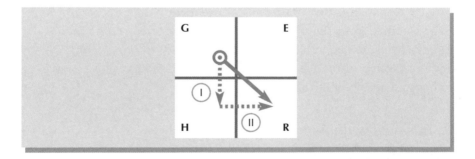

Appendix 4A

Formulation of vision statement

The task of formulating a vision statement is quite daunting. Certainly, it is achieved rarely by taking executives away on a weekend retreat to debate the future of the organization. Our experience over years of empirical work with top management teams is that a template is required when embarking on this undertaking. This, combined with a facilitated real-time environment, is the only way to achieve a meaningful, yet practical, vision statement. We have developed a vision template through working with hundreds of management teams over a decade; it has four components as indicated below, all of which are essential.

1. Contextual

The first component of our vision template is the context within which the particular organizational unit is operating. Leaders need to consider the role or unique contribution that the unit makes to the larger organization. The idea is to test whether or not the organization has an on-going role in which a vision is indeed appropriate. In many cases organizations struggle to pass this first hurdle and consequently doubt is cast on long-term viability from the outset. Typically, the internal contributions of supply chains will be in terms of cash generation, working capital reduction, ownership of the pipeline through which products move to market and custodianship of the inventory.

2. Business definition

In the second component, the organization needs to describe clearly what the business of the organization is now and is likely to be in the future.

Too many vision statements fail at this point because they describe the business in terms of what the organization does from day to day – and that may change. However, there is only one way to describe the business or boundary of the organization, and that is in terms of the needs the organization has set out to satisfy, for either internal stakeholders or external customers. If organizations follow this method, their definition of the business will remain constant over time. Contrary to popular opinion, the fundamental needs of customers do not change over time; only the way organizations go about satisfying those needs. That usually has something to do with the ever-changing technology landscape. However, technology and geography, combined with customers' needs, may also be used as part of the 'boundary' definition. So, the vision statement can be thought of as a 'boundary' or 'positioning' statement. This view is consistent with the *dynamic alignment* concept that we use to anchor all our supply chain work. It is also consistent with our view that organizations have supply chains plural rather than one supply chain as envisaged by previous writers. To understand this concept, think in terms of several conveyor belts running through an organization, all at different speeds and with different operating characteristics. The same product can travel down any conveyor or pathway.

3. Distinctive competence

Distinctive competence is the third component of our vision statement template and is perhaps the most difficult to understand and operationalize. Internal to the organization, distinctive competence attempts to identify the essential skills, capabilities and resources that underpin current and future success. It involves identifying those things that the organization does particularly well compared to competitors in the same business domain. Generally, a true distinctive competence is not easy to copy or emulate in the short to medium term.

Clearly, you must look for potential distinctive competencies among an organization's strengths. In our experience, most organizations lack this 'silver thread' or 'essence' running through the business, and this is one of the reasons why they are seemingly always struggling to achieve differential advantage in the marketplace; distinctive competencies underpin differential advantages.

If the conclusion is that no such unique competence exists, then try to define what competence you want to build and start the long process of growing it organically within the business. In the rare case where a genuine distinctive competence is uncovered, then the required action is to nurture and develop it further. Unfortunately, there have been many cases over the last few decades where distinctive competencies have been ignored and lost through neglect, very often as an outcome of mergers and acquisitions. In these examples, the business cases on which the mergers/acquisitions were approved will not be delivered.

A defensible distinctive competence, according to Quinn, Doorley and Parquette (1990) in the *Harvard Business Review*, usually derives from outstanding depth in human skills, logistics capabilities, knowledge bases, brand loyalty and other intangibles that competitors cannot easily replicate, and which lead to demonstrable value for the customer.[1] In any event, distinctive competencies can either be grown organically over time or bought as part of an acquisition, albeit with due care in the latter case. The most difficult distinctive competencies to compete against are those that are qualitative rather than quantitative, for example, a company's culture, or tacit knowledge. In both examples, the competence is deeply embedded in the organization and almost impossible to unbundle and extract.

Finally, unlike physical assets, Prahalad and Hamel (1990) have observed, a distinctive competence can be used simultaneously in several applications, does not wear out and can be combined in various ways to create new opportunities.[2] Indeed, a distinctive competence can be used to screen or filter any new opportunities being considered and, in this way, it helps the organizations' maintain focus.

4. Future indicators

This final component in the vision statement template is designed to give the overall statement a dynamic character, as it is the only component of the four that is likely to change materially from year to year. Future indicators are designed to provide a sense of future direction and the initiatives likely to be pursued in the medium term. In effect, future indicators are a catalogue of the organization's major strategies and are important enough to be included in the vision statement. Over time, the organization will modify these directional statements gradually as it weaves a path through its operating environment.

This then completes the template. As indicated, the 'personality' of the organization is best captured in the flavour of its vision statement, and the flavour should ideally reflect the dominant logic of the operating environment. At least four flavours of vision statement are possible, and the one chosen will be embedded eventually in the predominant culture of the organization.

Examples of supply chain vision statements

The supply chain groups of several large organizations in Australia and New Zealand have developed vision statements for their supply chains. The statements illustrate the depth of thinking involved in formulating a vision. While they might look relatively long at first, remember that once the hard graft of formulating a statement is achieved and the vision has been internalized by those involved, the statement can be shortened. Through this process, people will think of the full weight and content of the longer statement when they see the slogan. Both companies involved in the 1994 examples below have since changed through acquisition.

Myer Grace Department Store's (MGDS) supply chain vision

The logistics function within MGDS is the custodian of the supply chain (or pipeline) that links customers with suppliers. Supply Chain is charged with the professional management of those considerable resources that participate in the complex task of moving merchandise through the pipeline, i.e., facilities, systems, personnel and capital. The actual merchandise in the pipeline remains the 'property' of the merchandise function, but we are the facilitators. In effect, Supply Chain is an internal contractor, which has the potential to influence significantly the Department Stores Group overall profit by optimizing the service/cost equation. The Supply Chain function has several 'stakeholders', and in meeting their respective needs we effectively define our business. For example:

Suppliers: look to Supply Chain to fulfil elements of the strategic partnership arrangements entered into with the merchandise function for the purpose of achieving mutual profitability.

Merchandise function: is an internal client that requires Supply Chain to shorten the strategic lead-times that merchandise inventory is in the pipeline to Stores. Management of this lead-time has tremendous leverage on the group's overall profitability. We collaborate with merchandise personnel at the interface with suppliers, and manage the merchandise on their behalf from that point on.

Stores function: is another internal client which requires Supply Chain to deliver merchandise to every store according to previously agreed service levels, and in some cases to arrange final delivery to, and installation in, customers' premises. We also liaise with stores on a range of matters that affect the management of merchandise, such as packaging, price-marking, allocations, storage, facilities design and handling practices at the back door.

We liaise with marketing in regard to promotional campaigns, packaging and other special conditions that influence the flow of merchandise. Finally, it is our ultimate aim to contribute to customer satisfaction by collaborating with all internal functions, as well as suppliers. Our scope of operations is Australia and New Zealand. Supply Chain owns the methodologies and procedures that facilitate the cost-effective flow of merchandise from suppliers to stores and on to customers. These methodologies include leading edge physical and information systems, supported by a logistics orientation among all our personnel. Because we are responsible for the operation of such a comprehensive network of facilities, we can make things happen. For the future, the supply chain function intends to develop and implement a blueprint for quantum change that will take MGDS to the forefront of supply chain practice in department stores, worldwide. To achieve this we must institute and manage major changes in the way we currently do things. Our task is to ensure that no competitor out-performs MGDS in a supply chain sense, that stock in the 'pipeline' is managed expeditiously and that the entire supply chain (including the supplier component) comes under our influence – all of which adds up to a competitive advantage for MGDS at the point-of-sale. We are determined to realize most, if not all, the potential savings available through improved supply chain practices.

For this reason measurement systems and corresponding standards will be established along the supply chain. Technology will be applied as appropriate in the form of hardware and software. In regard to the latter, optimization models and other decision support systems will be a priority, as will Internet links with suppliers. We are mindful that Supply Chain manages major elements of the company's assets and as such we will seek to ensure acceptable rates of return on these investments. As an additional incentive, we propose to operate the function as a profit centre, servicing its various stakeholders to pre-arranged service levels for a predetermined cost to them.

DHL Airways Express Logistics Vision

DHL Airways Express Logistics exists to enhance and complement DHL Airways' current business, and to tap new emerging opportunities in the international express distribution market. DHL Airways is committed to expanding its service offering to selected customers and we have an important role in this expansion programme. In the process, DHL Airways Express Logistics will increase in sophistication – which will have a positive spin-off on the core business, increase competitiveness, build customer loyalty and contribute to corporation profits. However, it is important that our management remains fully cognizant of the impact that the logistic operation may have on existing network facilities and other key resources servicing the core business.

Our business is to facilitate the cost-effective, time definite movement of product through customers' supply chains, worldwide. In this, we effectively reduce the risk and complexity for our customers, thus allowing them to focus on their respective business(es). For our part, it is essential that we gain an in-depth understanding of customers' businesses and adopt a consultative selling approach, supported by advanced decision support technology, when formulating appropriate response(s). Such an approach will be able to change the 'rules' in the marketplace and dilute the current preoccupation with transport rates.

We have a truly global company at our disposal, providing an international network of express shipping, pick-up and delivery capabilities, interconnected with a reservoir of local knowledge about individual country-markets worldwide. We also have an adaptive culture, capable of flexible responses to customers' needs and a desire to access further competencies relevant to our business (e.g., relationship management of other suppliers of specialist services in the supply chain).

For the future, it is important that we position DHL Airways Express Logistics in that part of the overall third party logistics services spectrum which best protects and, leverages our evolving core competencies. This will involve careful market segmentation and, ultimately, selection of customers with genuine international requirements – which we feel we can meet within specified resource limitations – and whose products have handling and market characteristics, which align with our capabilities. Development of our logistics services portfolio will be evolutionary, consistent with our experience curve. It is important that we avoid the 'over-customizations trap', and instead develop a portfolio of standard service products which are capable of being combined in unique ways to satisfy the individual needs of our customers.

In that it is likely that we will necessarily have to enter into and play the lead role in developing strategic relationships with key suppliers, we should continue to develop our sourcing and relationship management skills.

Notes

1 Quinn, James Brian, Doorley, Thomas L. and Paquette, Penny C. (1990) 'Beyond products: services-based strategy', *Harvard Business Review*, March/April, Vol. 68, No. 2, pp. 58–67.
2 Prahalad, C.K. and Hamel, Gary (1990) 'The core competence of the corporation', *Harvard Business Review*, May /June, Vol. 68, No. 3, pp. 79–91.

Appendix 5A

Supply chain relationship *enablers*

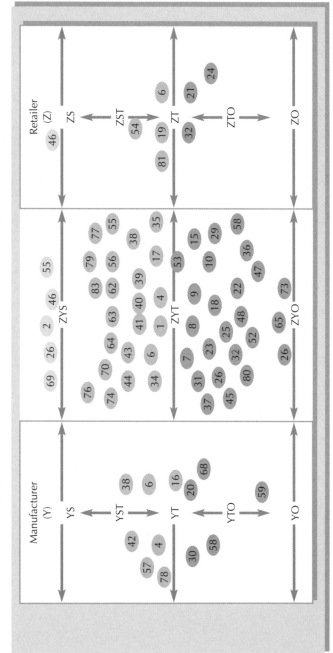

Source Barratt, Mark A. (2002) 'Exploring relationships and information exchange in grocery supply chains', unpublished PhD thesis, Cranfield School of Management, Cranfield University, UK

STRATEGIC		OPERATIONAL	
2	Board to board dialogue	7	Common objectives and goals
26	Multiple level relationships	8	Common philosophies
46	Senior management commitment	9	Communication
55	Communicable strategy	10	Communication mechanisms
69	On-going board level dialogue	15	Identifying communication channels
		18	Integrated SC plan
TACTICAL		20	Internal communication
1	Advanced problem notification	21	Internal understanding
4	Capability to share information	22	Joint replenishment decisions
6	Collaborative/information-based culture	23	Jointly defined processes
16	Information critical mass	24	Long-term commitment
17	Information quality	25	Mean what is said
19	Interdependency recognition	26	Multiple level relationships
34	Mutual understanding	30	Mutual honesty
35	Mutual agreed processes	31	Mutual recognition
38	Openness	32	Mutual respect
39	Opportunism v. collaboration	36	On-going partner recognition
40	People relationship skills	37	On-going trust development
41	Proactive approach	45	Seeking industry best practice
42	Problems not symptoms	47	Share future plans
43	Relationship commitment	48	Shared KPIs
44	Relationship manager	52	Understanding partner's issues
54	Benefit demonstration	58	Customer implants
55	Communicable strategy	59	Customer team clusters
56	Context dependent relationship	65	Integrated SC operations
57	Creative thinking	68	Maintain current information
62	Full process review	73	Solving operational issues
63	Individual chemistry	80	Understanding role of people
64	Integrated relationships		
70	People relationship facilitators		
74	Supply chain manager		
76	System enabled processes		
77	Understanding buying behaviour		
78	Understanding demand aggregation		
79	Understanding information requirements		
81	Understanding role of suppliers		
83	Vendor managed inventory		

Source Barratt, Mark A. (2002)

Supply chain relationship *inhibitors*

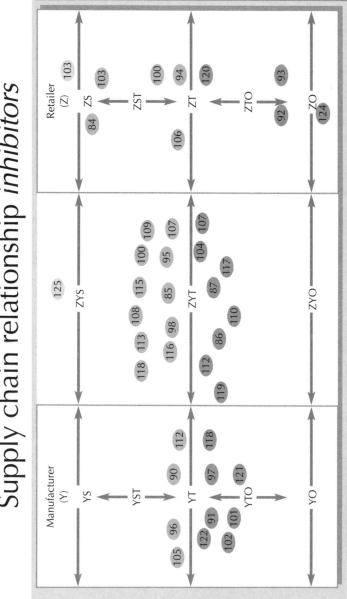

Source Barratt, Mark A. (2002)

	STRATEGIC		OPERATIONAL
103	Mechanistic relationship behaviour	86	Cost-focused
125	Poor strategic relationships	87	Cultural differences
		91	Forecast driven production
	TACTICAL	92	Functional-based teams
84	Adopting a 'customer' mentality	93	Functional silo mentality
85	Commercial pressures	97	Information starved
90	Forecast driven DC	101	Managing change
94	Increasing competitive environment	102	Managing promotions
95	Information exchange accuracy	104	Misunderstanding decision
96	Information overload		implications
98	Joint initiative resources	107	Perceived supplier performance
100	Lacking senior management	110	Product lead-times
	commitment and support	112	Role of EPOS
105	Not sharing future production plans	117	Underestimating the scale of
106	Panic-buying behaviour		change required
107	Perceived supplier performance	118	Collaboration slippage
109	Poor personal relationships	119	Differing trading strategies
112	Role of EPOS	120	Functional management style
113	Short-term focus	121	Information location
116	Timeliness of information exchange	122	Organizational size
118	Collaboration slippage	124	Poor in-house logistics

Source Barratt, Mark A. (2002)

Appendix 5C

'Strategic partnering' technique

No matter how much the world changes, buyers, sellers and third parties will always need each other. (Anon)

Perhaps the single most strategic issue facing companies today is the overhaul and consequent re-design of their supply chains, i.e., the commercial and physical arrangements made with other parties in order to provide consumers or corporate users with access to products and services. This pressure for change has been brought about through rapid developments in most marketplaces.

Unfortunately, in most industrial situations the conflict between the various parties in distribution channels and supply chains continues, generally with a 'zero-sum' result. Often conflict arises because buyers and suppliers have different expectations of each other's role in the value-adding process of selling and distribution. Conflict can also arise when one member in a supply chain introduces innovations which ensure the benefits remain with the innovator, while corresponding costs flow to the parties in other parts of the chain.

However, perhaps the major source of conflict between supply chain parties is the lack of understanding each has of the other's business and respective market positioning. Usually, one party is more sophisticated than the other, and consequently a 'mis-communication gap' can easily arise between the two. Strategic partnering can help close this gap and get the two parties relating to each other in a much more positive fashion. Our experience is that in such situations, resources are better allocated and a 'win–win' condition arises wherein **both** parties achieve additional profitability – to their mutual satisfaction.

The important thing here is that two parties in a given supply chain commit to a **unique** rather than **exclusive** relationship, and that this relationship is systematized rather than simply relying on more fragile personal contacts.

Customer/supplier loyalty – the key to success

Enlightened enterprises throughout the world are recognizing the value of developing sustained cooperation with other supply chain members. Enduring cooperative relationships are the key to successful marketing in the new millennium, below as indicated, in a modified version of Raphael's ladder of loyalty. Too often we work tirelessly to move a customer (or supplier in the reverse case) up through the various phases of customer loyalty, as depicted, only to lose them at the Advocate stage. Often getting them back on the bottom rung of the ladder is much more costly in time and money than careful 'maintenance' of the relationship would have been in the first instance. But by then it's too late.

Raphael's ladder of loyalty

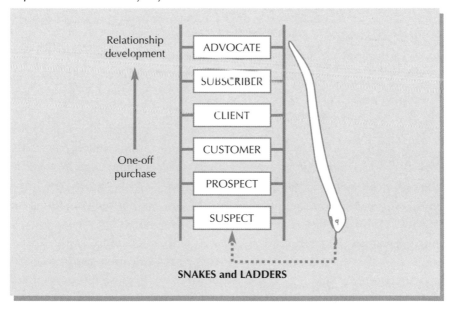

Upgrading the relationship

Our experience indicates that many of the problems which arise between buyers and suppliers occur because managers take a low-level and generally unplanned approach to the relationship, i.e., solving operational problems as they arise. However, the secret is to set the correct context early – at the highest possible managerial level – and then cascade the understanding

which arises from this meeting of minds downwards through the two collaborating organizations via a series of horizontal communications between the
two. The workshop-driven methodology we have developed to achieve this is
described below and depicted diagrammatically on p. 312.

Process methodology

Step 1 Vision formulation

This step produces vision (or philosophical) 'what we stand for' statements
from both parties. The process significantly reinforces the awareness of the
necessity to understand each other's business position and aspirations. It
also prepares the way for an understanding of any conflict points wherein
the companies may not fundamentally share the same objectives, *yet both
exist to serve the same end-user or consumer.*

Step 2 Environmental scan

This step seeks to flush out and understand the various elements of the
economic, government, consumer and organizational environment which
do, or would, influence the proposed 'partnership'.

Step 3 Issues formulation

This step solicits and documents critical issues from both individual
companies and jointly held perspectives. These issues are seen to be significant in as much as they can have a major impact on performance in a
pre-determined time frame.

Step 4 Issues identification and definition

This step 'tests' each issue with pressure questions in an attempt to understand the rationale for its selection. The objective is to sort out clearly
symptoms and causes.

Step 5 Issues prioritization

This step determines and graphically documents the position of the issues on
an impact/urgency matrix to ensure that the resources available are

allocated correctly. It also provides the key to the on-going monitoring of issues which require attention when further resources become available.

Step 6 Issues break-out

This step translates the issues (those selected as critical, given the resources) into:

- Assumptions
- Objectives
- Strategies
- Action plans
- Time frames
- Budgets
- Monitor points
- Responsibilities.

And it ensures that both partners in the 'partnership' understand and agree on what is to be done, by whom, and by when, to achieve the jointly agreed results. This very process has the effect of more closely binding the two parties together in a mutually beneficial partnership.

Strategic partnership technique

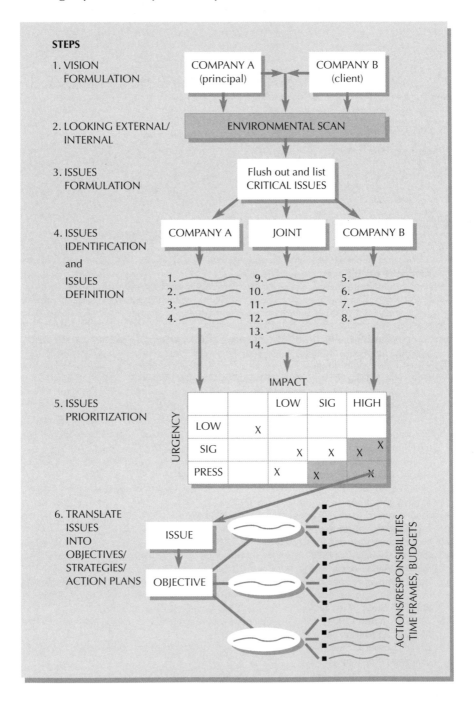

Notes

Chapter 1

1 Surowiecki, James (1998) 'Dark days at Sunbeam', *The Motley Fool*, posted Friday April 17 at 12:30am ET, www.slate.com/id/2650.

2 I am indebted to Emeritus Professor Malcolm McDonald who coined this term.

3 CFROI = [(Cash flow from operations / capital   capital charge], generally expressed as a percentage. CFROI percentage spread correlates positively with share price and market capitalization.

4 The business units that comprised Goodman Fielder at the time were: Ingredients, Meadow Lea Foods, Milling & Baking, Steggles and Uncle Tobys.

5 Kirby, Julia (2003) 'Supply chain challenges: building relationships', a conversation with Scott Beth, David N. Burt, William Copacino, Chris Gopal, Hau L. Lee, Robert Porter Lynch and Sandra Morris, *Harvard Business Review*, July, pp. 64–73.

6 This is the author's own assessment based on more than 100 consulting assignments.

7 Jackson, Tony (1998) 'Melding of minds to master the intangibles – management sharing knowledge', *Financial Times*, 15 June, 15 Online edition, sourced from http://global.factiva.com.simsra.cl.net.ocs.mq.edu.au/ha/default.aspx.

8 Friedman, Thomas, L. (2005) *The World is Flat: A Brief History of the Twenty-first Century*, Farrar, Strauss & Giroux, NY.

9 Neuschel, Robert P. (1967) 'Physical distribution – forgotten frontier', *Harvard Business Review*, March–April, Vol. 45, No. 2, pp. 125–34.

10 Stolle, John F. (1967) 'How to manage physical distribution', *Harvard Business Review*, July–August, Vol. 45, No. 4, pp. 93–100.

11 *See Signature Concepts* at www.johngattorna.com.

12 Porter, Michael E. (1979) 'How competitive forces shape strategy', *Harvard Business Review*, March–April, Vol. 57, No. 2, pp. 137–45.

13 Advertisement for one-day national management conference in Dublin and Manchester, in *business life*, the in-house magazine published by British Airways, September 2004.

14 'Siberian Siren', *The Sunday Times*, Singapore, 11 July 2004, p. 31.

15 Chessell, James (2005) 'Lion boss eschews champagne tastes', *Sydney Morning Herald*, Monday 23 May, p. 34.

16 Bryan, Lowell L. and Joyce, Claudia (2005) 'The 21st-century organization', *McKinsey Quarterly*, No. 3, pp. 25–33.

17 Akumatsu, K. (1962) 'A historical pattern of economic growth in developing countries', *Japanese Economic History 1600–1962*, Vol. 1, pp. 1–23. Akumatsu applied the wild geese analogy to economic theory, specifically the adoption of new technology by Asian nations.
18 Photograph from Getty Images in article by: Ryan, Melissa (2004) 'Australia wins 4000m team pursuit gold', *Sydney Morning Herald*, 24 August.
19 Coase, R.H. (1937) 'The nature of the firm', an essay in *4 Economica NS*, pp. 386–405, quoted in Williamson, O.E. and Winter, S.G. (eds) (1991) *The Nature of the Firm*, Oxford University Press, New York, NY, pp. 19–31.
20 Labovitz, G. and Rosansky, V. (1997) *The Power of Alignment: How great companies stay centred and accomplish extraordinary things*, John Wiley & Sons, New York, NY.
21 Chorn, N.H. (1987) 'The relationship between business-level strategy and organizational culture', unpublished PhD thesis, Witwatersrand University, Johannesburg.
22 Gattorna Strategy Consultants Pty Ltd, Sydney, Australia, 1985–95.
23 See Adler, G., Fordham, M. and Read, H. (eds) (1971) *The Collected Works of CG Jung Volume 6: Psychological Types* (translated by R.F.C. Hull), Bollingen Series 20, Princeton University Press, Ewing, NJ.
24 Adizes, Ichak (1979) *How to Solve the Mismanagement Crisis*, 1st printing, Dow-Jones-Irwin; 5th Printing (1985), Adizes Institute, Santa Monica, CA.
25 Gerard W. Faust, President, Faust Management Corporation, Poway, CA (previously President of the Adizes Institute).
26 This diagnostic tool will provide a single overall assessment of the alignment between your enterprise and its marketplace. However, to obtain detailed assessments of alignment against specific customers and customer segments, the 'quick' behavioral segmentation diagnostic outlined in Appendix 2C must first be undertaken.
27 Gosfield, Josh and Lopez, Nola (1996) 'Levi's changes everything', *Fast Company*, No. 3, June/July.
28 Huckboy, Jamie (2005) 'Queen B', in *Harper's Bazaar*, September, pp. 118–20.
29 Fly-by-wire technology is an electronically managed flight system, which uses computers to make the aircraft easier to handle, while further enhancing performance and safety. More details can be found at www.airbus.com. See also Gattorna, J. (ed.) (1998) *Strategic Supply Chain Alignment: Best practice in supply chain management*, Gower Publishing, Aldershot, pp. 633–4.
30 An observation frequently made to the author during his research and consulting.

Chapter 2

1 These additional building blocks include 'fit' of personnel in the organizational structure, internal communications, performance measurement regimes and incentives, planning systems, training and development initiatives, recruitment and role modelling.
2 Holweg, Mattias and Pil, Frits K. (2001) 'Successful build-to-order strategies start with the customer', *MIT Sloan Management Review*, Vol. 43, No. 1, Fall, pp. 74–83.
3 Davenport, Thomas H., Harris, Jeanne G. and Kohli, Ajay K. (2001), 'How do they know their customers so well?', *MIT Sloan Management Review*, Vol. 42, No. 2, Winter, p. 63.
4 Ibid.
5 Ings-Chambers, Edwina (2004) 'In the mood', *Financial Times*, 30–31 October, p. W14.
6 Nunes, Phil F. and Cespedes, Frank V. (2003) 'The customer has escaped', *Harvard Business Review*, No. 81, Issue 11, November, pp. 96–105.
7 Ibid., p. 105.

8 Fisher, Marshall L. (1997) 'What is the right supply chain for your product?', *Harvard Business Review*, Vol. 75, No. 2, March–April, pp. 105–16.

9 Ibid., p. 106.

10 Ibid., p. 109.

11 Lee, Hau L. (2002) 'Aligning supply chain strategies with product uncertainties', *California Management Review*, Vol. 44, No. 3, Spring, pp. 105–19.

12 Ibid., p. 119.

13 Johnson, Alan (2004) 'Decision time for consumer manufacturers', *Manufacturing Monthly*, May, p. 26.

14 Booz Allen Hamilton (2003) *Smart Customization: Profitable Growth Through Tailored Business Streams*, White Paper, 7 pp.

15 Ibid., p. 1

16 Byrnes, Jonathan (2005) 'You only have one supply chain?', *Working Knowledge*, Harvard Business School, 1 August. Sourced from http://www.hbswk.hbs.edu.

17 Ibid.

18 Ibid.

19 Ibid.

20 A.T. Kearney (2004) *How Many Supply Chains Do You Need?*, 13 pp., A.T. Kearney, Chicago, IL.

21 Godsell, Janet (2005) 'Demand chain strategy: the missing link', *Management Focus*, Cranfield School of Management, No. 22, Spring, pp. 4–7.

22 Ibid., p. 7.

23 Anderson, David (2005), 'Quick-change supply chain', *ASCET*, Vol. 7, 13 September, 6 pp. Sourced from http://www.ascet.com/documents.asp?d_ID=3432.

24 Ibid., p. 1.

25 Nunes, Phil F. and Cespedes, Frank V. (2003) 'The customer has escaped', *Harvard Business Review*, Vol. 81, No. 11, November, pp. 96–105.

26 Ibid., p. 100.

27 As defined by Hofstede, who was one of first to extensively research the influence of national cultures on work-related values. One of his early articles: Hofstede, Geert (1983) 'National cultures in four dimensions', *International Studies of Management and Organization*, Vol. 13, No. 1/2, Spring/Summer, pp. 49–74.

28 Adapted from original work first published by Gattorna Strategy Consultants Pty Ltd, (1991) 'Pathways to Customers: reducing complexity in the logistics pipeline', *Strategy Spotlight*, Vol. 1, No. 2, October, pp. 21–30.

29 *Zara* (2003) 'Case Study', written by Ferdows, K., Machuca, J.A.D. and Lewis, M. Available from The European Case Clearing House, Cranfield University, England and USA, 15 pp.

30 Lee, H.L (2004) 'The Triple-A Supply Chain', *Harvard Business Review*, Vol. 83, No. 1, October, pp. 102–12.

31 Ibid., p. 112.

32 McAdam, R. and Brown, L. (2001) 'Strategic alignment and the supply chain for the steel stockholder sector: an exploratory case study analysis', *Supply Chain Management: An International Journal*, Vol. 6, No. 2, pp. 83–94.

33 August, B. (2002) 'Aligning the supply chain to anticipate developing market trends', unpublished conference paper, delivered at the Kenan Institute, Asia, March.

34 Evans, Simon (2005) 'New Foster's unit flexes muscle', *Australian Financial Review*, 30 May, p. 16.

35 Ibid.

36 Gettler, Leon (2005) 'Foster's has a big ambition, a very big ambition', *The Age*, 28 September, p. 14.

37 After Kim, W. Chan and Mauborgne, R. (2005) *Blue Ocean Strategy: How to create uncontested market space and make the competition irrelevant*, Harvard Business School Press, Boston, MA.

38 For example, in a market with just a few major customers, each customer in effect can be equivalent to a market. In these situations more sophisticated techniques are required to identify the different buying behaviours present inside each major customer.

39 SLIM, designed at MIT by Professor Jeremy Shapiro and associates.

40 Wagner, Stephen N., Bolton, Jamie M. and Nuthall, Linda (2003) 'Supply chain network optimization modeling', Chapter 2.1 in Gattorna, John L. (ed.), *Handbook of Supply Chain Management*, Gower Publishing, Aldershot, pp. 89–104; and Jimenez, Sue, Brown, Tim and Jordan, Joe (1998) 'Network-modelling tools: enhancing supply-chain decision making', Chapter 19 in Gattorna, John (ed.), *Strategic Supply Chain Alignment*, Gower Publishing, Aldershot, pp. 302–24.

Chapter 3

1 Anders, George (2003) 'The Carly Chronicles', *Fast Company*, February, p. 70.

2 Coutts, Louis (2004) 'Culture clubs', *Business Review Weekly*, July 22–28, p. 57.

3 Schien, Edgar H.(1992) *Organizational Culture and Leadership*, 2nd edn, Jossey-Bass., San Francisco, CA, p. 12.

4 Hofstede, Geert (1993) 'Cultural constraints in management theories', *Academy of Management Executive*, Vol. 7, No. 1, pp. 81–94.

5 Gattorna, J.L. (2003) *Handbook of Supply Chain Management*, 5th edn, Gower Publishing, Aldershot, pp. 14–17 for a formula to draft a meaningful vision statement.

6 Slagmulder, R. and Grottoli, D. (2003) *Sainsbury's (A) Transforming the Supply Chain*, INSEAD, 13 pp.

7 Hofstede, Geert (1980) *Culture's Consequences: International Differences in Work-Related Values* (Cross Cultural Research and Methodology), Sage Publications, Newbury Park, CA.

8 Firoz, Nadeem M., Maghrabi, Ahmad S. and Kim, Ki Hee (2002) 'Think globally manage culturally', *International Journal of Commerce and Management*, Vol. 12, Nos. 3 & 4, pp. 32–50.

9 Hofstede, Geert & Associates (1998) *Masculinity and Femininity: The Taboo Dimension of National Cultures*, Sage Publications, Newbury Park, CA.

10 Fonterra behavioural segmentation analysis carried out in 2000/01.

11 First mentioned in a *Fortune* article by an executive of Texas Instruments, in the 1980s.

12 'Revinventing Motorola', *Business Week*, 9 August 2004, p. 98.

13 Neilson, Gary L. and Pasternack, Bruce A. (2005) 'The cat that came back', *strategy+business*, No. 40, Fall, pp. 32–45.

14 Petronius, AD 66, Roman Centurian.

15 General Accident (UK), parent company of New Zealand Insurance (NZI), merged in 1998 with Commercial Union (CU) to form the CGU Insurance Group (UK).

16 Stevens, Greg (2003) 'Changing a culture to become more innovative – faster than ever before', *inKNOWvations*, February, 4 pp.

17 Ibid., p. 2.

18 Ibid.

19 Evans, Simon (2005) 'New CEO wants Amcor out of the silo', *Australian Financial Review*, Thursday 25 August, p. 19.

Chapter 4

1 Kotter, John P. (1990) 'What leaders really do', *Harvard Business Review*, May–June, pp. 103–11.

2 Ibid., pp.105 and 107.

3 Ibid., p. 103.

4 Hanley, Mike, (2005) 'Really, truly – forget charisma. The latest leadership gift is authenticity. And if it doesn't come naturally, you can learn to be real', *Australian Financial Review BOSS*, May, pp. 52–5. Article based on a forthcoming book by Goffee, Rob and Jones, Gareth (forthcoming) *Why Should Anyone Be Led by You*, Harvard Business School Press, Boston, MA.

5 Ibid., p. 52.

6 Clarke, John (2005) *Working with Monsters: how to identify and protect yourself from the workplace psychopath*, Random House Australia, Sydney.

7 Ibid., pp. 56–7.

8 Cromie, Ali (2005) 'The Big Profit' Interview with Chip Goodyear, CEO BHP Billiton, on *Business Sunday*, Nine Network, Australia, 28 August.

9 Hilb, Martin (2005) 'New corporate governance: from good guidelines to great practice', *New Corporate Governance*, Vol. 13, No. 5, September, pp. 569–81.

10 The Myers-Briggs Type Indicator or MBTI® is the original and best known instrument in its category. It is the registered trademark of Consulting Psychologists Press, California.

11 Burrows, Peter (2005) 'The new broom starts to sweep at HP', *Australian Financial Review*, 25–26 June, p. 30.

12 Burrows, Peter (2001) 'The radical: Carly Fiorina's bold management experiment at HP', *BusinessWeek*, February 8; online edition www.businessweek.com.

13 Ibid.

14 Salter, Chuck (2004) 'And now the hard part; JetBlue is cool. Can David Neeleman make it great?', *Fast Company*, May, pp. 66-75.

15 Lee, Hau L. (2004) 'The Triple-A Supply Chain', *Harvard Business Review*, October, pp. 102–12.

16 Ibid, p. 112.

17 See Gattorna, John L. and Tang, M. (2003) 'Formulating a supply chain vision', Chapter 1.2 in Gattorna, John L. (ed.) *Handbook of Supply Chain Management*, 5th edn, Gower Publishing, Aldershot, pp. 11–35.

18 Van Lee, Reggie, Fabish, Lisa and McGaw, Nancy (2005) 'The value of corporate values', *strategy+business*, No. 39, pp. 1–14.

19 'In praise of Peter Drucker', *The Guardian*, Thursday 17 November 2005, p. 34.

Chapter 5

1 Clark, Theodore H. (1994) 'Campbell Soup Company: a leader in continuous replenishment innovations', Case Study 9-195-124, Harvard Business School, 14 October, 21 pp.

2 I am indebted to Bill Gill, Managing Director, Joe White Maltsters, for this example of a *continuous replenishment* supply chain.

3 Anthony Burgmans, CEO Unilever, speaking at the 6th ECR (Efficient Consumer Response) Conference, Edinburgh, 2001.

4 Mitchell, Sue (2002) 'Super market forces', interview with Roger Corbett in *AFR BOSS* magazine, *Australian Financial Review*, 2 January, pp. 43–4.

5 Barratt, Mark A. (2002) 'Exploring relationships and information exchange in grocery supply chains: a case study of enablers and inhibitors', unpublished PhD thesis, Cranfield University.

6 Refer to Appendix 5A for a list of the 83 cultural *enablers*.

7 Refer to Appendix 5B for a list of the 34 cultural *inhibitors*.

8 Bartlett, Christopher, A. and Ghoshal, Sumantra (1990), 'Matrix management: not a structure, a frame of mind', *Harvard Business Review*, July–August, pp.138–45.

9 Garvin, David A. and Levesque, Lynne C. (2004) 'Executive Decision Making at General Motors', Case Study 9-305-026, Harvard Business School, revised February 2005, 21 pp.

10 I am indebted to Corey Loehr, Intel Australia, for his help with the Systems/IT sections in Chapters 5–8.

11 This suite of software applications is proprietary to the SAS Institute.

12 Details from SAS presentation by approval of Dev Mookerjee, August 2005.

13 Kaplan, Robert S. and Norton, David P. (1992) 'The balanced scorecard: Measures that drive performance', *Harvard Business Review*, Vol. 70, No. 1, January/February, pp. 71–9.

14 Kaplan, Robert S. and Norton, David P. (2005) 'Managing alignment as a process', *Balanced Scorecard Report*, Harvard Business School Publishing, July–August, 6 pp.

15 Liker, Jeffrey, K. and Choi, Thomas, Y. (2004) 'Building deep supplier relationships', *Harvard Business Review*, December, pp. 104–13.

16 Howell, R. and Heskett, J. (2004) 'Shouldice Hospital Limited', Case Study 9-805-002, Harvard Business School, 14 pp. And refer to website www.shouldice.com.

17 Humphries, Andrew S. and Wilding, Richard D. (2004) 'Long term collaborative business relationships: the impact of trust and C^3 behavior', *Journal of Marketing Management*, Vol. 20, pp. 1107–22.

18 See Lambert, Douglas M. and Knemeyer, Michael A. (2004) 'We're in this together', *Harvard Business Review*, December, pp. 114–22.

Chapter 6

1 Vitasek, Kate, Manrodt, Karl B. and Abbott, Jeff (2005) 'What makes a lean supply chain?', *Supply Chain Management Review*, October, pp. 39–45.

2 Womack, James P., Jones, Daniel T. and Roos, Daniel (1990) *The Machine that Changed the World: Based on the MIT 5-million dollar Study on the Future of the Automobile*, Rawsons Associates, New York, NY.

3 Hill, T. (2004) 'Designing service delivery systems', Chapter 5, *Operations Management*, 2nd edn, Palgrave Macmillan, p. 117.

4 Chandrasekhar, Ramasastry and Menor, Larry (2004) *Dabbawallahs of Mumbai (A)*, Case 9B04D011, Richard Ivey School of Business, 22 pp.

5 Comment made by Don Meij, CEO/Managing Director of Domino's Pizza Australia and New Zealand (16 May 2005) at MGSM Networker meeting, Sydney, Australia; www.mgsmnetworker.net.

6 SCOR (supply chain operations reference) model was developed by the Supply Chain Council, a not-for-profit organization that commenced in 1996-97. SCOR is a process model designed to improve efficiency and productivity through the use of best practices, standardized terminology, a cross-functional framework along with common metrics. For more information go to www.scor.com.

7 EDLP was a concept developed by Wal-Mart and Procter & Gamble at the end of the 1990s. It has not become a universal practice, although many retail organizations have tried to mimic this arrangement.

8 I am indebted to James Gibson for the insights he has provided on this emerging area of BPMS, May 2005.
9 I am indebted to Deborah Ellis, Principal of Carpenter Ellis, for this example, August 2005.
10 Cowley, Mark (2005) 'BlueScope Steel – a case study in adapting to a global manufacturing market', a paper presented by Mark Cowley at the Smart Conference, Sydney, 2 June.

Chapter 7

1 See IBM Australia's advertising campaign (commenced in March 2003) to communicate its vision of 'e-business on demand' to a wider business community.
2 This is where customer account profitability regimes come in.
3 Fonterra placed embargoes on certain production from certain of its processing factories so that production allocated against forecasts for 'collaborative' customers would not be interfered with.
4 I am indebted to Professor Donald Sull, London Business School, for this example, Chantilly, 7 October 2005.
5 Sull, Donald H. with Yong Wang (2005) *Made in China*, Harvard Business School Press, Boston, MA.
6 Fine, Charles, H. (2005) 'Are you modular or integral? Be sure your supply chain knows', *strategy+business*, No. 39, Summer, pp. 499–506.
7 Ibid., p. 502.
8 Ibid., p. 503.
9 Ibid.
10 Gupta, Vivek and Radlika, A. Neela (2005) 'Li & Fung: the global value chain configurator', Case ref. 305-052-1, ICFAI Center of Management Research, Hyderabad, 28 pp.
11 These are days when one section of the system, e.g., the port, is closed for maintenance. The new approach is for all participants in this supply chain to undertake maintenance on the same day to reduce overall system down-time.
12 'Ship Ahoy', aired on *60 Minutes* programme in Australia on 21 August 2005; reporter, Richard Carleton.
13 I am indebted to Terry O'Connor, General Manager Corporate Services Director, ABB Grain, for this enlightening example, 7 December 2005.
14 Plant, Robert, Feeny, David and Mughal, Hamid (2000) 'Land Rover vehicles: the CB40, a project in nimbleness and flexibility', Case 600-001-1, Templeton College Publication, European Case Clearing House, Templeton College, Oxford, 19 pps.
15 I am indebted to Mike Bernon of the Cranfield Centre for Logistics and Supply Chain Management for his insights on this project.
16 Ritter, Ronald C. and Sternfels, Robert A. (2004) 'When offshore manufacturing doesn't make sense', *McKinsey Quarterly*, online journal of McKinsey & Co., No. 4; www.mckinseyquarterly.com
17 Ibid.
18 Ibid.
19 Ibid.
20 'Haier's aim: "Develop our brand overseas"', *BusinessWeek* online, 31 March 2004, p. 2; http://search.businessweek.com.
21 Cienski, Jan (2005) 'Asia forces rethink for Polish clothing makers', *Financial Times*, Wednesday 26 October, p. 4.
22 Salter, Chuck (2001) 'This is one fast factory', *Fast Company*, No. 49, August, pp. 32–4.

Chapter 8

1 The concept of two variants in a *fully flexible* supply chain and their characteristics/names were developed by Kate Hughes, PhD scholar, Macquarie Graduate School of Management (MGSM), Sydney, Australia.

2 Steinberg, Jessica (2003) 'Driving in the valley of the shadow of death', *Fast Company*, No. 74, September, p. 88.

3 Murray, Sarah (2005) 'How to deliver on the promises: supply chain logistics', *Financial Times – Business Life*, 7 January, p. 9.

4 Dr Chris Morgan, Lecturer at Cranfield Centre for Logistics and Supply Chain Management, Cranfield University.

Chapter 9

1 Porter, Michael E. (1990) *The Competitive Advantage of Nations*, Free Press, New York, NY.

2 A form of 4PL® is taking shape among some leading members of the Australian publishing industry.

3 A 3PL-driven collaborative model exists in Australia to service the retail and wholesale tobacco markets.

4 Sydney Mascot International Airport has a system for aviation fuel where provider companies share the cost of infrastructure on a time-share basis. This means natural competitors are still competing, while collaborating to reduce costs in a specific area of their supply chains.

5 Hardman, Doug, Messinger, David and Bergson, Sara (2005) 'Virtual scale: alliances for leverage', *strategy+business*, 14 July, Booz Allen Hamilton, p. 1; published online at http://www.strategy-business.com/resiliencereport/resilience/rr00021?pg=0.

6 Based on my own assessment over the last two decades of consulting.

7 Where the returns generated are consistently greater than the cost-of-capital.

8 Expressed as an equation, CFROI = [(Cash flow from Operations / Capital Employed) – Capital Charge]

9 Litman, Joel and Frigo, Mark L. (2004) 'When strategy and valuation meet; five lessons from return driven strategy', *Strategic Finance*, August, pp. 31–9.

10 Magretta, Joan (1998) 'Fast, global and entrepreneurial: supply chain management, Hong Kong style. An interview with Victor Fung', *Harvard Business Review*, Vol. 76, No. 5, September/October, pp. 102–14.

11 Kissel, Mary, (2005) 'Li & Fung may be more valuable than its profit measure shows', 'Heard in Asia' column, *Wall Street Journal*, Tuesday 25 October, p. 19.

12 Litman, Joel and Frigo, Mark L. (2004), 'When strategy and valuation meet: five lessons from return driven strategy', *Strategic Finance*, August, pp. 31–9.

13 I am indebted to Will Lock of Accenture (UK) for his help in clarifying the various financial ratios mentioned in the text for assessing the performance of business enterprises.

14 Then called Andersen Consulting.

15 See Gattorna, John (1998) 'Fourth-party logistics: en-route to breakthrough performance in the supply chain', Chapter 27 in John Gattorna (ed.) *Strategic Supply Chain Alignment: best practice in supply chain management*, Gower Publishing, Aldershot, pp. 425–45.

16 1994 Andersen Consulting Survey of 250 UK companies. The industries surveyed were: consumer, retail, oil, gas and chemical, industrial and utilities.

17 Alpha Research Consortium (2004) *Characteristics, Strategies and Trends for 3PL/4PL in Australia*, Logistics Association of Australia, March, p. 86.

18 For more detailed information on the 4PL® model, see Chapter 27 in John Gattorna, (ed.) (1998) *Strategic Supply Chain Alignment*, Gower Publishing, Aldershot.

19 Petroleum Development of Oman (PDO) issued such an RFQ in 2003.

20 Vogel, Jochen (2001) *4PL Report*, March, Lehman Bros, London.

21 EV / EBITDA, i.e., Economic Value/Earnings before Interest and Tax Depreciation and Amortization.

22 M-co developed after the deregulation of New Zealand's power industry. Company information can be found at www.nz.m-co.com.

23 I am indebted to Barry Mellor, Chief Executive, NHS Logistics Authority, for permission to use this case.

24 See also John Gattorna (1998) 'Fourth-party logistics; en-route to breakthrough performance in the supply chain', Chapter 27 in John L. Gattorna (ed.) *Strategic Supply Chain Alignment*, Gower Publishing, Aldershot, pp. 425–45.

25 For example: Corprocure in Australia; Transora in the United States.

26 Breene, Tim and Nunes, Paul F. (2004) 'High-performance business – is bigger always better?', *Outlook*, Accenture, No. 3, pp. 19–25.

27 Ibid., p. 25.

28 Alpha Research Consortium (2004) *Characteristics, Strategies and Trends for 3PL/4PL in Australia*, Logistics Association of Australia, 30 March.

29 Ogulin, Robert (2005) 'Coordination in networked supply chains', PhD thesis work-in-progress, Macquarie Graduate School of Management, Sydney.

30 Petroleum Development of Oman (PDO) has attempted to form a 4PL® by tender for the task of moving exploration equipment; the winning company has encountered early difficulties, which are now being addressed.

31 This was the experience with the Thames Water – Accenture Connect 2020 venture, which although successful, was unable to attract other utilities to join and bring with them additional volume that would have driven the experience curve down at an even faster rate than was achieved with just the one major principal.

Chapter 10

1 McGee, Kenneth, G. (2004) *Heads Up: How to anticipate business surprises and seize opportunities first*, Harvard Business School Press, Boston, MA.

2 Gattorna, John L. (1991) 'Exocets and Equilibrium', Strategy Spotlight, the in-house journal of Gattorna Strategy Consultants Pty. Ltd., Vol. 1, No. 1, February, pp. 8–12.

3 Holliday, Charles, O. Jr., Schmidheiny, Stephan and Watts, Philip (2002) *Walking the Talk: the Business Case for Sustainable Development*, Case Study 38, Berrett-Koehler Publishers, San Francisco, CA, p. 22.

4 'No writing on the wall?, Sustainable Development as a Business Principle in the Supply Chain, a discussion paper by The Nordic Partnership, 2003, p. 2. See http://www.nordicpartnership.org.

5 Comment made in conversation between Dr Ian Woods and myself at a University of Wollongong Supply Chain Forum, Sydney, 29 June 2005. AMP Capital Investors writes research papers on issues affecting the Socially Responsible Investments (SRI) industry. See www.ampcapital.com.au.

6 Demos, Telis (2005) 'Managing beyond the bottom line', *Fortune*, October 3, pp. 70–5.

7 Fittipaldi, Santiago (2004) 'When doing the right thing provides a pay-off', *Global Finance*, January, pp. 18–22.

8 Hall, James (2005) 'Designer Companies', *Australian Financial Review BOSS*, January, p. 40.

9 Ibid., p. 41.

10 Birchall, Jonathan (2005) 'Wal-Mart sets out stall for a green future', *Financial Times*, Wednesday 26 October, p. 17.

11 Holliday, Charles, O. Jr., Schmidheiny, Stephan and Watts, Philip (2002) *Walking the Talk: the Business Case for Sustainable Development*, Case Study 38, Berrett-Koehler Publishers, San Francisco, CA, pp. 170–1.

12 Ibid., Case Study 21, pp. 118–20.

13 'The Nike factory challenge', *Ethical Corporation*, News Release, 16 May 2005, p. 1.

14 Latest research in risk in the supply chain is being undertaken at Cranfield School of Management by Omera Khan, email omera.khan@cranfield.ac.uk.

15 Adapted from Chopra, Sunil and Sodhi, ManMohan S. (2004) 'Managing risk to avoid supply-chain breakdown', *MIT Sloan Management Review*, Fall, p. 54.

16 Ibid., p. 53.

17 Lee, Hau L. and Wolfe, Michael (2003) 'Supply chain security without tears', *Supply Chain Management Review*, January/February, pp. 12–20.

18 Sheffi, Yossi (2005) *The Resilient Enterprise; overcoming vulnerability for competitive advantage*, MIT Press, Cambridge, MA.

19 Ibid., p. 255.

20 Booz Allen Hamilton (2001) 'Out of Sorts with Outsourcing', New York, 25 July.

21 Deloitte Consulting (2005) *Calling a Change in the Outsourcing Market*, April, p. 2.

22 Ibid., p. 3.

23 Internal paper prepared by Ming Tang, Partner, Asia-Pacific Supply Chain Practice, 2003.

24 Drucker, Peter F. (1974) 'New templates for today's organizations', *Harvard Business Review*, January–February, pp. 45–51.

25 George, M., Freeling, A. and Court, D. (1994) 'Reinventing the market organisation', *McKinsey Quarterly*, No. 4, pp. 43–62, p. 59.

26 This was a new organizational format that McKinsey & Co. tried out with various clients in the early 1990s, but it has not been widely adopted.

27 Sull, Donald N. (2005) *Made in China: what Western managers can learn from trailblazing Chinese entrepreneurs*, Harvard Business School Press, Boston, MA, p. 107.

28 Ibid.

29 Ashby, W.R. (1956) *An Introduction to Cybernetics*, Chapman & Hall, London; and by the same author: (1954) *Design for a Brain*, 2nd edn, John Wiley, New York, NY.

30 Cohn, Jeffrey M., Khurana, Rakesh and Reeves, Laura (2005) 'Growing talent as if your business depended on it', *Harvard Business Review*, October, pp. 62–70.

31 See Miller, Ron (2005) 'The evolution of knowledge management', November, *EContent*, pp. 38–41.

32 Lowell, Bryan L. and Joyce, Claudia (2005) 'The 21st-century organization', *McKinsey Quarterly*, No. 3, pp. 24–33.

33 Mangan, J. and Christopher, M. (2005) 'Management Development and the supply chain manager of the future', *International Journal of Logistics Management*, Vol. 16, No. 2, pp. 178–91.

34 Taken from press release, 'Outsourcing in the new supply chain environment', Supply Chain Management Forum, Athens Hilton, Athens, 25–26 November 2005. See www.scmforum.org.

35 Senge, Peter, Scharmer, C. Otto, Jaworski, Joseph and Flowers, Betty Sue (2005) *Presence: Exploring Profound Change in People, Organizations, and Society*, Nicholas Brealey Publishing, London, p. 7.

36 See De Geus, Arie (1997) *The Living Company*, Nicholas Brealey Publishing, quoted in Senge, P. *et al.*, *Presence*, p. 7.

37 Ibid.

Select bibliography

Adizes, Ichak, *How to Solve the Mismanagement Crisis*, 1st printing, Dow-Jones-Irwin, 1979; 5th printing, Adizes Institute, Santa Monica, CA, 1985.

Adler, G., Fordham, M. and Read, H. (eds), *The Collected Works of C.G. Jung Vol. 6: Psychological Types* (translated by R.F.C. Hull), Bollingen Series 20, Princeton University Press, Ewing, NJ, 1971.

Ashby, W.R., *An Introduction to Cybernetics*, Chapman & Hall, Boston, MA, 1956.

Ashby, W.R., *Design for a Brain*, 2nd edn, John Wiley, New York, NY, 1954.

Bacon, Terry R. and Pugh, David G., *The Behavioral Advantage: What the Smartest, Most Successful Companies Do Differently to Win in the B2B Arena*, AMACON, New York, NY, 2004.

Barker, Joel A. and Erickson, Scott W., *Five Regions of the Future: Preparing Your Business for Tomorrow's Technology Revolution*, Penguin, New York, NY, 2005.

Beck, John C. and Wade, Mitchell, *Got Game: How The Gamer Generation is Reshaping Business Forever*, Harvard Business School Press, Boston, MA, 2004.

Benfari, Robert with Knox, Jean, *Understanding Your Management Style: Beyond the Myers-Briggs Type Indicators*, D.C. Heath, Lexington, MA, 1991.

Berger, Andrew J. and Gattorna, John L., *Supply Chain Cybermastery: Building High Performance Supply Chains of the Future*, Gower Publishing, Aldershot, 2003.

Bossidy, Larry and Charan, Ram, *Execution: The Discipline of Getting Things Done*, Crown Business, New York, NY, 2002.

Brooks, Frederick P. Jr, *The Mythical Man-Month: Essays on Software Engineering*, Addison-Wesley Longman, Boston, MA, 1995.

Christopher, Martin, *Logistics and Supply Chain Management: Creating Value-Adding Networks*, 3rd edn, FT Prentice Hall, London, 2005.

Christopher, Martin and Peck, Helen, *Marketing Logistics*, 2nd edn, Elsevier Butterworth-Heinemann, Oxford, 2004.

Clarke, John, *Working with Monsters: How to Identify and Protect Yourself from the Workplace Psychopath*, Random House, Sydney, 2005.

Cohen, Shoshannah and Roussel, Joseph, *Strategic Supply Chain Management: The Five Disciplines for Top Performance*, McGraw-Hill, New York, NY, 2005.

Cokins, Gary, *Performance Management: Finding the Missing Pieces (to Close the Intelligence Gap)*, John Wiley, New York, NY, 2004.

Conner, Daryl R., *Managing at the Speed of Change: How Resilient Managers Succeed and Prosper Where Others Fail*, Villard, New York, NY, 1992.

Conner, Daryl R., *Leading at the Edge of Chaos: How to Create the Nimble Organization*, John Wiley, New York, NY, 1998.

Cranfield School of Management, *Supply Chain Vulnerability*, Report on behalf of DTLR, DTI and Home Office, 2002.

Davenport, Thomas H. and Prusak, Laurence with Wilson, H. James, *What's The Big Idea? Creating and Capitalizing on the Best Management Thinking*, Harvard Business School Press, Boston, MA, 2003.

De Geus, Arie, *The Living Company: Habits for Survival in a Turbulent Business Environment*, Harvard Business School Press, Boston, MA, 1997.

Friedman, Thomas L., *The World is Flat: A Brief History of the Globalized World in the 21st Century*, Penguin Books, London, 2005.

Fritz, Robert, *Corporate Tides: The Inescapable Laws of Organizational Structure*, Berrett-Koehler Publishers, San Francisco, CA, 1996.

Gabel, Jo Ellen and Pilnick, Saul, *The Shadow Organization in Logistics: The Real World of Culture Change and Supply Chain Efficiency*, Council of Logistics Management, Oak Brook, IL, 2002.

Gattorna, J.L. and Walters, D.W., *Managing the Supply Chain: a Strategic Perspective*, Macmillan Business, London, 1996.

Gattorna, John (ed.), *Strategic Supply Chain Alignment: Best Practice in Supply Chain Management*, Gower Publishing, Aldershot, 1998.

Gattorna, John L., *Handbook of Supply Chain Management*, 5th edn, Gower Publishing, Aldershot, 2003.

Goldratt, Eliyahu M., *Theory of Constraints: and How it Should be Implemented*, North River Press, Great Barrington, MA, 1990.

Goold, Michael and Campbell, Andrew, *Designing Effective Organizations: How to Create Structured Networks*, Jossey-Bass, San Francisco, CA, 2002.

Handy, Charles, *The Elephant and The Flea: Reflections of a Reluctant Capitalist*, Harvard Business School Press, Boston, MA, 2001.

Herzlinger, Regina, E., *Market-Driven Health Care: Who Wins, Who Loses in the Transformation of America's Largest Service Industry*, Perseus Books, Cambridge, MA, 1997.

Hofstede, Geert, *Cultures Consequences: International Differences in Work-Related Values (Cross Cultural Research and Methodology)*, Sage Publications, Newbury Park, CA, 1980.

Hofstede, Geert, *Cultures Consequences: Comparing Values, Behaviors, Institutions, and Organizations Across Nations*, 2nd edn, Sage Publications, Newbury Park, CA, 2001.

Hofstede, Geert and Hofstede, Gert Jan, *Cultures and Organizations: Software of the Mind*, 2nd edn, McGraw-Hill, New York, NY, 2005.

Hofstede, Geert & Associates, *Masculinity and Feminity: The Taboo Dimensions of National Cultures*, Sage Publications, Newbury Park, CA, 1998.

Holliday, Charles O. Jr, Schmidheiny, Stephan and Watts, Philip, *Walking the Talk: The Business Case for Sustainable Development*, Berrett-Koehler Publishers, San Francisco, CA, 2002.

Horne, Alistair, *The Age of Napoleon*, Modern Library, New York, NY, 2004.

Ibarra, Hermina, *Working Identity: Unconventional Strategies for Reinventing Your Career*, Harvard Business School Press, Boston, MA, 2003.

Itami, Hiroyuki with Roehl, Thomas W., *Mobilizing Invisible Assets*, Harvard University Press, Cambridge, MA, 1987.

Jung, C.G., *Memories, Dreams, Reflections*, Fontana Paperbacks, London, 1983.

Kaplan, R.S. and Norton, D.P., *The Balanced Scorecard*, Harvard Business School Press, Boston, MA, 1996.

Kim, W. Chan and Mauborgne, Renee, *Blue Ocean Strategy: How to Create Uncontested Market Space and Make the Competition Irrelevant*, Harvard Business School Press, Boston, MA, 2005.

Labovitz, George and Rosansky, Victor, *The Power of Alignment: How Great Companies Stay Centered and Accomplish Extraordinary Things*, John Wiley, New York, NY, 1997.

Lencioni, Patrick, *The Five Temptations of a CEO: a Leadership Fable*, Jossey-Bass, San Francisco, CA, 1998.

Low, Jonathan and Kalafut, Pam Cohen, *Invisible Advantage: How Intangibles Are Driving Business Performance*, Perseus Publishing, Cambridge, MA, 2002.

Management Today Series, *The Power of Culture: Driving Today's Organisation*, Australian Institute of Management, McGraw-Hill, Sydney, 2004.

Mant, Alistair, *Intelligent Leadership*, Allen & Unwin, Sydney, 1997.

Marsh, Nick, McAllum, Mike and Purcell, Dominique, *Strategic Foresight: The Power of Standing in the Future*, Crown Content, Melbourne, 2002.

MacFarlane, Hugh, *The Leaky Funnel: Earn More Customers by Aligning Sales and Marketing to the Way Businesses Buy*, Bookman Media, Melbourne, 2003.

McGee, Kenneth, G., *Heads Up: How to Anticipate Business Surprises and Seize Opportunities First*, Harvard Business School Press, Boston, MA, 2004.

Messner, Reinhold, *Moving Mountains: Lessons on Life and Leadership*, Executive Excellence Publishing, Provo, UT, 2001.

Morrell, Margot and Capparell, Stephanie, *Shackleton's Way: Leadership Lessons From The Great Antarctic Explorer*, Nicholas Brealey, London, 2001.

Nadler, David A. and Tushman, Michael L., *Competing by Design: The Power of Organizational Architecture*, Oxford University Press, New York, NY, 1997.

Neilson, Gary L. and Pasternack, Bruce, A., *Results: Keep What's Good, Fix What's Wrong, and Unlock Great Performance*, Crown Business, New York, NY, 2005.

Pandya, Mukul and Shell, Robbie, *Lasting Leadership: What you Can Learn from the Top 25 Business People of Our Times*, Wharton Publishing and Pearson Education, Upper Saddle River, NJ, 2005.

Penrose, Edith, *The Theory of the Growth of the Firm*, 3rd edn, Oxford University Press, Oxford, 1995.

Pitelis, Christos (ed.), *The Growth of the Firm: The Legacy of Edith Penrose*, Oxford University Press, Oxford, 2002.

Porter, Michael E., *The Competitive Advantage of Nations*, The Free Press, New York, NY, 1990.

Roberts, John, *The Modern Firm: Organizational Design for Performance and Growth*, Oxford University Press, New York, NY, 2004.

Rudzki, Robert A., Smock, Douglas A., Katzorke, Michael and Stewart, Shelley, Jr, *Straight to the Bottom Line: An Executive Roadmap to World Class Supply Management*, J. Ross Publishing, Fort Lauderdale, FL, 2006.

Rummler, Geary A. and Brache, Alan P., *Improving Performance: How to Manage the White Space on the Organization Chart*, 2nd edn, Jossey-Bass Publishers, San Francisco, CA, 1995.

Samuels, Martin, *Command or Control: Command, Training and Tactics in the British and German Armies, 1888–1918*, Frank Cass, London, 1995.

Senge, Peter, Scharmer, C. Otto, Jaworski, Joseph and Flowers, Betty Sue, *Presence: Exploring Profound Change in People, Organizations, and Society*, Nicholas Brealey, London, 2005.

Sheffi, Yossi, *The Resilient Enterprise: Overcoming Vulnerability for Competitive Advantage*, MIT Press, Cambridge, MA, 2005.

Sull, Donald N., *Revival of the Fittest: Why Good Companies Go Bad and How Great Managers Remake Them*, Harvard Business School Press, Boston, MA, 2003.

Sull, Donald N., *Made in China: What Western Managers Can Learn From Trailblazing Chinese Entrepreneurs*, Havard Business School Press, Boston, MA, 2005.

Sveiby, Karl Erik, *The New Organizational Wealth: Managing and Measuring Knowledge-Based Assets*, Berrett-Koehler Publishers, San Francisco, CA, 1997.

Towill, Denis and Christopher, Martin, *International Journal of Logistics: Research Applications*, Vol. 5, No. 3, 2002, pp. 233–309; www.tandf.co.uk/journals.

Williamson, Oliver E. and Winter, Sidney G. (eds), *The Nature of The Firm: Origins, Evolution, and Development*, Oxford University Press, New York, NY, 1993.

Womack, James P., Jones, Daniel T. and Roos, Daniel, *The Machine that Changed the World: Based on the MIT 5-million Dollar Study on the Future of the Automobile*, Rawsons Associates, New York, NY, 1990.

Index

About the Author

Dr John Gattorna has spent a lifetime working in supply chains, from the early days of 'Physical Distribution Management', through the '80s and '90s as the 'Logistics' concept emerged and developed, to the current 'Supply Chain' era. He worked for a number of multi-national companies before forming his own consultancy in the mid-1980s, specializing in marketing and logistics strategy. In 1995 he was invited by Andersen Consulting (now Accenture) to establish their logistics strategy (and subsequent supply chain) practice in Australia, New Zealand, and South-East Asia. He built this practice into the largest of its type in the Asia Pacific Region and in 2002 retired to pursue his interests in teaching, research, and writing. John now regularly teaches and consults in the UK, France, North and South Asia, and the Middle East. His books have been published in Chinese, Japanese, and Russian language editions, and this book represents the culmination of decades of problem-solving and insights gleaned from working continuously in the field.

Invitation for feedback from the reader

I invite feedback and comment on the ideas and content in this book. Please contact me on my email: john@johngattorna.com and feel free to visit my website: www.johngattorna.com or the Financial Times Prentice Hall website: www.pearsoned.co.uk